MW00773064

THE

PORCH AND THE
MIDDLE CHAMBER

THE BOOK OF THE LODGE

Albert Pike

ISBN 1-56459-308-8

Request our FREE CATALOG of over 1,000

Rare Esoteric Books

Unavailable Elsewhere

Alchemy, Ancient Wisdom, Astronomy, Baconian, Eastern-Thought, Egyptology, Esoteric, Freemasonry, Gnosticism, Hermetic, Magic, Metaphysics, Mysticism, Mystery Schools, Mythology, Occult, Philosophy, Psychology, Pyramids, Qabalah, Religions, Rosicrucian, Science, Spiritual, Symbolism, Tarot, Theosophy, *and many more!*

Kessinger Publishing Company
Montana, U.S.A.

THE PORCH
AND
THE MIDDLE CHAMBER

— — —

THE BOOK
OF
THE LODGE

SECRET WORK

INTRODUCTION

Albert Pike's The Book of the Lodge was published in 1872, in a limited edition. It has been our finding that, outside of the vaults of the Supreme Councils for the Southern and Northern Jurisdictions of the United States, and several Grand Lodge libraries, this document is not to be found. Of the "Secret Work," no complete copies appear to exist outside of the Supreme Councils.

As Brother Pike noted (p 14, Book of the Lodge) "This Ritual is intended for instruction only, in the States of the Southern Jurisdiction, where there are no Lodges working the Ancient and Accepted Scottish Rite; to be studied and understood before investiture with the fourth degree. For, without it, the system of that Rite is incomplete, and even like a fabric without foundation."

It may be correctly assumed that Pike had intended this Ritual of the first three degrees of the Ancient and Accepted Scottish Rite, Southern Jurisdiction, as a supplement to the "American Rite" Degrees 1 through 3, and not a replacement for it. This to provide that "post-graduate" instruction so necessary to allow an effective transition from the one Rite to the other.

Due to a prevailing provincial mentality that exists among the hierarchy of Freemasonry today, the fear that Pike's Ritual would supplant the existing American Rite Degrees, has effectively buried this important document in the hope that its implied "threat" would somehow disappear. But such is not to be the case.

It is with great pleasure that we, who are student's of Albert Pike's philosophy, and of the Ancient Mysteries in general, publish Albert Pike's The Book of the Lodge.

The Secret Work, as provided here, to these three degrees has been faithfully reconstructed from fragments of the original document, plus esoteria from French, Spanish, and Latin American manuscripts that existed from 1830 through 1880. In determining the nature of the esoteria and how best to apply it, we adopted methodologies used by Albert Pike in his Degrees 4-32. It is our contention that this Secret Work is true to the intent of Pike's Ritual, and that any variances (unless otherwise noted) are purely unintentional.

DEGREE 1
APPRENTICE

0.1.

[p 38]

There must also be a third room, styled the "Chamber of Reflection". It should be a story below the lodge room; and, if possible, underground, with no window. The floor must, in any case, be of earth. On the walls should be brief sentences of morality, and maxims of austere philosophy, written as if with charcoal. Among them must be these:

0.2.

[p 38]

Over the door of the vault is a transparency in the shape of the top of a coffin painted in black, on which the following words, made to appear luminous with a blood-red light, at the proper time, by means of a lamp, introduced from the outside, through a small wicket.

Over the pile of bones is written:

"The vile remains of a perjured traitor!"

Over the skeleton:

"Death, avenger of perjury and treason!"

On the coffin, over the breast of the supposed corpse:

"An Apprentice faithless and erased!"

The door should have a large, heavy iron lock, like that of a dungeon, with a huge bolt.

In the center of the room is placed a small wooden table. Next to it, a rock or mound of earth, which is the only seat. On the table are placed a single light, set in a human skull, a small bell, a small loaf or roll of bread, a basin of water, containers of salt, sulphur and mercury; and paper, pens and ink.

On the floor near the table is a coffin (with only the head of the corpse showing). In one corner stands a skeleton, complete, holding in one hand an arrow, in the other a dagger. In another corner a skull and other human bones lie in a confused head on the ground.

O.3.

[p 49]

SW: Brothers Senior and Junior Deacons [or Expert and Assistant Expert], you will determine if all present are Masons.

(1 rap) Brethren, to order as Masons.

O.4.

[p 50]

VM: Brother Senior Warden, are you a Mason?

SW: My brothers recognize me as such.

VM: Who is a Mason?

SW: A free man of good morals, equally a friend of the poor and the rich, who is virtuous.

VM: What have you come here to do?

SW: To learn to overcome my passions, to subdue my will, and to make new progress in Masonry.

VM: What are the fundamental precepts of a Mason?

SW: Fraternal love, relief, and truth.

VM: What is Freemasonry?

SW: A fraternal system of morals, illustrated by symbols, in association with honest brothers, who seek the perfection of human morals.

VM: What is the work of a Mason?

SW: To dig pits for vice and to raise temples to virtue.

VM: How should I recognize you to be a Mason?

SW: By my signs, a word, and the grip.

VM: What brings you here?

SW: My obligation.

VM: What do you bring here with you?

SW: Love for my brethren and zeal for the interests of the Ancient and Accepted Scottish Rite.

0.5.

[p 50]
The Venerable Master raps two times and all officers stand.

0.6.

[p 52]
The Venerable Master rises and approaches the Senior Deacon [Expert]. Both make the sign of the degree and then clasp right hands. The Master whispers the Sacred Word of an Apprentice to the Senior Deacon [Expert]. They then step back.

VM: Brother Senior Deacon [Expert], carry the Sacred Word of the First Degree to the Senior Warden.

The Senior Deacon [Expert] approaches the Senior Warden's station, who rises and receives the word in the same way. The Senior Warden in turn gives the word to the Junior Deacon [Assistant Expert] and orders him to carry it to the Junior Warden. The Deacons [Experts] return to their stations.

0.7.

[p 54]

The Junior Warden raps three times, followed by the Senior Warden, who raps three times, followed by the Venerable Master, who raps three times.

VM: My brethren, let us return thanks to the Grand Architect of the Universe for the many blessings with which He has surrounded us, and implore His aid to enable us to perform our duties.

PRE: Sovereign Author of the Universe, we pay you the sincere homage of our fervent gratitude for all the blessings which your infinite goodness has bestowed upon us. We implore you to purify our hearts by the sacred fire of your love, and to guide and direct us in the ways of virtue. Let peace and charity form the chain of our union. Cause us in this lodge faintly to imitate the state and condition of your elect in Your holy and spiritual kingdom. Enable us in all things to discern and adopt the good and reject the evil. Let us not be deceived by pretended zeal and devotion, nor deceive ourselves as to our weakness and errors. Aid us in advancing the purposes and attaining the objects of the true and genuine Masonry, and thus enable us to serve our fellows and assist in carrying forward your great designs. Amen.

ALL: So mote it be.

VM: With me, my brethren.

All give, the Venerable Master leading, the battery (3 x 3). This is followed by the Sign three times, each time saying:

ALL: Huzza!

0.8.

[p 58]

VM: (3 raps) To order, my brethren.

All stand under the Sign of Order for the degree.

VM: From whence come you?

MC: A visitor, from the Lodge of Saint John of Scotland [or, the Holy Saints John].

The Master of Ceremonies gives the name and lodge of the visitor(s).

[*The French Ritual adds the following:*]

VM: What do you bring with you to this place?

MC: Obedience to the Venerable Master, love, gladness, health and welfare to all my brethren.

VM: What it done in the Lodge of Saint John?

MC: Wreaths are twined and temples are erected for virtues.   While dungeons are carved out and chains fashioned for vice.

VM: What have you come here to do?

MC: Conquer my passions, subdue my desires, and make further progress in Masonry.

0.9.

[p 64]
The Deacon [Expert] meets with the candidate in the retired room.   He relieves the brother in waiting and proceeds to prepare the candidate by blindfolding him, saying:

JD: Mister {A.B.}, I cover your eyes with this blindfold, not to prevent your observing your surroundings, but to shut out any distractions which might occur along this short journey.

It is my duty to conduct you to a room known as the Chamber of Reflection, where, in silence and solitude, you will have opportunity to meditate in silence.

As they descend, there should be the sound of dripping water and the squealing of rats.

The Deacon [Expert] conducts the candidate to a seat in the Chamber of Reflection.   The Deacon [Expert] withdraws silently, and a brother (as the Preparer) enters.   He is clothed in a long black domino, with a broad-brimmed slouched hat, and his face covered by a mask of black silk, with a sword by his side.   The Preparer says:

0.10.

[p 65]
The Preparer exits, closes the door, and knocks 3 times.

0.11.

[p 66]
After a minute, or so, the sound of chains will be rattled without, and cries, groans and moans will be heard, followed by a great crash. There are cries, as of pain and terror, and then dead silence.

Then light will be introduced, making the writing on the transparency legible.

0.12.

[p 70]
The Deacon [Expert] prepares the candidate by divesting him of all metal, giving him a garment to wear; right foot, knee, arm, and breast bare; blindfolded with a rope (cabletow) three times around his neck.

0.13.

[p 70]
The Pursuivant or Junior Deacon places the point of his sword against the naked breast of the candidate.

PUR: Who is this audacious one who attempts to force entry into the temple?

SD: Calm yourself, my brother. Mister {A.B.} has no intention of penetrating, in spite of you, into this sacred enclosure. The man who comes and knocks is a candidate desiring to receive light, and who humbly entreats of our venerable lodge.

PUR: Is he a free man and of good repute?

SD: He is.

PUR: Is he properly prepared?

SD: He is.

The Pursuivant or Junior Deacon closes the door, turns and reports:

0.14.

[p 72]
The Pursuivant or Junior Deacon opens the door, and says:

PUR: Enter.

The Senior Deacon conducts the candidate to a point between the two columns (about five feet inside the lodge room) and stops. He is met by the "Terrible Brother" (one who has been selected to act as such from among the brethren). The Terrible Brother places the point of the sword on the naked breast.

TB: Mister {A.B.}, what do you feel?

CAN: (PROMPTED) The point of a weapon.

TB: Mister {A.B.}, the steel, whose point you feel, is a symbol of the remorse which will tear at your heart if disgraced, at some future date, by your becoming a traitor against this august society, which has received you into our bosom, because you are a man of honor.

The sword is removed.

TB: What do you see?

CAN: Nothing.

TB: The blindfold that covers your eyes is a symbol of the blindness in which man finds himself, when dominated by the passions and submerged in ignorance and superstition.

VM: Mister {A.B.}, what is your opinion of Masonry?

CAN: (ANSWER)

VM: Is it your intention to become a Mason?

CAN: It is

VM: Is it of your own free will, without any compulsion or persuasion, that you present yourself?

0.15.

[p 76]
Just inside the door, a large wooden frame stands, in which the empty space is filled by a paper "screen". The whole being supported by brothers on each side.

BR1:   What shall we do with the profane?

BR2:   Shut him up in the cavern!

Two brethren seize the candidate and throw him through the paper screen into the arms of two other brethren who stand ready to receive him. The outer door, previously left open, is shut with great noise.

BR3:   The incubation is complete!

BR4:   It is time. Make the profane come forth from the mystic chaos in which he exists!

The candidate is assisted up and conducted to the Senior Warden's station.

0.16. [0.14.]

[p 94]
The Venerable Master raps 3 times and all brethren stand.

The Senior Warden proceeds to the altar and places in the hands of the candidate a cup without a handle and divided into two parts. In one part is water sweetened with honey. In the other water made bitter with gentian or some other harmless herb or drug; or there may be two cups precisely alike in shape.

SW: Mister {A.B.}, you will repeat the words which I am about to say, exactly.

SW/
CAN: I, {A.B.}, in the presence of the Great Architect of the Universe, and of the brethren now here assembled, do most solemnly and sincerely promise and swear, that I will never reveal any of the secrets and mysteries which may hereafter be entrusted to me, forever hereafter, in respect to all the tests, whether my initiation be completed or remain

incomplete, to any person in the world, who shall not be entitled at the time to receive them.

I furthermore promise and swear that I will battle to control unrestrained passions, in myself as in others; and that I will practice the virtues of kindness, generosity and beneficence, especially with my brethren; giving advise and counsel when requested, and providing for their necessities when in need.

To all of which I most solemnly and sincerely promise on my honor of silence.

A Deacon [Expert] places the candidate's right hand over his heart, while the candidate takes a drink of the sweetened water. The Senior Warden takes the cup, and the following is said:

SW: Mister {A.B.}, you will continue to repeat the words after me.

SW/
CAN: And, if I should ever violate my obligation, I consent to this which the sweetness of this beverage changes itself to bitterness, and to this which its beneficial effect becomes for me that of a subtle poison.

The Senior Warden returns the cup (bitter side to the candidate, or a second cup with bitter water) to the candidate. The candidate's right hand still over his heart, when he is told to take a drink from the cup.

SW: Mister {A.B.}, your expression changes. Is the sweet already become bitter? Perhaps your conscience belies your words?

The Senior Warden then takes the cup and places it on the altar.

LITURGY A.

[p 96, Liturgy p 59]
VM: From the earliest times, the initiate into the Mysteries was subjected to physical trials if his courage and endurance. Pythagoras imposed on his disciples five years of silence. Wherever the Mysteries were practiced, and under whatever name, the good faith, devotion and manhood of the candidate were tested, and complete assurance of them had, before he was irradiated by the light of truth.

In the middle ages, when the church of Rome, sitting on the ruins of the fallen empire, reigned supreme over consciences, Masonry, claiming as its patron Saint John the Evangelist, needed to require similar tests and trials. Like the early Christian mysteries, it was a "secret discipline." For, during whole centuries, a word, the least indiscretion, a gesture, was a death warrant. The miter and crown were then in league together against man.

The Inquisition classed Masons with Jews and heretics, and dealt with them by the tender mercies of torture. To be a Mason then, was to expose one's self to the same dangers as surrounded the Christian under Nero and Domitian. The existence of the entire Masonic body was involved in every initiation.

Masonry comes more directly from the mysteries of the sun, and those of Mithra, in Persia. There the aspirant commenced by easy tests, and arrived by degrees at those that were most cruel, in which his life was often endangered. No one can be initiated, says Suidas, until after he has proven, by the most terrible trials, that he possesses a manly soul, exempt from the sway of every passion.

Masonry has softened, but has not chosen to dispense with, the ancient tests; for it is not in free countries only that she exists; nor is it in them that she plays the most important part. Neither, even in these, is there any guarantee of the eternity of freedom, or that the powers of government may not be usurped by those to which masonry might become dangerous, and would be hostile, unless false to its mission.

O.17.

[p 97]
VM: Terrible Brother, you will seat the candidate upon the stone of reflection.

The candidate is conducted to the east where the Rough Ashlar is situated. The Terrible Brother returns to his station.

VM: Withdraw, my brethren, that this man may be left to his conscience and to that darkness which covers his eyes.

Four or five brethren, make noise of people exiting the lodge, closing the door noisily, etc. Then absolute silence is maintained for about two minutes.

O.18.

[p 97]

The Terrible Brother approaches the candidate and says:

TB: Get up!

The Brother conducts the candidate THREE times around the lodge, beginning in the northwest, proceeding first East, then south (past the Master's station), then west, then north (in front of the Senior Warden), then east, and so forth, and ending in front of the Junior Warden.

During this first journey, there is much noise as various brothers argue back and forth. Blocks of variously sized wood are placed randomly along the candidate's path, so that he may occasionally stumble. Equipment should be placed, on the route, to generate electrical arcs that noisily (though harmlessly) crackle. Large heavy balls are rolled on the floor to imitate thunder.

During the first circuit, two brothers hold a Deacon's staff, horizontally, about five feet off the ground. This, the candidate must pass under:

TB: We are approaching an arch... lower your head... stoop down... proceed slowly.

During the second circuit, two more brothers hold a staff, horizontally, about six inches off the ground. This, the candidate must pass over:

TB: There is an obstacle ahead... go slow... life up your right foot and pass over... now lift up your left foot.

During the third circuit an incline, made of heavy 3'x8' plywood, raised about a foot at one end, is placed on the candidate's path. Meanwhile, several brothers, holding large fans, blow air onto the candidate. The candidate is made to slowly climb the incline and then told to jump [NOTE: In older rituals, the candidate was required to climb a ladder of seven steps. Once at the summit, he was then told to jump. A mattress was so placed for his landing]:

TB: Go slowly and have courage, we are at the summit of the journey. Stop!... Now jump into space!

Upon landing, the candidate is given a light shock with and electrical device.

The candidate is conducted to in front of the Junior Warden. The Terrible Brother stamps on the floor with his foot three times. The Junior Warden gets up immediately and applies his gavel to the candidate's chest.

JW: Who comes here?

TB: This is a profane who requests to be accepted as a Freemason.

JW: By what right does he dare to make this request?

TB: Because he is free and of good morals.

JW: Since he is thus, he may pass.

The brother reconducts the candidate back to the two columns, turns and faces the east.

TB: Venerable Master, the first journey has been completed.

0.19.

[p 102]
The Terrible Brother conducts the candidate THREE times around the lodge, beginning in the south, proceeding first west, then north (in front of the Senior Warden), then east, and south, and ending in front of the Senior Warden. During this second journey, the brethren rattle and clash swords. The candidate's path is clear with no obstacles.

The Terrible Brother stamps on the floor three times. The Senior Warden gets up immediately and applies his gavel to the candidate's chest.

SW: Who comes here?

TB: This is a profane who requests to be accepted as a Freemason.

SW: By what right does he dare to make this request?

TB: Because he is free and of good morals.

SW: Since he is thus, he may pass and be purified by water. He will now wash in the ancient spirit of leaving all passions, vice and falsehood behind, that he may enter, as the neophyte, into the ancient Mysteries, cloaked only in clean and white garments.

A basin of water is brought before the candidate, and he is to immerse his left hand in the water three times. The candidate's hands are dried and the Brother reconducts the candidate back to the two columns, turns and faces the east.

TB: Venerable Master, the second journey has been completed.

LITURGY B.

[p 103, Liturgy p 64]
VM: In the Druidical Mysteries, among the trials of the candidate, he was placed in a boat and sent out to sea alone, having to rely on his own skill and presence of mind to reach the opposite shore in safety. If the candidate declined it, he was dismissed with contempt. If he made it and succeeded, he was termed "thrice-born," was eligible to all the dignities of the state, and received complete instruction in the philosophical and religious doctrines of the Druids.

When the aspirant was initiated into the Mysteries of Isis, he was conducted to the nearest baths, and after having bathed, the priest first solicited forgiveness of him of the gods, and then sprinkled him all over with the clearest and purest water, and conducted him back to the temple. It was required of every initiate that his heart and hands be free of every stain. It was represented that, except for the gravest sins, there was opportunity for expiation; and the tests of air, water, and fire were represented, by means of which, during the march of many years, the soul could be purified, and rise toward the ethereal regions. The ascent being more or less tedious and laborious, according as each soul was more or less clogged by the gross impediments of its sins and vices.

In the Mithriac Mysteries, the candidate was purified with water and fire, and went through seven stages of initiation. Ablutions were required in all the mysteries, symbolical of the purity necessary to enable the soul to escape from its bondage in matter.

Sacred baths and preparatory baptisms were used, lustrations, immersions and purifications of every kind. At Athens, the aspirants bathed in the Ilissus, which subsequently became a sacred river. Before entering the Temple of Eleusis, all were required to wash their hands in a vase of lustral water, placed near the entrance. Apuleius bathed seven times in the sea, symbolical of the seven spheres which the soul must reascend. The Hindus must bathe in the sacred River Ganges. Menander speaks of a purification by sprinkling three times with salt and water. Water nourishes and purifies. The urn from which it flowed as thought worthy to be a symbol of the Deity, as of the Osiris-Canobus, who with living water irrigated the soil of Egypt; and also an emblem of hope. That should cheer the dwellings of the dead. In the terrible and dangerous tests of some of the old Mysteries, the candidate was made to swim a river.

0.20.

[p 104]

The Terrible Brother conducts the candidate **THREE** times around the lodge, beginning in the west, proceeding first north, then east, then south and west, to in front of the Venerable Master. During this third journey, there is absolute silence and no obstructions block the path of the candidate.

The Terrible Brother stamps on the floor three times. The Venerable Master gets up immediately and applies his gavel to the candidate's chest.

VM: Who comes here?

TB: This is a profane, baptized, who requests to be accepted as a Freemason.

VM: By what right does he dare to make this request?

TB: Because he is free and of good morals.

VM: Since he is thus, he may pass by the purifying flames, in order that nothing of his past profane life may remain.

A candle is brought before the candidate, and he is to pass his right hand slowly over the flame three times (being careful not to inflict damage).

[*NOTE: In older rituals, a blast of flame was blown into the face of the candidate by use of a long metallic tube having at one end a mouth-piece and at the other a spirit-lamp, surrounded with wire gauze. The tube contained lycopodium or arcanson in powder, which, when blown upon the spirit-lamp would cause a harmless flash of flame.*]

The Brother reconducts the candidate back to the two columns, turns and faces the east.

TB: Venerable Master, the third journey has been completed.

0.21.

[p 106]
VM: Terrible Brother, conduct the candidate to the Brother Surgeon. (DONE)

Brother Surgeon, do your duty.

A brother, who has been appointed as Surgeon, steps up and addresses the candidate:

Surgeon: Mister {A.B.}, it gives me great pleasure to congratulate you upon the progress you have made in your search for light and truth, and upon the possession of that fortitude which has sustained you in your journeys, pursued by so many good and true men before you.

Courage has been ever deemed a prerequisite to Masonic advancement. You have been tested by earth, air, water and fire. At each step of your advancement, a degree of fortitude was demanded. You will not, then, be surprised to learn that a further test awaits you, not only of fortitude but of sincerity.

Coursing through your arteries and veins is a crimson fluid essential to life. So precious is it to every man that he who sheds his blood in defense of a cause, or in the line of duty, proves in the most decisive manner his devotion thereto.

I propose here, in the presence of the brethren, to take from you the amount of blood that you may voluntarily offer to sacrifice. The whole amount of blood in the human body is about 1/13 of the body's weight. In the bountiful provision of nature several pounds of this vital fluid may be lost and again restored. But, should the limit of safety be passed and your physical life be lost, your name will be enrolled among the gods, and you will be immortal. The worthy Mason surmounts all difficulties; surpasses all obstacles, and, to fear, becomes a hardened statue.

Terrible Brother, you will bare the right arm of the candidate. Place your staff in his right hand. (DONE)

TB: Brother Surgeon, the candidate has been prepared.

The Brother holds the arm of the candidate. Meanwhile, the Surgeon ties a cord around the arm, and when the vein is raised, he passes the point of a needle (clean) or penknife against a small point on the arm of the candidate. At the same time, a syringe filled with tepid water, is placed above the "scratch" on the arm, and water is allowed to trickle on the arm, the liquid falling to a bowl. After about 10-15 seconds, stop! Wipe the candidate's arm dry and place a bandage over the supposed cut.

VM: Mister {A.B.}, you probably can tell that you have been mock bled. This was done, not to trifle with your feelings, but to test your courage. It has been one of the landmarks of this institution, that the courage should be thus tested; and should any prove to be recreant to their promise, they would immediately be led out of the chamber without ever once beholding the beauties of our institution. I am satisfied that you possess the necessary courage, fortitude, manhood and perseverance to entitle you to receive the secrets of our ancient rite.

MISSING PAGE

[p 110]
...to give it deprives you of some luxury or comfort, and truly makes you poorer than before, it is the widow's mite, as acceptable in the sight of heaven as the rich man's costly offerings would be. Your gift is received and accepted by the lodge with grateful thanks.

0.22.

[p 111]
VM: Terrible Brother, seat the candidate.

The candidate is seated in a chair in front of the east.

VM: Soon, Sir, you are to reap the harvest of the trials you have endured. We are disposed to reward the sense pf beneficence you have just displayed. However, it is my duty to consult once more those with whom I am about to associate you to learn if there be no objection to present against your admission.

Any brother present may now ask through his Warden for leave to speak, either to object or defend the candidate from an objection. However, in each instance, the candidate having received a clear ballot, these objections are to be unwoundingly friendly and frivolous.

The Venerable Master must keep strict control. No real objection may be presented now. Such must have been made privately to the Master before the candidate was first brought in.

When all discussion has finished, the Venerable Master will say:

0.23.

[p 111]

On the altar, to the east, in front of the Bible, is placed the mannequin head representing "John the Baptist."

The candidate is again blindfolded and conducted into the lodge room via the preparation room door, stopping between the two columns.

VM: Brother Guide, you will deliver the candidate into the hands of the Senior Warden, so that he may teach him to make the first step in the angle of an oblong square. After that, conduct Him to the east, in order that he may consent to his obligation.

SW: Mister {A.B.}, you will approach the altar in the following manner: Stand erect. Advance your left foot. Now advance the right, bringing the heel of the right to the heel of the left, forming the angle of a square. Now repeat this step two more times.

The Senior warden Returns to his seat.

SW: Venerable Master, the candidate has taken the required steps.

VM: Place the candidate to the altar.

The Conductor causes the candidate to kneel on both knees. Both of the candidate's hands are placed on the Holy Bible, over which a square and a compasses are resting on the altar.

The Venerable Master raps three times and all brethren stand.

VM: Mister {A.B.}, the engagement which you have contracted contains nothing offensive with respect to your duty to God and to good morals, nor to the obedience you owe to the laws. This obligation is a serious matter and because of that it will be necessary that you consent of your own free will. Therefore, do you consent?

CAN: (ANSWER)

VM: You will repeat the words which I am about to say, exactly.

VM/
CAN: I, {A.B.}, in the presence of the Great Architect of the Universe, and of the brethren now here assembled, do most solemnly and sincerely promise and swear, that I will never reveal any of the secrets of Freemasonry that may be confided in me to any person in the world, who shall not be entitled at the time to receive them.

I furthermore promise and vow that I will bear true allegiance to the Supreme Council of the Inspectors General of the 33rd Degree, and will pay due obedience to its regulations, statutes and edicts; and that I will obey and abide by the by-laws, rules, and regulations of the Lodge of Apprentices to which I may belong, so long as I continue a member thereof.

Further, I promise to love my brethren, to succor them, and to aid them in their need, according to my ability.

To all of which I do most solemnly pledge my faith and honor; and if I should ever fail my obligation, may I be disgraced by my brothers, as if having my throat cut and be buried in the sands of the sea, that the ebb and flow bear me into eternal oblivion. May the Great Architect of the Universe aid me to keep and perform the same.

VM: Brother Senior Deacon, you will remove the cabletow from this new brother as he is now bound to us by his obligation.

The cabletow is removed as instructed. Terrible Brother then helps the candidate to rise and they return to a point between the two columns.

VM: My brothers, do your duty!

0.24.

[p 111]
The Venerable Master raps three times slowly. On the third rap, the Junior Warden removes the blindfold from the candidate. In the dim light he sees the head of "John the Baptist" in front of him.

VM: However horrible this scene may appear to you, let no fears arise in your mind.

0.25.

[p 116]
VM: If light, let it be so.

Wisdom excels folly as far as light excels darkness. The light shines in the darkness and the darkness has not overcome it. And the universe was without form and confused, and darkness brooded on the face of the abyss, and the spirit of God moved on the expanse of waters, and God said, "Let there be light." And, there was light.

The Master raps three times slowly. On the third rap, the guide removes the blindfold from the candidate. A puff of flame near the face of the candidate in provided by a blowpipe-like device. The Venerable Master raps three times on the head of the compasses.

VM: My brother, learn, by the precision of the compasses, to direct all your movements towards good.

O.26.

[p 119]
Then, over the neophyte's head, the Master strikes three blows, at equal
intervals, with his mallet, on the blade of his sword.

VM: Arise, my brother.

O.27.

[p 121]
VM: There are two signs: The Sign of Order is made
by standing and placing the flat of the right hand under
the throat, bent slightly toward the carotid artery of the
left, the four fingers pressed and the thumb separated in
the form of a square, and the left arm hanging out. This
Sign has an allusion to the penalty of your obligation is you
should ever violate it.

The Sign of Recognition is made after you have
been placed in order, by placing horizontally your right
hand near the right shoulder, and by a movement that
simulates the act of cutting your throat, then immediately
allowing your right hand to fall the length of the body. You
will find that you have, by this sign, depicted a square
upon yourself. This is also called the Guttural Sign.

The March of an Apprentice is made in three
steps in the following manner: Stand erect. Advance your
left foot. Now advance the right, bringing the heel of the
right to the heel of the left, forming the angle of a square.
Now repeat this step two more times. The first step
addresses the Venerable Master, the second, the Brethren in
the North, and the third, the Brethren in the South. This
march is to be used when entering the lodge and
approaching the altar and is to be followed by the Sign of
Recognition.

The Grip is made by engaging the right hand of
the one whom you wish to be acquainted with. You place
your thumb on the first knuckle of his index finger, and
then you tap lightly three times in the hollow of his hand.
This Grip, when given by a brother, is, at the same time, the
demand of the Sacred Word.

The Sacred Word, or "the Word", is not ever to be pronounced, much less written. In order to communicate it between Masons, they spell it by letter, the one to the other, orally, as follows:

(TO THE SENIOR DEACON)   Give me the Sacred Word.

SD: The Sacred Word cannot be pronounced.

VM: How will you give it?

SD: We may only spell it. I will give you the first letter and you will give me the second.

            B.

VM: O.

SD: A.

VM: Z.

This word signifies "force." You see the first letter on the column to the north. Remember, when one demands of you the Sacred Word of a Freemason, you shall respond: "The Sacred Word cannot be pronounced. We may only spell it. I will give you the first letter and you will give me the second."

[*The French ritual continues:*]

VM: The Battery of a Mason is made by slowly clapping the palms of the hand, three times, thus... You will repeat the battery with me. (DONE)

The Battery of Applause is made by clapping the hands three times in the same manner and stamping with the left heel at the third clap.

My brother, the things that you see us do will become familiar to you. We do all things in the "square" and that the number "3" is, to us, a mysterious number. Thus, when a brother asks you your age, you should reply that you are "three years of age". Do you understand?

CAN: (ANSWER)

MC: The president of this lodge is titled the Venerable Master. You will now respond by giving that title.

CAN: Venerable Master.

VM: This is good. I recognize you to be an Apprentice Mason.

0.28.

[p 122]
This section cannot be determined from resources available. It is unique to the Pike work. It undoubtedly refers to differences in Sacred Words and their pronunciations, as well as structural differences in each respective Rite's work. For example:

The Sacred Word of this degree is "boaz", but is variously pronounced as "bohaz" and "booz." In the Grand Orient of France, the Sacred Word of an Apprentice is "jakin (jachin)". In addition, the Rites in Europe make use of a "Word of the Semester" to be used as a password.

The March of an Apprentice is on the left foot. In the Grand Orient of France, the March is the same with the exception that it is on the right foot.

The Battery of this Degree is "* * *", but in the Grand Orient of France it is "** *".

Differences between this Work and the York (American) Rite equivalent degrees should already be known.

0.29.

[p 132]
...entering into a new life. you were made to wear the clothes of an initiate. All metals were removed from you, and you were deprived of the use of your sight.

By taking away all metals, we taught you of the condition of man before civilization in a state of nature; while the darkness presented to you man in complete ignorance.

[p 137]
A sword

0.30.

[p 150]
The Venerable Master and brethren clap (3 X 3). This is followed by the
acclamation three times:

All: Huzza!

0.31.

[p 150]
If he takes the pen and proceeds to write, the Master of Ceremonies will
strike a blow on the table with his sword. The Venerable Master, striking
another with his mallet will say:

VM: Have you so soon forgotten, or did you not
understand your obligation! Repeat that part of your
obligation!

If the candidate cannot, the Venerable Master will repeat it for him, then
continue:

0.32.

[p 150]
If the candidate refuses to write, the Venerable Master will commend him
for his prudence and memory of his obligation.

0.33.

[p 160]
VM: (1 rap) Brother Senior Warden, what age are
you?

SW: Three years.

VM: What is the length of time that masons work?

SW: From high noon until midnight.

VM: What is the hour?

SW: It is midnight.

VM: Since it is midnight and this is the hour in which Masons end their labor, brothers Senior and Junior Wardens, invite the brethren of the two columns to join with you and me in closing this Lodge of Apprentices.

JW: Brethren in the south, this lodge is about to be closed.

SW: Brethren in the north, this lodge is about to be closed.

The Venerable Master raps 3 times and all the brethren stand

VM: In the name of God and of Saint John of Scotland, and under the auspices of the Supreme Council (Mother-Council of the world), of the 33d and last degree of the Ancient and Accepted Scottish Rite of Free-masonry, for the Southern Jurisdiction of the United States, and by virtue of the authority in me vested as Venerable Master of this Lodge of Apprentice Masons, I declare it to be duly closed. With me, my brethren.

All give, the Venerable Master leading, the battery (3 x 3). This is followed by the Sign three times, each time saying:

All: Huzza!

The Junior Warden raps 3 times, followed by the Senior Warden, and then the Venerable Master, each rapping 3 times.

VM: The lodge is closed, my brethren. Go in peace, but first swear to keep profoundly secret every thing here done and transacted this night, not proper to be revealed.

Beginning with the Senior Warden, all brethren pass in procession in front of the Venerable Master, who, standing at the entrance of the Orient, holds out the hilt of his sword. Each, in turn, lays his right hand on the hilt, saying:

BR: I vow.

END DEGREE 1 SECRET WORK

DEGREE 2
FELLOW CRAFT

✝1.

[p 185]

SW: Brothers Senior and Junior Deacons [or Expert and Assistant Expert], you will determine if all present are Fellow-Craft Masons.

(1 rap)   Brethren, to order as Fellow-Craft Masons.

The officers remain at their stations, and they and the brethren remain seated, under the Sign of the order. Beginning in the east, the Senior Deacon [Expert] receives the password from the brethren on the north, while the Junior Deacon [Assistant Expert], likewise, receives the pass from the brethren on the south.

If either Deacon [Expert] fails to receive the password, or does not recognize a particular person as such, he directs him, by gesture to rise. If any brother knows the person rising to be a Fellow-Craft Mason in good standing, he will rise and so declare. It is not enough to have sat in a lodge with him. If no one vouches for the party, he will be required to withdraw to the Preparation Room for examination.

When none remain but Fellow-Craft Masons, and the Expert and Assistant Expert are satisfied, they will return to their places, and standing, the Junior Deacon [Assistant Expert] will say:

JD: Brother Senior Deacon, all on the column of the south are Fellow-Craft Masons.

SD: Brother Junior Warden, all on both columns are Fellow-Craft Masons.

JW: Brother Senior Warden, all present are Fellow-Craft Masons.

SW: Venerable Master, I have satisfied myself that all present are Fellow-Craft Masons.

VM: Then, in the name of God and St John the Apostle, let us proceed.

The Venerable Master raps once and all sit.

VM: Brother Senior Warden, are you a Fellow-Craft Mason?

SW: I have seen the Flaming Star.

VM: What brings you here?

SW: My obligation.

VM: What have you learned as a Fellow Craft?

SW: To acquaint and to correct myself with the chisel of morals.

VM: At what hour should we open our lodge?

SW: At high noon.

VM: What is the hour?

SW: It is high noon.

VM: Then, since it is the hour at which we open for labor, let us resume our work, for the benefit of our fellows, our country and mankind.

The Venerable Master rises and approaches the Senior Deacon [Expert]. Both make the Sign of the degree and then clasp right hands. The Master whispers the Sacred Word of a Fellow-Craft to the Senior Deacon [Expert]. They then step back.

VM: Brother Senior Deacon [Expert], carry the Sacred Word of the Second Degree to the Senior Warden.

The Senior Deacon [Expert] approaches the Senior Warden's station, who rises and receives the Word in the same way. The Senior Warden in turn gives the Word to the Junior Deacon [Assistant Expert] and orders him to carry it to the Junior Warden. The Deacons [Experts] return to their stations.

JW: (1 Rap)   Venerable Master, all is just and perfect.

VM: (1 rap)   It being high noon, and all being just and perfect, be pleased, brethren Senior and Junior Wardens to proclaim, on your respective columns, that I am about to open the labors of the respectable Lodge ...., No. ......, in the Second Degree.

SW: (1 Rap)   Brother Junior Warden, brethren who grace the column of the north, the Venerable Master announces to you that he is about to open the labors of the respectable Lodge ...., No. ......, in the Second Degree.

JW: (1 Rap)   Brethren who grace the column of the south, the Venerable Master announces to you that he is about to open the labors of the respectable Lodge ...., No. ......, in the Second Degree.

        (1 Rap)   It is proclaimed on the column of the south, brother Senior Warden.

SW: (1 Rap)   Venerable Master, it is proclaimed on both columns.

The Venerable Master raps three times and all brethren stand.

VM: To order, my brethren.

The Venerable Master takes off his hat, and says:

†2.

[p 185]
VM: With me, my brethren.

All give, Venerable Master leading, the battery (3 x 3). This is followed by the sign of the degree three times, each time saying:

All: Huzza!

†3.

[p 189]
The Deacon [Expert] prepares the candidate by divesting him of all metal, removing his jacket or coat; left foot, knee, arm, and breast bare; with a rope (cabletow) three times around his waist. The candidate is <u>not</u> blindfolded.

The room is darkened, with essentially the light of candles, illuminating the lodge room. The Deacon [Expert] conducts the candidate (who is holding a 24-inch gauge) to the Preparation Room door into the Lodge where he is required to rap (* * *).

SW: (1 rap) Venerable Master, an Apprentice knocks at the door of the temple.

VM: (1 RAP) See who this Apprentice is.

SW: (1 RAP) Brother Junior Warden, see who this Apprentice is that knocks at the door.

JW: (1 RAP) Brother Junior Deacon, see who this Apprentice is that knocks at the door.

NOTE: If there is a Pursuivant, the Junior Deacon will pass this and future orders to him, and he will reply to the Junior Deacon, what is set down for the latter, he then replying to the Junior Warden. This will be continually understood hereafter in all the Degrees.

The Junior Deacon or Pursuivant will entirely open one leaf of the door, if it have two.

PUR: Who comes here?

SD: Brother {A.B.}, an Apprentice who has worked the due time.

PUR: Is his master satisfied with him?

SD: He is.

PUR: Is this of his own free will and accord?

SD: It is.

The Pursuivant or Junior Deacon closes the door, turns and reports:

---

†4.

[p 194]
On reaching this position, the candiate will use the mallet and chisel upon
the rough stone (Ashlar), and then pass the chisel slightly over the smooth
stone (Perfect Ashlar).

†5.

[p 200]
...have my throat cut across...

†6.

[MISSING]

†7.

[p 206]
The candidate lays down his instruments. With his right hand, he lifts a
small stone and then uses the lever in moving a larger one.

†8.

[p 211]
The candidate will then lay down his tools and, at the trestle board, place
his right hand flat, so that this thumb and index finger may form a right
angle.

†9.

[p 220]
The Master of Ceremonies does as instructed. Then he conducts the
candidate (free-handed) once around the lodge room, as before. As they
pass the Venerable Master's station he raps (*** **), then each Warden raps
(*** **). They stop at the Venerable Master's station.

✝10.

[p 220]
The Venerable Master presents a sword to the candidate.

✝11.

[p 229]
The Master of Ceremonies hands the candidate the gavel, and leads him to the Rough Ashlar, on which he strikes with the gavel THREE blows at equal intervals.

MC: Venerable Master, the candidate has done his last work as a faithful Apprentice.

The candidate is conducted to in front of the Tracing Board of this degree. The Mysterious Star and Sacred Letter are illuminated in the east over the Venerable Master's station.

✝12.

[p 235]
As the Master of Ceremonies and candidate advance, the Senior Warden rises and leaves his station. The candidate is placed, facing east, about 6 feet west of the altar.

SW: Brother {A.B.}, you will approach the altar in the following manner: Stand erect. Advance your left foot. Now advance the right, bringing the heel of the right to the heel of the left, forming the angle of a square. Now repeat this step two more times. Now advance your left foot forward and to the right. Bring the heel of the right foot to the heel of the left. Now advance your left foot forward and to the left. Bring the heel of the right foot to the heel of the left.

Venerable Master, the candidate has taken the required steps.

VM: Brother Master of Ceremonies, place the candidate at the altar.

The Master of Ceremonies causes the candidate to kneel on both knees. The Conductor places in the candidate's hands on the holy bible, over which a square and a compasses are resting on the altar.

The Master raps three times and all stand.

VM: My brothers, about and to order with your sword in hand. the candidate is prepared to take the obligation of a Fellow Craft.

        Brother {A.B.}, your toils as a Fellow Craft are now about to begin. You have completed your work as an Apprentice. Your obligation as a Fellow Craft will not only bind you to secrecy, but also to the performance of the chief duties of brotherhood. it will contain nothing at variance with your duties to your God, your country, or your family. Are you ready to assume it?

CAN: (ANSWER)

VM: You will repeat the words which I am about to say, exactly.

VM/
CAN: I, {A.B.}, in the presence of the Great Architect of the Universe, and of the brethren now here assembled, do most solemnly and sincerely promise and swear, that I will never reveal any of the secrets of the degree of Fellow Craft that may be confided in me to any person in the world, who shall not be entitled at the time to receive them.

        I furthermore promise and vow that I will bear true allegiance to the Supreme Council of the Inspectors General of the 33d Degree, and will pay due obedience to its regulations, statutes and edicts; and that I will obey and abide by the by-laws, rules, and regulations of the Lodge of Fellow Crafts to which I may belong, so long as I continue a member thereof.

        Further, I will act as a true and faithful craftsman, to answer signs and obey summons, and to maintain the principles inculcated in the former degree.

        To all of which I do most solemnly pledge my faith and honor; and if I should ever fail my obligation, may I be disgraced by my brothers, as if having my heart torn out, my body burned and my ashes cast to the wind that there remain no more memory of me among the Masons. May God aid me to keep and perform the same.

VM: Brother {A.B.}, what you have repeated may be considered a serious promise, and as a pledge of your fidelity, and to render it a solemn obligation binding on you so long as you shall live, you will seal it on the Holy Bible with your lips.

The candidate kisses the Bible.

VM: Brother Senior Warden, as you are of the first column of this temple, since the candidate has demonstrated patience and steadfastness, and has served five years as an Apprentice, do you judge him worthy of being admitted among us?

SW: Yes, Venerable Master.

VM: Brother Junior Warden, do you, likewise, judge him worthy of being admitted among us?

JW: Yes, Venerable Master.

VM: Your progress in Masonry is marked by the position of the square and compasses. When you were made an Apprentice, both points of the compasses were hid. In this degree one is disclosed, implying that you have completed your work as an Apprentice and that your toils as a Fellow Craft are now to begin. You are now halfway between the things of earth and those of heaven; between the moral and political, and the philosophical and spiritual.

The Venerable Master grips the saber with his left hand and positions the strip of metal on the head of the kneeling candidate. Taking the gavel with his right hand and prepares to rap on the sword.

VM: To the Glory of the Grand Architect of the Universe, and under the auspices of the Supreme Council of the Ancient and Accepted Scottish Rite, and in virtue of the powers that are mine to confer, I, Venerable Master of this lodge, create, (RAPS SWORD) accept, (RAPS SWORD) and constitute (RAPS SWORD) Fellow-Craft Mason, Second Degree of the Scottish Rite, and member of this lodge.

Arise, my brother. (DONE)

The Master raps once and all brothers (excluding the Senior Deacon and Master of Ceremonies) return to their stations and sit.

VM: My brother, there are two signs of a Fellow Craft Mason: the Sign of Order is made by standing and placing the right hand, half-open, palm upwards, on the heart, the four fingers curved and the thumb raised in the form of a square.   At the same time the left hand, fully open, is raised to the height of the head, the palm in advance, and the fingers clenched with the thumb raised in a square, the elbow close to the body.   This sign has an allusion to the penalty of your obligation is you should ever violate it.

The Sign of Recognition is made after you have been placed in order, by returning the right hand horizontally across the heart, from left to right, then permitting both the right and left hands to drop simultaneously to their respective thighs.   You will find that you have, by this sign, depicted a square upon yourself. This is also called the Pectoral Sign.

The March of a Fellow Craft is made with the three steps of an Apprentice.   Now advance your left foot forward and to the right.   Bring the heel of the right foot to the heel of the left.   Now advance your left foot forward and to the left.   Bring the heel of the right foot to the heel of the left forming the angle of a square.

The Grip is made by engaging the right hand of the one whom you wish to be acquainted with.   You place your thumb on the first knuckle of his middle finger, and then you tap lightly five times in the hollow of his hand. This Grip, when given by a brother, is, at the same time, the demand of the Sacred Word.

The Sacred Word, or "the Word", is not ever to be pronounced, much less written.   In order to communicate it between Masons, they spell it by letter, the one to the other, orally, as follows:

(TO THE MASTER OF CEREMONIES) Give me the Sacred Word.

MC: The Sacred Word cannot be pronounced.

VM: How will you give it?

MC: We may only spell it. I will give you the first letter and you will give me the second.

        J.

VM: A.

MC: C.

VM: H.

MC: I.

VM: N.

This Word signifies "establish." You see the first letter on the column to the south. Remember, when one demands of you the Sacred Word of a Fellow Craft, you shall respond: "The Sacred Word cannot be pronounced. We may only spell it. I will give you the first letter and you will give me the second."

The Password of a Fellow Craft is SHIBBOLETH, which means "an ear of corn", or "a branch of an olive tree". It is to be given at the opening of a Lodge of Fellow Crafts.

The Battery of a Fellow Craft is made by slowly clapping the palms of the hand, five times, thus: (* * * *). You will repeat the battery with me. (DONE)

When a brother asks you your age, you should reply that you are "five years of age".

Brother Senior Deacon, you may return to your station. (DONE)

†13.

[p 239]

The Venerable Master approaches the candidate and makes a Tau Cross on his forehead, saying:

VM: I sanctify you to your work by the sign of the cross.

†14.

[p 241]

The candidate is conducted to a point in front of the Master's station. On cue, the Master of Ceremonies alters the appearance of the apron.

VM: My brother, you will wear your apron with the flap turned down, and the left corner tucked in the form of a triangle to contain the tools of your labor. This is the distinguishing badge of a Fellow Craft, and marks the progress that you have made in the science.

The new Fellow Craft is conducted to the pointed cubical stone, and is required to approach it by the five steps of the degree. His Conductor hands him a mallet and the candidate is required to make FIVE equally timed raps on the stone.

MC: Venerable Master, the candidate has done his first work as a new Fellow Craft.

†15.

[p 242]

VM: (1 rap) Brother Senior Warden, what age are you?

SW: Five years.

VM: What have you learned during this time?

SW: To be intelligent, honest, courageous, prudent, and charitable.

VM: What is the length of time that Masons work?

SW: From high noon until midnight.

VM: What is the hour?

SW: It is midnight.

VM: Since it is midnight and this is the hour in which Fellow Crafts end their labor, brothers Senior and Junior Wardens, invite the brethren of the two columns to join with you and me in closing this Lodge of Fellow Crafts.

JW: Brethren in the south, this lodge is about to be closed.

SW: Brethren in the north, this lodge is about to be closed.

The Venerable Master raps three times and all the brethren stand.

VM: In the name of God and of Saint John of Scotland, and under the auspices of the Supreme Council (Mother-Council of the world), of the 33d and last degree of the Ancient and Accepted Scottish Rite of Free-masonry, for the Southern Jurisdiction of the United States, and by virtue of the authority in me vested as Venerable Master of this Lodge of Fellow-Craft Masons, I declare it to be duly closed. With me, my brethren.

All give, the Venerable Master leading, the battery (3 x 3). this is followed by the Sign three times, each time saying:

All: Huzza!

The Junior Warden raps (*** **) times, followed by the Senior Warden, and then the Venerable Master, each rapping (*** **) times.

VM: (1 rap) The lodge is closed, my brethren. Go in peace, but first swear to keep profoundly secret every thing here done and transacted this night, not proper to be revealed.

Beginning with the Senior Warden, all brethren pass in procession in front of the Venerable Master, who, standing at the entrance of the Orient, holds out the hilt of his sword. Each, in turn, lays his right hand on the hilt, saying:

BR: I vow.

†16.

[p 243]
All give, the Venerable Master leading, the battery (3 x 3). This is followed by the sign three times, each time saying:

All: Huzza!

The Junior Warden raps (*** **), followed by the Senior Warden, and then the Venerable Master, each rapping (*** **).

VM: (1 RAP) My brethren, labors of this Lodge of Fellow Crafts is now suspended, and labor has been resumed in the degree of Entered Apprentice.

END DEGREE 2 SECRET WORK

DEGREE 3
MASTER MASON

*1.

[p 247]
...a human skeleton, a crown on its head, a dagger in its right hand, and a
gilt cup or goblet in its left.

*2.

[p 247]
...a white dove, just killed, its feathers stained with blood.

*3.

[p 248]
...sword, skull and two human thigh bones crossed.

*4.

[p 249]
...a coffin with a shroud, an apron, and a branch of acacia.

...coffin...

*5.

[p 249]
The head of the coffin it towards the west. At the foot of it is a square,
and at the head the compasses. Under the coffin is a sunken place in the
floor, in the shape of a grave.

*6.

[p 249]

The Senior Deacon [Expert] will spread the tracing board of the third degree on the floor.

When all are clothed, and in their places and stations, the Worshipful Master will say:

WM: (1 rap) Brother Senior Warden, what is the first duty of a Warden in the lodge?

SW: To assure himself that the temple is duly tiled, Worshipful Master.

WM: Be pleased to assure yourself of that, my brother, and cause the tiler to be informed that we are about to open this Lodge of Master Masons for the dispatch of business, that he may tile accordingly.

SW: (1 rap) Brother Junior Warden, be pleased to ascertain if the temple is duly tiled, and cause the Tiler to be informed that we are about to open this Lodge of Master Masons for the dispatch of business, that he may tile accordingly.

JW: (1 rap) Brother Junior Deacon [Assistant Expert], be pleased to ascertain if the temple is duly tiled, and inform the Tiler that we are about to open this Lodge of Master Masons for the dispatch of business, that he may tile accordingly.

The Junior Deacon [Assistant Expert] draws his sword, examines whether the key of the door is right, places it on the altar, opens the door, communicates the order to the Tiler on the outside, closes the door, raps on it 3 times at equal intervals, the Tiler answering with the same, and then again 3 times at equal intervals, which is repeated by the Tiler. And lastly, the Deacon raps once, which is repeated once by the Tiler.

The Junior Deacon [Assistant Expert] returns to his place, sheaths his sword, and says to the Junior Warden:

JD: Brother Junior Warden, the temple is duly tiled.

JW: (1 rap) Brother Senior Warden, the temple is duly tiled.

SW: (1 rap)   Worshipful Master, the temple is duly tiled.

WM: (1 rap) How tiled, my brother?

SW: With secrecy and brotherly love, by a worthy brother Master Mason, without the door, with a drawn sword.

WM: His duty there?

SW: To guard against the approach of all cowans and eaves-droppers, on the hills or in the vales, and to see that none enter here, except such as are duly entitled, and have the permission of the Worshipful Master.

WM: It is well, my brother. What is the second duty of the Senior Warden in the lodge?

SW: To know, with certainty, that all present are Master Masons.

WM: Be pleased, my brother, calling to your assistance the brother Junior Warden, to obtain that assurance, the brother Senior Deacon and Junior Deacon [Expert and his Assistant] demanding the password of a Master Mason from all.

SW: Brothers Senior and Junior Deacons [or Expert and Assistant Expert], you will determine if all present are Master Masons.

        (1 rap) Brethren, to order as Master Masons.

The officers remain at their stations, and they and the brethren remain seated, under the Sign of the order. Beginning in the east, the Senior Deacon [Expert] receives the password from the brethren on the north, while the Junior Deacon [Assistant Expert], likewise, receives the pass from the brethren on the south.

If either Deacon [Expert] fails to receive the password, or does not recognize a particular person as such, he directs him, by gesture to rise. If any brother knows the person rising to be a Master Mason in good standing, he will rise and so declare. It is not enought to have sat in a lodge with him. If no one vouches for the party, he will be required to withdraw to the preparation room for examination.

When none remain but Master Masons, and the Expert and Assistant Expert are satisfied, they will return to their places, and standing, the Junior Deacon [Assistant Expert] will say:

JD: Brother Senior Deacon, all on the column of the south are Master Masons.

SD: Brother Junior Warden, all on both columns are Master Masons.

JW: Brother Senior Warden, all present are Master Masons.

SW: Worshipful Master, I have satisfied myself that all present are Master Masons.

WM: Then, in the name of God and St. John the Apostle, let us proceed.

The Worshipful Master raps once and all sit.

WM: Brother Senior Warden, are you a Master Mason?

SW: I know the acacia.

WM: Where is it?

SW: At the grave of our brother Master Hiram.

WM: What does the acacia symbolize?

SW: Immortality, by its eternal green color.

WM: What is immortality?

SW: Enlightened thought that possesses merited divinity.

WM: From where to you come as a Master Mason?

SW: From the Middle Chamber.

WM: What is done in the Middle Chamber?

SW: The memory of our Master Hiram is kept in honor, and measures are taken to punish his assassins.

WM: What have you come here to do?

SW: To recover the Master's Word.

WM: How?

SW: By passing from the square to the compasses, over the tomb of our Master Hiram, by the aid of a branch of acacia.

WM: What brings you here?

SW: My obligation.

WM: How many compose a Lodge of Master Masons?

SW: Three, five, seven, or nine.

WM: When composed of nine, of whom does it consist?

SW: The Worshipful Master, the Senior and Junior Wardens, the Orator, the Almoner, the Treasurer, the Secretary, and the Senior and Junior Deacons.

WM: At what hour should we open our lodge?

SW: At high noon.

WM: What is the hour?

SW: It is high noon.

WM: Then, since it is the hour at which we open for labor, let us resume the work of the Middle Chamber, for the benefit of our fellows, our country and mankind.

The Worshipful Master rises and approaches the Senior Deacon [Expert]. Both make the sign of the degree and then clasp right hands. The Master whispers the Sacred Word of a Master Mason to the Senior Deacon [Expert]. They then step back.

WM: Brother Senior Deacon [Expert], carry the Sacred Word of the Third Degree to the Senior Warden.

The Senior Deacon [Expert] approaches the Senior Warden's station, who rises and receives the Word in the same way. The Senior Warden in turn gives the word to the Junior Deacon [Assistant Expert] and orders him to carry it to the Junior Warden. The Deacons [Experts] return to their stations.

JW: (1 Rap)   Worshipful Master, all is just and perfect.

WM: (1 rap)   It being high noon, and all being just and perfect, be pleased, brethren Senior and Junior Wardens to proclaim, on your respective columns, that I am about to open the labors of the respectable Lodge ...., No. ......, in the Third Degree.

SW: (1 Rap)   Brother Junior Warden, brethren who grace the column of the north, the Worshipful Master announces to you that he is about to open the labors of the respectable Lodge ...., No. ......, in the Third Degree.

JW: (1 Rap)   Brethren who grace the column of the south, the Worshipful Master announces to you that he is about to open the labors of the respectable Lodge ...., No. ......, in the Third Degree.

           (1 Rap)   It is proclaimed on the column of the south, brother Senior Warden.

SW: (1 Rap)   Worshipful Master, it is proclaimed on both columns.

The Worshipful Master raps three times and all brethren stand.

WM: To order, my brethren.

The Worshipful Master takes off his hat, and says:

WM: My brethren, let us return thanks to the Grand Architect of the Universe for the many blessings with which he has surrounded us, and implore his aid to enable us to perform our duties.

*7.

[p 250]
WM: With me, my brethren.

All give,Wworshipful Master leading, the battery (3 x 3). This is followed by the sign three times, each time saying:

All: Huzza!

*8.

[p 252]
The last Master raised is placed in the coffin in the lodge room, his feet
to the east, his left arm forming a square, his right hand on his heart. A
black cloth covers the body.

*9.

[p 255]
The candidate is prepared by being divested of all metal, giving him a
garment to wear; left foot, knee, arm, and breast bare; blindfolded, with a
rope three times around his waist. His apron is that of a Fellow Craft.

*10.

[p 263]
A cloth is suddenly flung over the candidate's head and he is seized.

SW: Are you guiltless? Lay, then, your right hand
upon the breast of this corpse.

          Oh, apostle of liberty, equality and fraternity, if
this man be not guiltless, let your wounds bleed afresh and
convict him of perjury.

The candidate is made to place his right hand as directed. After a few
seconds, he removes it.

*11.

[p 263]
The the Junior Warden conducts the candidate to the west side of the altar
and causes him to knee on two knees. The arrow from the hand of the
skeleton is placed in the candidate's left hand, with the point aimed at
his left breast.

WM: Brother Senior Warden, present to the Fellow
Craft the cup of obligation.

The Senior Warden proceeds to the altar and places the cup of obligation,
containing wine, in the candidate's right hand.

The Worshipful Master raps three times and all brethren stand. The Wardens and armed brethren form a Roof of Steel over the candidate.

WM: Brother {A.B.}, you will repeat the words which I am about to say, exactly.

WM/
CAN: I, {A.B.}, in the presence of the Grand Architect of the Universe, and of the brethren now here assembled, do most solemnly and sincerely promise and swear, that I am a true and loyal Fellow-Craft Mason, and am not the spy, emissary or an instrument of temporal or spiritual tyranny.

        I furthermore promise and swear, that in seeking to be raised from the square to the compasses, I am motivated strictly by a desire for instruction and of perfection in Masonry.

        In token of the truth and sincerity, and as a pledge of secrecy and fidelty, I do now drink this cup, praying that if I am now false and insincere, that which I take from it may become to me the most deadly poison; and that if I prove false hereafter, the arrows of death shall pierce my heart. So help me God.

WM: You will now drink of the cup.

The candidate takes a drink of wine.

WM: Brother {A.B.}, you may now arise.

The Worshipful Master raps onnce and all the brethren return to their stations. The Master of Ceremonies and candidate remain standing at the altar.

WM: Brothers Senior and Junior Wardens, how do you find the candidate?

*12.

[P 267]
The candidate arises, and is conducted three times around the lodge room by the Master of Ceremonies and the Senior Deacon. Both the officers place their swords, in a arch, over the candidate's head. On passing the Junior Warden, Senior Warden, and Worshipful Master's stations, each respective office raps once. The Worshipful Master is always the last to rap his

gavel on a given circuit. The following lesson is read during the three circuits:

LITURGY C.

[p 269, Liturgy p 164]

VM: God, in the Hebrew writings, is continually symbolized by LIGHT. The sun was regarded as His visible image. The "Word of God" is explained by Philo in Eusebius, to be the universal and invisible light, SOURCE substance or essence of the light recognizable by the senses, and which shines forth from the planets and stars. The word LIGHT was used to express this essence, of which visible light is the manifestation. The Deity was better expressed, as the mysterious essential FIRE, of which FLAME is the action, LIGHT is the outflowing or manifestation.

The worship of fire and light was the basis of all the religions of antiquity. Agni, the fire, and Indra, the light, were the highest deities of our ancestors the Aryans. And when Zarathustra, among the Bactro- or Irano-Aryans, imagined a spiritual God, Ahura Mazda, superior to these, and author and creator of the universe, with his seven emanations, the Amesha-Çpentas, the second of these was Asha-Vahista, the spirit of fire; and fire is continually called in the Zend-Avesta, the son of Ahura-Mazda. The Persian Mithra was the sun, but the original Bactrian and Iranian Mithra was the morning star.

In the Vedic hymns, composed at least 4,000 and probably 5,000 years before the birth of Christ, the sun, moon, planets and stars are bodies by which Agni and Indra, fire and light, manifest themselves. They are, all, Agni and Indra, in act, limited and defined by form and body.

The Avesta calls the sun the body of Ahura-Mazda. The Indo-Aryans had the same idea. By the Helleno-Aryans, the sun was regarded as the visible image of the Deity.

The Seven Amesha-Çpentas, or DIVINE EMANATIONS, known to the Hebrews by their median captivity, became the seven Archangels, of which one was assigned to each of the seven bodies, formerly called "the planets". They were still emanations or rays from the invisible essential light, which was the very Deity,--rays by which the Deity was manifested and shone forth, each being the Deity manifested in one mode and characteristic.

Accordingly, each Archangelic name has a reference to this light, which is the Deity. Tsaphiel, means the Splendor of Al. Raphael, the Healing of Al, reminding us of "the sun of righteousness rising with healing in his wings." Hamaliel, the Benignity of Al. Zarakiel, the Rising of Al. Auriel, the Light of Al. Gabriel, the Potency of Al. And Michael, the Image of Al.

On all the monuments of Mithra, we see by the side of that god seven altars or pyres, consecrated to the seven planets. And these and the seven candlesticks represented the seven spheres or vessels that shed abroad in the universe the ethereal light. By these altars the seven angels are seen. Sometimes, instead of the altars are seen seven stars, symbolized by the seven gates of the Mithriac cave, through which the initiates passed; and which passages are presented by your journeys.

The ancients thought that the natural home of the soul of man was in the highest regions of the universe, in the sphere of the fixed stars. Hence it was held to have descended through the seven planetary spheres, to illumine the body, to communicate to it form and movement, to vivify and animate it; in the same manner as, when the universe of matter was a shapeless chaos, the breath of God moved on the surface of the abyss.

The soul tends to reascend, as soon as it can free itself from the impediment of matter. The reascension of each soul would be more or less tedious and laborious, according as it was more or less clogged by the gross impediments of its sins and vices.

Except for the gravest sins there could be expiation; and by penance, repentance, acts of beneficence and prayer, symbolized by the tests of water, air and fire, the soul could be purified, and rise toward the ethereal region. But grave crimes were mortal sins, beyond the reach of such remedies.

The visible world is the image of the invisible world. The essence of the human soul is the image of God; and its home is above the stars. The equinoxes were the gates through which souls passed to and fro, between the hemisphere of light, and that of darkness. Near each of these gates passed the galaxy; and it was termed "the Pathway of the Souls."

The symbolic image of this passage among the stars, was a ladder reaching from earth to heaven, divided into seven steps or stages, to each of which was a gate, and at the summit an eighth, that of the fixed stars. You have already seen this Mystic Ladder in a former degree, though there it was represented as having three steps. It is by knowledge as well as morals the soul ascends toward the stars, and climbs the skies to its home.

An emanation of the ethereal fire, exiled from the luminous starry region, it descended through the planetary gates, and by the equinoctial and solstitial doors, along the Milky Way, to be immured in the prison-house of matter. There the body is its prison, until it shall at last return to its place of origin, its home, through the constellations and planetary spheres.

Through the gate of Capricorn, along the galaxy, and by the way of the seven spheres it must ascend. To reascend to the unity of its source, it must pass through a series of trials and migrations. The scene of these is the grand sanctuary of initiations, the world. Their primary agents are the elements; the means, are the sorrows, the trials and the calamities of life.

Thus the theories of the ancients were not mere barren speculations; but a study of the means for arriving at the great object proposed, the perfecting of the soul, and, as a consequence, that of morals and society and the state. The earth, to them, was not the soul's home, but its place of exile. Its home and birth-place was Heaven. To purify this soul of its passions, and weaken the empire of the body over it, to give him true happiness here below, and expedite his reascension to his home, was the object of initiation.

*13.

[P 285]
The Senior Warden rises and approaches the candidate.

SW: Brother {A.B.}, you will approach the altar in the following manner: Stand erect. Advance your left foot. Now advance the right, bringing the heel of the right to the heel of the left, forming the angle of a square. Now repeat this step two more times. Now advance your left foot forward and to the right. Bring the heel of the right foot to the heel of the left. Now advance your left foot forward and to the left. Bring the heel of the right foot to the heel of the left.

Being now placed at the head of the coffin, you will leap over the end of it, to a point one-third forward and to the right of it. Now leap, from right to left, over the coffin, to a point two-thirds from the head. Finally, leap, once again, from the left to the bottom of the coffin, both feet forward, heels touching.

Worshipful Master, the candidate has taken the required steps.

WM: Fellow Craft, since this test of you has been favorable, our confidence has increased. We will shortly disclose to you the circumstances relating to the unprecedented crime that has cast consternation among us. Before we may proceed, it will be necessary that you give us the assurance that you will not disclose anything of that which you will learn, either to the uninitiated, or to apprentices, or the same to fellow crafts, your brothers.

You have been in search of light. If you still desire to advance toward it, you must now assume a solemn and binding obligation, from which no earthly power can ever free you. It will in no way conflict with any duties you owe yourself, your family, your friends, your country, the human family, or your God; but it will bind you to secrecy and fidelity, and to the performance of the great duties of brotherhood.

Are you willing to take upon yourself that obligation?

CAN: (ANSWER)

WM: Brother Master of Ceremonies, place the candidate to the altar.

The candidate is caused to kneel on both knees. The Conductor places in the candidate's hands on the Holy Bible, over which a square and a compasses are resting on the altar.

The Worshipful Master raps three times and all stand.

WM: My brothers, about and to order with your sword in hand. The candidate is prepared to take the obligation of a Master Mason.

You will repeat the words which I am about to say, exactly.

WM/
CAN: I, {A.B.}, in the presence of the Great Architect of the Universe, and of the brethren now here assembled, do most solemnly and sincerely promise and swear, that I will never reveal any of the secrets of the degree of Master Mason that may be confided in me to any person in the world, who shall not be entitled at the time to receive them.

I furthermore promise and vow that I will bear true allegiance to the Supreme Council of the Inspectors General of the 33d Degree, and will pay due obedience to its regulations, statutes and edicts; and that I will obey and abide by the by-laws, rules, and regulations of the Lodge of Master Masons, to which I may belong, so long as I continue a member thereof.

Further, I will bear friendship and loyalty to all brother Master Masons, their widows and orphans, and pledge to help them according to my abilities and their needs.

Further, I will maintain a Master Mason's honor, in his absence as though he were present, and carefully preserve it as my own; that I will not injure him, nor knowingly suffer others to do so, if within my power to prevent, but, will boldly repel the slanderer of his good name.

Further, I will venerate truth, source of all good; and flee falsehood, source of all evil.

Further, I will act as a true and faithful craftsman, adhering to the principles of the square and compasses, to answer signs and obey summons of a Lodge of Master Masons, and to maintain the principles inculcated in the former degrees.

Further, I will maintain and uphold the Five Points of Fellowship in spirit as well as word.

To all of which I do most solemnly pledge my faith and honor; and if I should ever fail my obligation, may I be disgraced by my brothers, as if having my body severed into two parts, and my bowels torn out and burned, and the ashes thereof scattered to the winds. May God aid me to keep and perform the same.

WM: Brother {A.B.}, what you have repeated may be considered a serious promise, and as a pledge of your fidelity, and to render it a solemn obligation binding on you so long as you shall live, you will seal it on the Holy Bible with your lips.

The candidate kisses the Bible.

WM: Brother Senior Warden, as you are of the first column of this temple, since the candidate has demonstrated patience and steadfastness, and has served seven years as a Fellow Craft, do you judge him worthy of being admitted among us?

SW: Yes, Worshipful Master.

WM: Brother Junior Warden, do you, likewise, judge him worthy of being admitted among us?

JW: Yes, Worshipful Master.

WM: Your progress in Masonry is marked by the position of the square and compasses. When you were made an Apprentice, both points of the compasses were hid. In the Second Degree one point was disclosed. In this degree both are exhibited, implying that you are now at liberty to work with both those points to render the circle of your Masonic duties complete.

Arise, newly obligated brother. (DONE)

*14.

[p 294]

Having finished his devotions, Hiram was returning by the south entrance, when he was accosted by the first of the villians, who for want of another weapon, had armed himself with a 24-inch gauge, and in a threatening manner demanded the secrets of a Master.

The candidate represents Hiram. The Junior Warden acts as Jubela and stands in front of, and facing, the candidate and his Conductor. The Conductor will answer for the candidate.

HIRAM: Craftsman, why are you not at work?

JUBELA: Master, I seek this time to talk with you. I have retained this inferior rank for too along a time, and I desire to be advanced. Admit me into the office of Master.

HIRAM: I cannot. I alone an unable to accord you this favor. It must be done with the assistance of my brothers, King Solomon and King Hiram, of Tyre, and only after you have completed your time and have been sufficiently instructed. I will pass on your request to the Council of Masters when we next meet.

JUBELA: I am well enough instructed. You will not pass me unless you give me the Word of the Masters.

HIRAM: You are insane! This is not the way to receive the Master's Word. Work and persevere, and you will be rewarded.

JUBELA: I want the Master's Word or I will take your life!

HIRAM: You cannot receive it!

Jubela taps on the throat of the candidate with the 24-inch gauge and steps aside.

*15.

[p 294]
The Senior Warden plays Jubelo and stands in front of, and facing, the candidate and his Conductor. Jubelo roughly grabs the candidate's shoulder.

JUBELO: Master Hiram, give me the Word of a Master!

HIRAM: It cannot be given!

JUBELO: I want the Word of a Master or you shall die!

HIRAM: I will not!

Jubelo taps on the left breast of the candidate with the square.

*16.

[p 295]

The Worshipful Master plays Jubelum and steps in front of the candidate and his Conductor, and seizes the candidate by the shoulder, pushing.

JUBELUM: Master Hiram, you will give me the Master's Word!

HIRAM: I cannot!

JUBELUM: You will give me the secrets of a Master or you shall die!

HIRAM: Rather death than to violate the secret which to me has been confided!

Jubelum taps on the forehead of the candidate with the setting maul. The candidate is gently pushed backward into the empty coffin. A funeral pall is placed over the candidate so that he can no longer see anything that is happening to him.

JUBELA: Is he dead?

JUBELUM: I do not know, nether do I care. You can examine for yourself.

JUBELO: There he lies. He is dead, and we have gained nothing.

JUBELA: Did he speak no words?

JUBELUM: Nothing, after he fell. As I struck him, he threw up his hands in front of his forehead, crying, "Oh Lord, My God, is there no help for the Widow's son!"

JUBELO: Though the earth drinks the blood, it will still cry to heaven from the ground, like that of Abel. Let it cry. What is the blood of man more than the blood of the beast. If the Avenger of Blood pursues, no city of refuge will protect us.

*17.

[p 296]

...the body (candidate) lies, and taking the coffin, they carry it three times around the lodge room. Then lowering the coffin to the ground, they cover all, except for the candidate's head, with a dark cloth or carpet.

*18.

[p 301]

..."Oh, that my throat were cut across and my tongue torn out by the roots, that I had been an accessory to so great a crime."

And the second voice said, "Oh, that my heart were torn out from by breast and thrown to the beasts of prey, that I should have conspired to take his life."

And the third voice added, "Oh, that my bowels torn out and burned to ashes, and the ashes scattered to the winds of heaven, that I should have murdered our Master Hiram."

*19.

[p 308]

Azariah and three brethren advance, bend down, and make as if removing the covering on the grave.

BR1:   Look! That which was the Architect! The one who came from God. Maobon!

BR2:   Makhba-nak! The place where the one murdered was hidden!

AZARIAH: Here lies the remains of the Master Hiram. Look, here is his jewel!

The veil, over the candidate's head, is parted. Solomon then gives the sign of horror then the sign of despair.

SOLOMON: Oh Lord, my God! Is there no help for the son of the widow? The Master Hiram is no more. But he died bravely, refusing to betray his trust, and shall ever be to Masons an emblem of fidelity and honor.

You will see by the nature of the tools abandoned in this pit, the class of workmen whom we must search for. The murderers cannot escape. The unseen Avenger of Blood pursues them.

Alas, my brethren, since the fatal moment that we have been deprived of our master Hiram, the world has stopped, in darkness most heavy. All the work has been suspended. In our grief we have nothing to venture, but to recover the light. We lament the wickedness of this crime. A brother of virtue so rare has succumbed; to him alone possessed the secret of the initiated work. Who will dare, this day, to introduce himself and follow after?

Solomon again gives the sign of horror then the sign of despair.

SOLOMON: Oh Lord, my God! Is there no help for the son of the widow! The Master's Word is lost!...

*20.

[p 309]

...the sign involuntarily given by brothers Adoniram and Tsadoc at first sight of the body shall be the Sign of Horror. And, as I have silently resolved, the first words which were spoken at the grave shall be substituted in lieu of the Master's Word, until three masters shall know and be able to communicate it on the Five Points of Fellowship.

My brethren, you are charged to be particularly careful in observing whatever casual sign, token or word might occur among you while engaged in this last sad tribute of respect.

*21.

[p 310]

ADON.: By the grip of an Apprentice.

The Junior Warden steps over the coffin, takes the index finger of the right hand of the candidate, and pulls lightly.

ADON.: Boaz!

The Junior Warden feigns to see the finger of the candidate slip. He raises his hands to the sky and then lets them fall with despair.

ADON.:   Oh Lord, my God! The flesh leaves the bone!

SOLOMON: Brother Tsadoc, how shall this brother be raised to the new life?

TSADOC: By the grip of a Fellow Craft.

The Senior Warden steps over the coffin, takes the middle finger of the right hand of the candidate, and pulls lightly.

TSADOC: Jachin!

The Senior Warden feigns to see the finger of the candidate slip. He raises his hands to the sky and then lets them fall with despair.

TSADOC: Oh Lord, my God! All has come asunder!

SOLOMON: My brethren, is it not so that you will succeed to raise the body of our Master. Do you not recall that union makes for strength, and that without the help of others, we are unable to do anything. My brethren, assist me.

The Worshipful Master (Solomon) places his feet next to the feet of the candidate, bends toward him, takes hold of him by the right hand, and draws him up, aided by the brethren. The Worshipful Master then places his left hand around the back of the candidate, at the neck, and assumes the position of the "Five Points of Fellowship: (foot to foot, knee to knee, breast to breast, hand to shoulder, head to head). In this position he passes the Sacred Word.

SOLOMON: Mah-hah-bone.

           Mah

CAN: Hah

SOLOMON: Bone.

Solomon steps back and raises his hands.

SOLOMON: The Grand Architect of the Universe be praised!

The Worshipful Master, taking his sword in hand, lays the naked blade on the candidate's head, and the Junior Warden holds the two points of the

compasses. The Worshipful Master strikes three times with his mallet on
the head of the candidate, saying:

WM: May remorse and self-contempt, symbolized by
the two points of the compasses, torture you until until
death if you should ever violate your Masonic obligations.

*22.

[p 310]
He then strikes three blows with his mallet on the blade of the sword, over
the candidate's head, saying:

WM: Loyalty, Honor, Truth!

I will now communicate the signs, grips and
words of this degree.

My brother, there are three signs of a Master
Mason: The Sign of Order is made by standing and bringing
towards the heart the open right hand, palm upward, the
fingers of which are separate and the thumb erect as much
as possible, holding the hand horizontally, the right arm
close to the body.

The Sign of Recognition is made after you have
been placed in order, by drawing the hand horizontally, as
if to cut the breast with the thumb raised. Raise the hands
to the height of the head, the ends of the fingers touching,
and say, "Oh Lord, my God!" Let the hands now fall on the
apron, in an attitude of surprise and astonishment. This is
also called the Sign of Horror and alludes to the shock of
finding the body of the Master Hiram.

The Sign of Distress is made placing, palms out,
the two hands on top of the head, or on the forehead, the
fingers of which are interlaced. Then say, "Come to my
assistance, you children of the widow!" To this cry or to
this gesture, all Masters who observe this Sign are obliged
to hasten to the aid of the brother so giving it. The Sign
of Distress, in certain situations, may be made simply and
quickly by the reversing of the hands on the head, and
without uttering the cry for help.

The March of a Master Mason is made with the
five steps of a Fellow Craft. Now raise the right leg in a
semi-circle partially right and step forward. Now raise the

left leg and turn partway to the left, and step forward, bring the leg high enough to avoid an imaginary obstacle. Finally, raise the right leg, and repeat the maneuver, moving forward and to the right. bring the left leg up, heel to heel, forming the angle of a square.

The True Grip of a Master is made on the Five Points of Fellowship. It is made by each brother approaching and placing their right feet, touching, side by side. Each brother then positions right knee to right knee, left hand on the other's right shoulder, breast to breast. Taking each other's right hand they make the Strong Grip of the Master, by gripping so that the four fingers grip the wrist of the other. In this position, they whisper in the ear of the other the Sacred Word.

The True Grip of a Master signifies that even if a brother has, by sin and shame, sunken, in his own estimation and that of the world, into the depths from which there seems to be no redemption, still you will endeavor to raise him from this death to a new life of manliness, honor, and virtue, not contenting yourself with one trial, nor with two, but using in the third every means and inducement in your power.

The Sacred Word, or "the Substitute Word", is not ever to be pronounced, much less written. In order to communicate it between Master Masons, they must whisper it by syllable, the one to the other, orally, as follows:

(TO THE SENIOR DEACON) Give me the Sacred Word.

SD: The Sacred Word cannot be pronounced.

WM: How will you give it?

SD: We may only syllable it. I will give you the first syllable and you will give me the second.

MAH.

WM: HAH.

SD: BONE.

WM: This word, as well as the French derivative "Makhbenak", signifies "the place where the body of the murdered one was hidden." Remember, when one demands of you the Sacred Word of a Master, you shall respond: "The Sacred Word cannot be pronounced. We may only syllable it. I will give you the first syllable and you will give me the second.

You received the Sacred Word on the Five Points of Fellowship. The Five Points of Fellowship you remember are foot to foot, knee to knee, breast to breast, hand to shoulder, and head to head.

The password of a Master Mason is TUBALCAIN, who was the son of Lamakh, and a worker in brass and iron.

The Battery of a Master Mason is made by slowly clapping the palms of the hand, seven times, thus: (*** *** *). You will repeat the Battery with me. (DONE)

When a brother asks you your age, you should reply that you are "Seven years of age and more".

Brother Senior Deacon, you may return to your station. (DONE)

**23.

[p 340]
The Five Points of Fellowship are foot to foot, knee to knee, breast to breast, hand to shoulder, and head to head.

Foot to foot...

Knee to knee...

Breast to breast...

Hand to shoulder...

Head to head...

*24.

[p 343]
JW: The better to observe the sun at his meridian
height; to send the workmen to their labors and recall them
from work to refreshment, that the Worshipful Master may
have honor and glory thereby.

WM: (1 RAP) Brother Senior Warden, where is your
station in the lodge?

SW: In the west, Worshipful Master.

WM: Why do you occupy the west?

SW: As the sun sets in the west to close the day, so
is the Senior Warden in the west to assist the opening and
closing of the lodge, to pay the workmen, and send them
away content and satisfied.

WM: Where is the Master's station in the lodge?

SW: In the east, Worshipful Master.

WM: Why in the east, my brother?

SW: As the sun rises in the east to begin his course
and open the day, so is the Worshipful Master in the east to
open the lodge, to direct it in its work, and to enlighten it
with his knowledge.

WM: Brother Senior Warden, what age are you?

SW: Seven years and more.

WM: Why do you say this?

SW: Seven years and more is an undetermined
number that expresses the age of wisdom and represents the
maturity of a Master Mason.

WM: What is the length of time that Masons work?

SW: From high noon until midnight.

WM: What is the hour?

SW: It is midnight.

WM: Since it is midnight and this is the hour, our work has ended in the Middle Chamber. Brother Senior and Junior Wardens, invite the brethren of the two columns to join with you and me in closing this Lodge of Master Masons.

SW: Brethren in the north, this lodge is about to be closed.

JW: Brethren in the south, this lodge is about to be closed.

The Worshipful Master raps three times and all the brethren stand

WM: My brethren, the Great Source and Origin of all that is, having allowed us to receive the Master's Word, let us, that it may ever remain engraved upon our hearts, and we be not again plunged into darkness, cleanse our souls of all impurities, and pray for his aid and support.

PRE: Grand Architect of the Universe, immortal and inexhaustible source of light and life, the workmen of this temple give you thanks, ascribing to you whatever that is good, useful, or glorious there may be in the works of this day. Continue to protect them. Guide them inward in the way that leads toward perfection, and let harmony, peace and concord ever cement their work. Let friendship and good works ever adorn this temple and here dwell and inhabit. Let generosity, loving kindness and courtesy always characterize the brethren of this lodge, and in the outer world help them to show by their words and conduct that they are true children of the light. Amen.

All: So mote it be.

WM: In the name of God and of Saint John of Scotland, and under the auspices of the Supreme Council, of the 33d and last degree of the Ancient and Accepted Scottish Rite of Free-masonry, for the Southern Jurisdiction of the United States, and by virtue of the authority in me vested as Worshipful Master of this lodge of Master Masons, I declare it to be duly closed. With me, my brethren.

All give, the Worshipful Master leading, the battery (3 x 3). This is followed by the sign three times, each time saying:

All: Huzza!

The Junior Warden raps (*** *** *), followed by the Senior Warden, and then the Worshipful Master, each rapping (*** *** *).

WM: (1 rap) The lodge is closed, my brethren. Go in peace, but first swear to keep profoundly secret every thing here done and transacted this night, not proper to be revealed.

Beginning with the Senior Warden, all brethren pass in procession in front of the Worshipful Master, who, standing at the entrance of the Orient, holds out the hilt of his sword.   Each, in turn, lays his right hand on the hilt, saying:

BR: I vow.

END DEGREE 3 SECRET WORK

הָאוּלָם וַהֲדַר הַתּוֹךְ

THE PORCH

AND

THE MIDDLE CHAMBER

ספל חככה.

ספר הסכרת.

THE BOOK

OF

THE LODGE.

Ἱεροδομ,

A∴ M∴ 5632.

INDEX.

GENERAL MATTERS, AND DEGREE OF APPRENTICE.

INTRODUCTORY.

This Ritual represents in its Ceremonies the peculiarities of a particular Masonic System.

It is therefore not to be regarded as a mere formula, that may be altered at pleasure.

Those portions which are of greater importance are to be distinguished from those of less moment. The former are sacramental, and must in all cases be strictly observed. With the latter, a departure from the stated forms of expression is allowable.

Of the portions which permit of no alteration are to be reckoned the forms of opening and closing the Lodge, and those parts of the ceremonial of preparation and initiation which apply immediately to the matter itself. The lessons of instruction may in part be omitted, and afterward given the Initiate to read; the prayers may be varied and departed from, when it appears proper. Still, it would not seem desirable, even as to these portions, to be too solicitous for new forms or expressions, as the Ritual itself offers sufficient variety. He who can be stimulated only by continual variations of phrase, shows thereby that the empty forms engage his attention far more than the meaning which the forms envelope. It is also exceedingly desirable that all the Brethren should, by frequent repetition, make themselves *thoroughly* conversant with the very terms and phrases used in the work; the uniformity and permanency whereof form, as it were, a force of cohesion, that binds together in unity all the Brethren of the Lodge.

The Rituals of these degrees of the Ancient and Accepted Scottish Rite are only to be found in the French language. But it seems evident that much of the formulistic portion of the

work is translated, not very literally or closely, from the English;
which was doubtless done when the first English Lodge was
established in France; and therefore, in re-translating, the old
and sacramental phraseology is retained in this Ritual as the
true equivalent of the French, though it does not always follow
it word for word.   On some points, where the *Rit Moderne* differs
from the Ancient and Accepted Scottish Rite, the variations are
given in notes.

In preparing this Ritual, the Sov.·. Grand Commander of the
Supreme Council at Charleston has used MSS. Rituals in his
possession, and the "*Guide des Maçons Ecossais*," a printed
work, for the Ancient and Accepted Rite; and MSS. Rituals, the
Régulateur Symbolique and the *Régulateur des Maçons*, for the
Rit Moderne. He has derived much assistance from the "*Thui-
leur Universel*," in MSS., of *de l'Aulnaye*, and the Abiman Re-
zon of Georgia, the work of Ill.·. Bro.·. ˙ROCKWELL; and is
also under obligation to the Ritual of Bro.·. V. A. DE CASTRO.
The old work is here much enlarged; and the lectures of instruction have been in part written and in part compiled by himself

I.

MASONRY.

MASONRY, more appropriately called FREE-MASONRY,—in French, *Franc Maçonnerie*,—has received many definitions.

The definition given of the Order by the Grand Orient of France is: "The Order of Frank Masons is an association of wise and virtuous men, whose object is to live in perfect equality, to be intimately connected by the ties of esteem, confidence, and friendship, under the name of Brethren; and to stimulate each other to the practice of the Virtues."

An English definition is, that "Free-Masonry is a system of Morality, veiled in Allegory and illustrated by Symbols."

Each definition is exceedingly imperfect. The Order of Free-Masons is, or ought to be, an association of intelligent, virtuous, disinterested, generous, and devoted men, regarding each other as Free, Equals, and Brothers, and bound by the obligations of Fraternity to render each other mutual assistance. And Free-Masonry is a system and school, not only of morals, but of political and religious philosophy, suggested by its Allegories and concealed under its Symbols. And, including in itself several degrees of Knighthood, it is also a Chivalric Order, requiring the practice and performance of the highest duties of the Man, the Citizen, the Patriot, and the Soldier.

The true definition of the Free-Masonry of the Ancient and Accepted Scottish Rite is this: It is an advance toward the Light; a constant endeavor, in all its Degrees, to elevate the Divine that is in Man, the Spiritual portion of his compound nature, his Reason and his Moral Sense, above, and make it dominant over, and master of, the human, earthly, and material portion of his nature, his passions, and his sensual appetites.

This Ritual is intended for *instruction* only, in the States of the Southern jurisdiction, where there are not Lodges working in the Ancient and Accepted Scottish Rite; to be studied and understood before investiture with the fourth degree. For, without it, the system of that Rite is incomplete, and even like a fabric without foundation.

II.

THE LODGE.

ITS OFFICERS, DECORATIONS, ETC.

The officers of a Lodge are twelve in number. They are, and rank, as follows:

⊙ .. 1. The Venerable Master............Le Vénérable Maître.
⊕ .. 2. The Senior Warden................Le Premier Surveillant.
○ .. 3. The Junior Warden...............Le Second Surveillant.
♉ .. 4. The Orator......................L'Orateur.
▢ .. 5. The Treasurer...................Le Trésorier.
△ .. 6. *The Secretary.................Le Sécrétaire.
♌ .. 7. The Almoner....................Le Hospitalier ou Aumonier.
♄ .. 8. The Senior Deacon or Expert......Le Premier Diacre ou l'Expert.
♃ .. 9. The Master of Ceremonies........Le Maître des Cérémonies.
♂ .. 10. The Junior Deacon or Assistant Expert.................Le Second Diacre ou Couvreur.
♀ .. 11. The Steward...................Le Maître des Réfections.
✗ .. 12. The Standard-Bearer............Le Porte-étendard.

There is also always a Tiler (Tuilleur) (†) on the outside of the entrance-door of the Lodge-room .

There may also be a Pursuivant (⚹), to be seated close to the door on the inside, and to attend to alarms there .

The Lodge is an oblong square or parallelogram, about one-fourth of which is separated from the other three-fourths by a railing, and its floor is higher than that of the body of the Lodge by three small steps. In the middle of the railing is an opening

---

* Sometimes the Secretariat is divided between two officers; the Keeper of the Seals and the Keeper of the Archives.

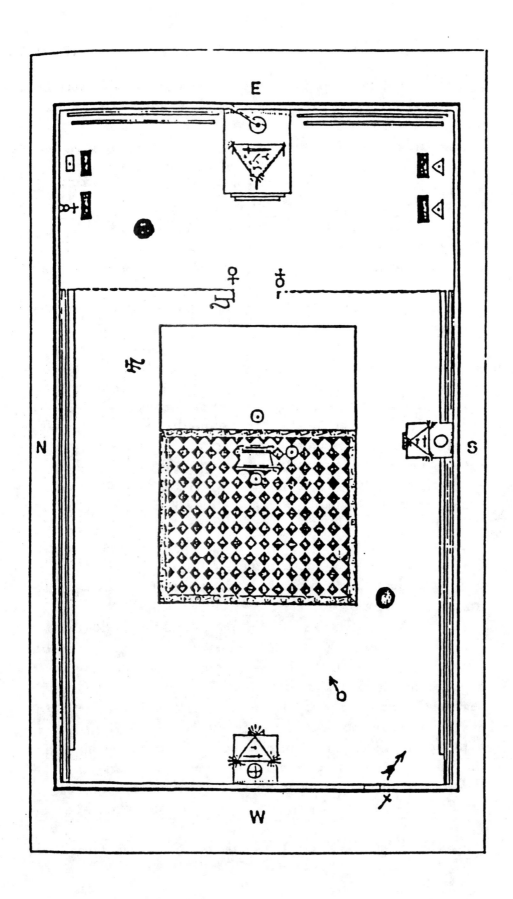

nine feet wide. The railing should be made with small gilt
rods and horizontal bars, from which light-blue curtains hang.
The height of these should not be more than five feet.

The part of the Hall so cut off from the rest, is, or is supposed to be, the Eastern part of it. It is therefore called "The
East," or "The Orient." The principal entrance to the Hall
is always at the opposite end, or in the West.

The floor of the body of the Lodge represents a Mosaic or
Tesselated Pavement, being composed of alternate lozenges of
black and white, with a wide bordering all round it, which,
accommodating itself to the indentations of the lozenges, is
of course "indented" or "denticulated." The color of this
bordering should be sky-blue.

At the extreme East is a platform, to which one ascends by
three steps. On this is an arm-chair for the Venerable Master.
In front of him is a triangular table, on which are to be a naked
sword, a mallet, three lights, and implements for writing.

On each side of the Master's table should be a light, slender,
fluted column, of the composite order, an arch springing from
one to the other. From the middle of the arch depends an
equilateral triangle of bars of yellow metal, in the centre of
which, fixed to invisible wires, is the old Hebrew letter ﬡ
[*Yud.*]

On the right of the Master, to the front, within the railing, is
the altar of incense, a short, truncated, fluted column; and between the door and the South is the altar of ablutions, a like
truncated column.

The Brethren at large sit on the North and South sides of the
Hall, the seats and Brethren on each side being styled the COL-
UMN of that side. The Senior Warden sits in the extreme West,
opposite the Master; and the Junior Warden on the South side
near to the wall, half-way the column of the South; or in the
West, on the South side of the Senior Warden. Each sits on
a platform raised one step, and has a table before him, like
the Master's, and on each table are a *sword*, a *mallet*, and *three
lights.* On each side the table of each is a column, those of
the Senior Warden, *Corinthian*, those of the Junior Warden,
Ionic.

All the tables, the altars, the seats, and the stool of the altar of obligation, are covered with bright blue cloth; and curtains of the same extend to the floor in front of the tables of the three Dignitaries. On each curtain of the Master's table is embroidered, in crimson, or painted, a SQUARE: on each of those of the Senior Warden's, a LEVEL: and on each of those of the Junior Warden's, a PLUMB.

Toward the East is spread on the floor, at the proper time, the TRACING-BOARD of the Degree in which the Lodge may be working; a square or oblong cloth, painted on which are the Symbols or Emblems of the Degree.

On the West side of the Tracing-Board is the Altar of Obligation, square and 3½ feet high, with a brazen plate covering the top, and horns or flames of brass at each corner. Upon this altar will always be the Hebrew Pentateuch, or a roll of parchment representing it, the Book of Constitutions, the SQUARE and the COMPASS, the latter always opened to 60 degrees.

On each of the East, South, and West sides of the altar, respectively, must always be a lighted candle, the three forming an equilateral triangle. Each *should* be long and large, and of blue wax, the candlesticks upon slender pedestals about three feet in height.

There is room for a person to pass between the wall and the seats of the Senior and Junior Wardens, respectively. The same is the case with the Master's seat.

The walls of the Lodge should be hung from ceiling to floor with light-blue cloth. This must at least be the case with the East.

On each side of the entrance is a column, proportioned according to the dimensions given in the Book of Kings, and consequently short and heavy in proportion to its diameter; these dimensions, as there given and corroborated by Ezekiel, being 18 cubits in height, and the capitals upon them 5 additional cubits, and the diameter 4 cubits.

The capitals should be carved as if formed of the seed-vessels of the lotus, covered with wreaths or chains, and lace or network, and surmounted by pomegranates. The one on the South is called YAKAYIN; that on the North, BAAZ, or BOAZ: [יכין and בעז]. They were undoubtedly, like those given on the next page, from an ancient Egyptian Temple.

In the centre of the Mosaic pavement is a five-pointed Star, emitting rays.

The capital (or chapiter) and upper portion of an Egyptian column next given, are also copied from Gau's Great Work on the Antiquities of Nubia, published by the French Government. In this there are three rows of imitations of the seed-vessel of the *lotus* or lily, which was the "lily-work" of the columns of the Temple of Solomon, and which the capital as a whole represents.

By measuring the height and diameter of the columns on this page, it will be seen that the proportions of these are the same, or nearly so, as those of the Temple at Jerusalem,

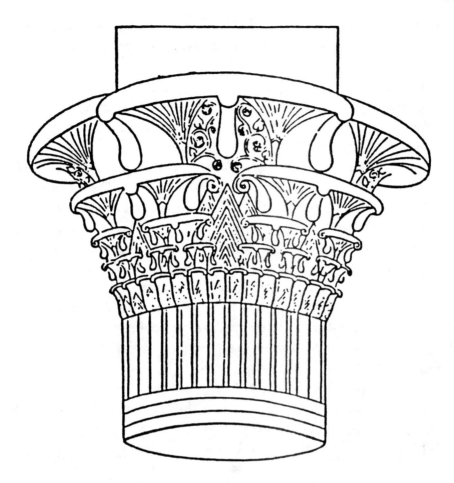

as given in the Book of Kings; and also that the proportion of the height of the capital to the height of the shaft is as stated in that Book.

Visitors, entitled to be so, are seated in the East, on either side of the Master.

The seats of the other officers will appear by the plan given above, in which each is designated by the character prefixed to each in the list. There are oblong tables for two Secretaries, or one and his assistant: and also one for the Treasurer and one for the Orator.

On the Altar of Incense are a tripod, censer, and cups containing perfumes for burning. On that of ablutions is a brazen laver always containing pure water.

On the North side of the Hall are four columns, two Tuscan and two Doric, of the same height as those of the Wardens.

In addition to the Altar lights, and those before the officers, there must be twelve movable lights, always ready for the reception of visitors.

The points of the Square upon the Altar must be toward the East; consequently, those of the Compass toward the West. If the Lodge possesses a regular Gavel of steel, it should also be on the Altar.

As the Tracing-Board or Painting contains the Symbols of Free-Masonry, it is always spread out when the Lodge is at work. The Deacons will spread it, while the Brethren are being clothed, before opening.

On the Treasurer's table will be two lights, implements for writing, the box of fraternal assistance or for contributions, and the clothing and insignia for the candidate.

On the Secretary's table, besides his books and papers, two lights, the Register of Visitors, the ballot-box, and the pouch Propositions, which is a bag of velvet or silk, attached to a small hoop, and with a short handle.

The ceiling will represent the Heavens. Over the East is painted a great Sun, shining; over the Senior Warden, a Crescent Moon; over the Junior Warden, a five-pointed Star.

All around the wall, just below the ceiling, is painted, in French Lodges, a knotted cord or rope (*la houppe dentelée*), about six inches in diameter, with tassels dependent from it at each corner. The knots are 81 in number. This is not used in this jurisdiction.

On the ceiling, also, particular Stars and Constellations are painted. In the centre, the three stars in the belt of ORION; and between them and the Northeast, the PLEIADES and HYADES, one of which is ALDEBARAN; half-way between ORION and the Northwest, REGULUS in Leo; in the North, URSA MAJOR; in the Northwest, ARCTURUS; West of Regulus, SPICA VIRGINIS; in the West, ANTARES; in the South, FOMALHAUT; over the East, also, is JUPITER, and over the West, VENUS; MERCURY, close to the Sun; and MARS and SATURN, near the centre of the ceiling. The Stars in the belt of *Orion* represent the number 3; the *Hyades* 5; the *Pleiades* and *Ursa Major*, 7. The five *royal Stars* are ALDEBARAN, ARCTURUS, REGULUS, ANTARES, and FOMALHAUT.

III.

TITLES, BADGES, CLOTHING, ETC.

In the first two degrees, the Master is styled VENERABLE: the other Dignitaries and Officers are styled, simply, BROTHER and BRETHREN.

In the third degree, the Master is styled WORSHIPFUL; the Wardens, MOST VENERABLE; and the Master Masons, other than the three Dignitaries, VENERABLE.

☞ It is not allowable, in addressing or speaking of an Officer or Brother, in the Master's Lodge, to omit his proper title. The terms *Dear*, and *Very Dear*, prefixed to the word *Brother*, or *Brethren*, in addressing an Officer or Brother, or Officers or Brethren, are represented in the Ritual by the Initials D∴ or V∴ D∴.

The jewels or badges of the Dignitaries and Officers are:

For the Master.................A Square.

For the Senior Warden..........A Level.

For the Junior Warden.........A Plumb.

For the Orator.................An Open Book, or a Roll.

For the Treasurer..............Two Keys, crossed.

For the Secretary..............Two Pens, crossed.

For the Almoner................An Open Hand.

For the Expert.................A Gavel.

For the Master of Ceremonies.....The Compasses, opened to 90 degrees in the Arc of a Circle graduated.

For the Assistant Expert........The 24-inch Gauge.

For the Steward................Two Wands, crossed.

For the Standard-bearer.........A Pennon.

For the Pursuivant.............An Arrow.

For the Tiler..................A Sword.

If the Secretariat is divided:

For the Keeper of the Seals.......A Signet-Ring.

For the Keeper of the Archives...Two Pens, crossed.

Each Jewel enclosed in a triangle; and the whole of Silver, and not more than two inches in length.

The dress should be a black coat, black pantaloons, and black or white vest. Master Masons wear their hats in each of the Lodges.

The *clothing* is a *square* apron of white lamb-skin (*not* of cotton or linen), tied by a blue silk cord, which ends in front with tassels. The apron is entirely plain, without any emblems or devices, lined with light-blue silk, and edged with light-blue ribbon, no more or less than half an inch wide. The flap is cut to a point in the middle, and lined and edged like the main apron. The width and depth of the apron, fourteen inches.

The Dignitaries alone wear scarfs of light-blue silk. All Officers and Brethren wear swords, steel-hilted, with light-blue belts round the body. The scabbard is of blue leather and steel-mounted.

All wear white gloves. These are part of the clothing. They should be of silk or white leather.

IV.

VISITORS AND HONORS.

EVERY Lodge has a Book, called The Register of Visitors. Before the Lodge opens, this book is taken to the ante-room, and no Visitor can be admitted until he has inscribed on the Register his name, his Lodge, if a member of one, and his Office or rank. When all are inscribed, the Book is taken into the Lodge.

Visitors in possession of other degrees and dignities than those of the Ancient and Accepted Scottish Rite, recognized in the State or country where the Lodge is held, as Masonic, if superior to those they hold in that Rite, may be received with the Honors appropriate, not of right, but by courtesy.

The scale of equivalents is as follows:

The American and English Royal Arch Degrees, and those of Royal and Select Master, are equivalent only to that of Perfection, or the 14th.

The degree of Templar, to that of Rose Croix.

The dignities of actual Grand Master of Masons of a State, or Grand High Priest of a State, or the Presiding Officer of a Grand Council of Royal and Select Masters of a State, and of Grand Commander of an Encampment of Templars of a State, are equivalent to that of Grand Commander of a Consistory of the 32d degree, other than that of the jurisdiction.

No Honors are rendered to past rank, outside of the Ancient and Accepted Rite.

Of these four, a Grand Master of Masons has precedence; a Grand Commander of Templars is next; a Grand High-Priest next; and a Presiding Officer of a Grand Council of R. and S. Masters, last.

The dignities of Grand King and Grand Scribe of a State Grand Royal Arch Chapter, and those of Generalissimo and Captain-General of a State Encampment of Templars, are equivalent to that of Prince of the Royal Secret.

Those of Grand Senior and Grand Junior Warden of a Grand Lodge, and of the Second and Third Officers of a Grand Council of R. and S. Masters, are equivalent to that of Kadosh. No Honors are paid to other Subordinate Officers of Grand Bodies.

The dignities of Grand Master of Templars of the United States or of any other nation, and of General Grand High-Priest of the United States, are equivalent to that of Sovereign Grand Inspector-General, not an active or Emeritus member of the Supreme Council.

The dignities of Generalissimo and Captain-General of Templars, of the United States, or of another nation, and of General Grand King and Scribe of the General Grand Chapter of Royal Arch Masons of the United States, are equivalents of that of a Commander-in-Chief of a Consistory of the 32d Degree.

Dignities of the Rite of Misraim, the Egyptian Rite, Rite of Memphis or Ancient and Primitive Rite, and the Rite of The Temple at Paris, are not recognized.

In receiving visitors, the lights taken out are termed STARS. Visitors are introduced in classes, and with the honors following.

Brethren of the first three degrees, the Brethren standing and under the Sign of order.

Masons of the 14th Degree, with two Stars and two Swords.

The Princes of Jerusalem, 16th Degree, with three Stars and three Swords.

Knights Rose Croix, Actual Masters of Blue Lodges, and Actual Presiding Officers of Lodges of Perfection and Councils of Princes of Jerusalem, with four Stars and four Swords.

Knights Kadosh and actual Presiding Officers of Chapters of Rose Croix, with five Stars and five Swords.

The Actual Commander of a Council of Kadosh, and Princes of the Royal Secret, with six Stars and six Swords, and Arch of steel.

The Commander-in-Chief of a Grand Consistory other than that of the Jurisdiction, with seven Stars and seven Swords, and Arch of Steel.

The Commander-in-Chief of the Grand Consistory of the Jurisdiction, and all Deputy Inspectors-General of the 33d degree, regularly commissioned by the Mother-Supreme Council, and all Sovereign Grand Inspectors-General, of the 33d degree, other than those hereinafter mentioned, with eight Stars and eight Swords, and Arch of Steel.

All Active and Emeriti Members of the Mother-Supreme Council, and her Special Representatives and Deputies, and Active Members of other Supreme Councils in alliance with the Mother-Supreme Council, with nine Lights and nine Swords, Steel Arch, swords clashing and mallets beating.

A Sovereign Grand Commander of another Jurisdiction, or a Past Sovereign Grand Commander of *any* Jurisdiction, with ten Stars and ten Swords, Steel Arch, swords clashing and mallets beating.

The Special Delegate and Proxy of the Sovereign Grand Commander of the Jurisdiction, or the Lieutenant Grand Commander of the Jurisdiction, with eleven Stars and eleven Swords, Steel Arch, swords clashing and mallets beating.

The Sovereign Grand Commander of the Jurisdiction, with twelve Stars and twelve Swords, Steel Arch, swords clashing and mallets beating.

But no honors are to be rendered to any Mason whose dignity or rank in the Ancient and Accepted Rite shall be inferior to that of the Presiding Officer; nor when the Commander-in-Chief of the Grand Consistory of the State shall already have been received and is present: except, in *any* case, when the Visitor is an *active* member of the Supreme Council, or a Sovereign or Past Sovereign Grand Commander, or the special Delegate or Proxy of the Sovereign Grand Commander.

While receiving visitors entitled to honors, all the Brethren and the Officers, except the Master, will be uncovered. He uncovers to no one.

———————

V.

PROPOSING AND ELECTING MEMBERS.

No Profane* can be admitted who has not attained the age of twenty-one years, or who is not free-born, of free and not servile condition, of respectable profession, trade, or employment; no atheist, nor in his dotage; or who is not master of his own person and actions, of some degree of education, at least able to read and write, of good character, and well recommended.

No domestic or servant of any class can be admitted; no professional gambler; no person without visible means of decent support; no one following any low, vile, abject employment.

No monk or Jesuit can be admitted; nor any tool or instrument of any unlawful tyranny or usurpation.

No person whatever can, under any pretext, ever be admitted to a degree without full payment of the regular fee.

The final vote on the question of admission cannot be taken until the third meeting of the Lodge after and including that at which he is proposed.

The interval between proposal and initiation will *regularly* be three months; but this may be reduced to forty-five days, if in that time there have been three meetings, with due notice of each to all the Brethren.

In every case, the Petition for admission of the Profane, written and signed by himself, will be presented, in the following form:

———————

* *Profanus*—a person *profano*, outside of the Temple—one not of "The Holy House of the Initiated." The word has no odious meaning.

" *To the Worshipful Master, the Most Ven∴ Wardens and Ven∴ Brethren of* ....*Lodge, No*......, *of the State of* ...., *of the Ancient and Accepted Scottish Rite of Freemasonry.*"

" I, A—— B——, being free by birth, and of the full age of twenty-one years, do declare that, unbiassed by any solicitation of friends or others, and uninfluenced by mere curiosity, or by mercenary or other unworthy motives, I freely and voluntarily offer myself for the Mysteries of Freemasonry; that I am prompted to do so by a favorable opinion conceived of the Fraternity, by the desire of knowledge, and a sincere wish to be serviceable to my fellow-creatures; and that I will cheerfully conform to all the ancient usages and established customs of the Order. I am .....years of age; was born at ...., in ...., am of the profession ['*trade*,' or '*employment*'] of ...., and reside at ....

A—— B——."

" *Recommended and vouched for by C—— D——,*
Member of the Lodge."

This petition is to be handed by the vouching brother to the Master, in private. The voucher must not be given without a full and intimate acquaintance with the character, habits, and disposition of the candidate; and it applies as well to his intellectual as to his moral character. No man who is not possessed of the mental strength and ability to understand and *value* the instruction conveyed, some education and some taste for study, and capacity for reflection, nor any perverse, pragmatical, or contentious person, ought to be allowed admission, even to the Lesser Mysteries. And if the voucher present a drunkard, gambler, seducer, cheat, or unfair dealer, he must himself be expelled from the Order. The plea of ignorance will not excuse him. Every one recommends and vouches as of personal knowledge, and accepts the risk.

The Master will, in the following form, propose the Profane in open Lodge, in the Apprentice's Degree, without in any manner naming or designating the Brother who presents and vouches for him:

⊙∴ ♪ My Brethren, the Profane, A.... B.....,

aged ...... years, by profession ["trade" or "employment"] a ...., born at ...., and residing at ...., is proposed, and desires to be initiated into our Mysteries, and to become a Member of this Lodge. My Brethren, Senior and Junior Wardens, announce this to your respective columns, and request the Brethren to procure information, by the next communication, in regard to this Profane; to the end that we may then consider whether a Committee shall be appointed.

⊕∴ ♪ Brother Junior Warden, Brethren who grace the column of the North, the Venerable Master proposes the Profane, A∴ .... B............, [repeating the particulars of age, etc.] to be initiated into our Mysteries and to become a Member of this Lodge ; and he requests us to inform ourselves, by the next communication, in regard to this Profane, to the end that we may then consider whether a Committee shall be appointed.

O∴ ♪ Brethren who grace the column of the South, the Venerable Master and the Brother Senior Warden propose, etc., [repeating the proposition in the same words] ♪ Brother Senior Warden, it is announced.

⊕∴ ♪ Venerable Master, it is announced.

At the next meeting (between which and the former fifteen days must have elapsed), the proposition will be taken up, and the Master will say :

O∴ ♪ Brethren Senior and Junior Wardens, invite the Brethren to communicate to us such information as they may have gathered touching the Profane A.......... B..........., who was proposed for initiation at the last communication.

⊕∴ ♪ Brother Junior Warden, Brethren who grace the column of the North, the Venerable Master invites you, etc.

○∴ ♪ Brethren who grace the column of the South, the Venerable Master invites you, etc.

♪ Brother Senior Warden, it is announced.

⊕∴ ♪ Venerable Master, it is announced.

If any Brethren have any remarks to make, they rise in succession, and ask the floor, by stretching out the right hand. The Warden on whose column they are, gives one rap with his Mallet, to which the other Warden replies by one rap, and then ⊙ by one, and the Warden of the Column says:

⊕∴ or ○∴ ♪ Venerable Master, a Brother on my column asks for the floor.

⊙∴ My Brother, you have permission to speak.

Brethren in the East, wishing to speak, will ask ⊙ for the floor.

This formula, according to which all announcements made in the Lodge pass up or down through the respective dignitaries, is sacramental under all circumstances, and determines the essential character of regular work. No one can address the Lodge or Master in any other way, at any time.

If more than one ask the floor at one time, the proper Warden will determine who first asked it or caught his eye, and so announce to the Master.

Any Brother may rise and demand a Committee, without giving a reason for it, in which case one is appointed without a ballot.

If no one rises, ○ says, in a low voice:

○∴ ♪ Brother Senior Warden, there are no remarks to be made on my column.

⊕ then says aloud:

⊕∴ ♪ Venerable Master, there are no remarks to be made on either column.

Then, or when the discussion is ended, ☉ says:

○∴ ♪ Brethren Senior and Junior Wardens, ascertain by the ballot whether any Brother demands that a Committee be appointed to make strict inquiry as to the Profane proposed.

⊕∴ ♪ Brother Junior Warden, it is the order of the Venerable Master that we ascertain, etc.

○∴ ♪ Brother Master of Ceremonies, that we may ascertain, etc., distribute the ballots.

♃ goes to the Secretary's table, and receives the ballot-box. It should have two drawers, one in which the ballots deposited are to fall, and one in which all are kept. He takes the former from the box, and shows ⊕ that it is empty. ☉ then requests the Members of the Lodge, of all the Degrees, to rise, and they are counted by ♃, ♄ and ♂ respectively. Their count agreeing, ♃ reports it to ⊕ and he to ☉, from his place. Then as many white balls and as many black ones are counted out by △ and ♃, and placed in the drawer where they are kept, which should have two compartments. The rest are retained by △.

Then ♃ goes round and gives each voter a white and a black ball. Then ☉ says:

☉∴ ♪ Brethren Senior and Junior Wardens, announce to your columns that the ballot is about to pass, to ascertain whether any Brother demands that a Committee shall be appointed to make strict inquiry as to the Profane proposed. A black ball will demand the Committee.

⊕∴ ♪ Brother Junior Warden, and Brethren who grace the column of the North, the ballot is about to pass, etc.

☉∴ ♪ Brethren who grace the column of the South, the ballot is about to pass, etc.

♃ now takes the box and receives the ballots. He goes first to ☉, then to ⊕, then to ◯, and then to the other officers in due succession, then to any Brethren entitled to vote, who may be in the East, and then places it on the Altar, and the BB∴ advance one by one, and vote, each first giving ☉ the sign. Then the Tiler is called in, the Pursuivant or a Brother relieving him, and he, being informed of the matter by ☉, deposits his vote, and retires again. In receiving the votes, ♃ must keep his hand before the opening of the box and turn away his head.

When all have voted, ♃ carries the box to ◯, then to ⊕, and then to ☉, each of whom examines the ballots. Then ☉ says :

☉∴ ♪ Brethren Senior and Junior Wardens, how stands the ballot ?

If the number of ballots and voters do not agree, ⊕ asks:

⊕∴ Brother Junior Warden, how is the ballot in the South ?

◯∴ Brother Senior Warden, the ballot is unequal and inexact.

⊕∴ ♪ Venerable Master, the ballot is unequal and inexact in the West, on the South and North.

☉∴ Brethren Senior and Junior Wardens, the ballot being unequal and inexact, in the South, North and East, ascertain, by another ballot, whether any Brother demands, etc.

PROPOSING AND ELECTING MEMBERS.

Another ballot is again taken and examined, as before.

If the ballot is unanimously white, and not unequal and in-exact, it is thus announced:

⊕∴ ♪ Brother Junior Warden, how is the ballot in the South?

○∴ ♪ Brother Senior Warden, the ballot is equal and exact, and *fair* in the South.

⊕∴ ♪ Venerable Master, the ballot is equal and exact, *fair* in the South, and *clear* in the North and West.

☉∴ ♪ The ballot is equal and exact, *fair* in the South, *clear* in the North and West, and BRIGHT in the East. Brethren Senior and Junior Wardens, announce to your columns, that no Brother demanding a Committee, none will be appointed, and the ballot, on the application of the Profane, will be passed at the next meeting of the Lodge.

⊕∴ ♪ Brother Junior Warden, Brethren who grace the column of the North, the Venerable Master informs you that, no Brother demanding, etc.

○∴ ♪ Brethren who grace the column of the South, the Venerable Master informs you, etc.

If the ballot shows a black ball, ○ will answer, when asked by ⊕ how the ballot is in the South:

○∴ ♪ Brother Senior Warden, the ballot is *dark* in the South.

⊕∴ ♪ Venerable Master, the ballot is *dark* in the West, on the South and North.

⊙∴ ♪ Brethren Senior and Junior Wardens, inform your columns that a Committee being demanded, one will be appointed, to report at the next meeting.

⊕∴ ♪ Brother Junior Warden, Brethren who grace the column of the North, the Venerable Master informs you that, etc.

⊙∴ ♪ Brethren who grace the column of the South, the Venerable Master informs you that, etc.

The Master will appoint the Committee, always of three, without making it known to the Lodge of whom it is composed; and any information desired by a Brother to be given to the Committee, must be communicated through the Master. The Master will designate the Chairman of the Committee.

At the next meeting, ♃, when directed by ⊙, will take round the Pouch of Propositions, first in the East, and then on the columns. He will present it to every Brother in succession; and every one must put in his hand, as if he intended to put something in without being perceived. Thus the Committee may put in their report, without any one knowing by whom it is done. It should be written on a thin square piece of paper, folded up into small compass, so that, when it is held in the hand, no one can see it. The Committee will thus remain unknown. The report will not be signed, and the Profane will be designated only by the initial-letter of his surname.

△ will make, on the minutes of proceedings of this communication, and of that when the Profane was proposed, only a general mention of him, without indicating his name, surname, profession, etc., age, or place of birth or residence. But on a separate sheet, sealed, and authenticated by at least three signatures, he will enter these particulars, and all action had on the proposition, such as the appointment of a Committee, the reference to it, the ballot, etc., up to the moment of admission, if that takes place. After admission he will transcribe into the Book of Architecture (Record), all that was committed to these "fugitive leaves."

The Committee will especially inquire, not merely into the life and morals of the person proposed, but into his disposition, whether it be genial, kind, equable, agreeable, etc., or morose, pragmatical, captious, petulant, and the like; into the nature of his leanings, his faults, and as to his intelligence, capacity, etc. And on all these points they will particularly and specially report, not simply recommending admission or rejection, or reporting favorably or unfavorably; a system which experience has proven to be too often a mere form.

If the whole Committee, or two of them, report against admission, the Master will so announce, and the matter ends.

If *all* report favorably, or if *two* of them do so, or if no Committee was demanded, the Master will say:

☉∴ My Brethren, in the communication of the ......day of............, the Profane, A........ B............, was proposed to be initiated into our Mysteries. Upon his application it was voted that a Committee should be appointed. I appointed a Committee of three to make the necessary investigations. The Committee has reported, to the effect that, in admitting this Profane we shall acquire a worthy Brother. [Or, upon his application, no Committee was demanded.] He persists in his wish to be received. The Brother Secretary will read the report. [It is read]: Brethren Senior and Junior Wardens, propose the Profane, A........... B..... ...., to the Brethren of your columns, and inquire if they desire to offer any remarks.

Each Warden makes the announcement, repeating the words of ☉, and following the formula of address already often given. If there are any remarks, they are heard.

Then ☉ directs it to be announced that the ballot will pass

on the question of receiving the Candidate, the white balls being for it. The vote is taken and the result announced, in all respects as already prescribed.

If the ballot is unanimous, ⊙ says:

⊙∴ ♪ Brethren Senior and Junior Wardens, announce to the Brethren of your columns, that the ballot being fair in the South, clear in the North and West, and bright in the East, the Profane, A.......... B.........., is duly elected to be initiated an Entered Apprentice Mason. At the same time, invite all the Brethren to join me in applauding the result.

⊕∴ ♪ Brother Junior Warden, Brethren who grace the column of the North, the Venerable Master informs you that the ballot. being, etc., and invites you, etc.

○∴ ♪ Brethren who grace the column of the South, the Venerable Master, etc.

The Plaudit is then given, as hereinafter described.

The announcement is that the Profane is elected to be initiated an Entered Apprentice Mason; for there must be a separate ballot for each Degree.

Then △ carries into his minutes of the day all that was on his fugitive leaves.

If there are *three* or more black balls, the Profane is definitively rejected, and the fugitive leaves are immediately burned.

If there are but *two*, the fact will be noted on the flying leaves, and the matter will lie over until the next regular meeting.

If, at that meeting, there are still *two* black balls on a ballot taken, the Profane is rejected. If there is but one, ⊙ will invite, and direct the Wardens to invite, aloud, the Brother who cast the black ball, to inform him, out of the Lodge, and under the Seal of Masonic Secrecy, of the reasons for his vote.

At this secret conference, if it takes place, ⊙ will be able to judge of the gravity of the reasons, and if he finds them frivolous or trivial, will endeavor to dissuade the Brother from persistence in his vote; but he must under no pretext endeavor to *constrain* him to yield his objection.

If, at the next meeting, there is still one black ball, the Profane is rejected.

If the objection is grounded solely on some statute or especial regulation of the Lodge, the Brother voting in the negative *may* rise, demand the floor, and state the ground, that the Lodge may consider it. In that case, whatsoever is determined by plurality of votes, upon the conclusions of the Orator, or on ballot, in the ordinary form, will govern.

If the Brother opposing the admission is unwilling to communicate his reasons to ⊙, either because he fears that he might create for himself an enemy, or because he objects, for the mere reason that he is unwilling to enter into the bonds of Brotherhood with the Profane proposed, he is entirely at liberty to decline making himself known to ⊙, and may quietly await the last ballot, when his one black ball will exclude.

The right of exercising one's judgment by the secret ballot is absolute. No Mason is bound to receive as his Brother, one whom he dislikes or suspects, or thinks unintelligent or likely to be indolent, indifferent, or pragmatical. To question him for his vote, is to deserve expulsion; and the Lodge should always be content to retain a tried Brother when it must virtually lose him to acquire a stranger, unknown to it as Masons know each other.

If there be one or more other Lodges, of any regular Rite, in the place, notice of an application for initiation will be given to each, as soon as it is made. Valid objections to a Profane may thereby become known, which would otherwise remain unrevealed.

Applications for Affiliation will be made by petition, and will, *in every case*, follow the same course as those for initiation.

VI.

REGULATIONS.

EACH Lodge will frame and adopt its own Regulations, and its Rules of Business and Order. These will be at once in force. But they must be, within a brief space, submitted to the Grand Consistory of the State, or, if there be none, then to the proper Active or Deputy Inspector-General, that if they contain anything contrary to the Grand Constitutions, or to the Laws, Statutes, Ordinances, Canons, or Regulations of the Supreme Council, or of the Grand Consistory if there be one, so much of them may be disapproved, and by such disapproval, when that is made known to the Lodge, cease to be of force, unless it be decided that such part or parts was from the beginning null and void.

The Regulations must provide that there shall be regular meetings of the Lodge on the days of the summer and winter solstice; that is, on the 24th of June, the Festival of the Nativity of St. John the Baptist, and on the 27th of December, the Festival of St. John the Evangelist. On these days the Brethren will dine together. The election of Officers will be held at the regular meeting next preceding the winter solstice, and they will be installed on that day.

The Officers of the Lodges will be elected for not less than three years. The first seven are Elective Officers. The others are appointed by the Master.

The right to Masonic burial cannot be denied to Fellow-Crafts and Entered Apprentices. They are Free-Masons. Nor can it be allowed to Masons long unaffiliated, and long neglectful of their duties. The Lodge always holds its honors under its control.

Either an Entered Apprentice's or Fellow-Craft's Lodge may be separately opened; but when a Lodge of Master Masons is opened, it *includes* in itself *both* the other Lodges, and the work of the first may be suspended, to commence or resume work in either of the others.

All the ordinary business of the Lodge is transacted in the

Apprentices' Lodge. The vote on an application for affiliation is taken there. The vote on an application for either Degree is taken in the Lodge of that Degree.

On an application for initiation, visiting Brethren are entitled to vote; for initiation creates duties on their part, as well as on those of the Brethren of the Lodge, and the *same duties*, toward the Initiate. For the same reason, they may vote on an application for the Second or Third Degree.

Any Brother can withdraw from a Lodge at his pleasure; but if he be under charges, the Lodge may refuse to accept his demission until after trial and acquittal; and if he be indebted to it, may refuse him a certificate of demission and good standing, until he pays it what he owes.

VII.

APARTMENTS CONNECTED WITH THE LODGE.

There must be a convenient and comfortable ante-room (*salle de pas perdus*) for the reception of visitors and other necessary purposes. It must be a *room*, one door opening into the Lodge-room, and with one other door for exit, that may be kept closed.

There must also be a Preparation-room, with a door opening into the Lodge-room, on the left of the Senior Warden. Here candidates will be prepared; and here also visitors may await admission.

In the ante-room must be a desk, with materials and implements for writing, on which desk the Register of Visitors will be laid. In this room, also, the wardrobe should be kept, and a book for subscriptions for banquets and festivals. It should be well supplied with chairs, and one or more tables for writing.

In the Preparation-room there will be no furniture except a single table, some chairs, and a book-case or cases containing the Library. The following sentences are painted on the wall, or are suspended, in large print, and framed, in a conspicuous place :

"*If mere curiosity brings thee hither, turn back; begone!*"

"*If thou fearest to see the faults and frailties of Humanity dissected, thou wilt find no satisfaction amongst us.*"

"*If thou valuest worldly goods and advantages alone, thou will find nothing here to aid thee in thy purpose.*"

"*If thou lackest confidence in us, advance no further.*"

"*If thy heart be pure, and thy intentions good, thou art welcome!*"

"*If thou perseverest, thou will be purified by the elements; thou will emerge from the abyss of darkness, and see the Light.*"

O. 1.   *   *   *   *   *   *   *

"*Dust we are, and unto dust we must return.*"

"*In the grave all men are equal.*"

"*He that goeth down to the grave shall come up no more.*"

"*The way of the wicked is as darkness. They know not at what they stumble.*"

"*He that walks with the wise shall be wise; but the companion of fools shall be destroyed.*"

"*He who stops his ears at the cry of the poor shall himself cry and not be heard.*"

"*Remove not the old landmarks; and enter not into the fields of the fatherless.*"

"*He that has no rule over his own spirit is a city dilapidated and without walls.*"

"*Hell and destruction are never full.*"

"*God small judge the righteous and the wicked.*"

"*The Glory of God is to conceal the Word.*"

O. 2.   *   *   *   *   *   *   *

VIII.

ORDER OF BUSINESS.

The regular Order of Business in every Lodge of the Rite is—

1st. The reading and signing of the Records of the previous communication or communications, as yet unread and unsigned, which are entered in a Book, called THE BOOK OF ARCHITECTURE. To insure the correctness of the entries, and avoid the necessity of defacement by erasures and interlineations, the minutes of each meeting are kept on loose sheets, called 'PLATES,' and are invariably to be read over, while in the rough, just before the closing of the communication at which they are taken, that any error or omission may at once be corrected, before the formal record is made up.

2d. Report from the Brother Almoner, of any special case or cases requiring relief or assistance.

3d. Reports from permanent or standing committees.

4th. Reports from special or select committees.

5th. Applications for initiation, reception, or admission to membership.

6th. Consideration of previous proposals for initiation or affiliation.

7th. Receptions.

8th. Motions and Resolutions.

After reports from Committees are received, their consideration, if they give rise to debate, may be postponed until after the initiations or receptions.

At every meeting the Secretary will place before the Master the "Order of the day," on which, under the above heads, will be stated the different matters to be considered and acted upon. The Lodge may postpone any matter, by "passing to the order of the day."

IX.

MISCELLANEOUS.

1st. All trials for offences must be held in open Lodge, before the whole Lodge, on regular charges and specifications, the vote on each of which will be taken separately, by yeas and nays, the youngest member not an Officer voting first, and so on up to the eldest, and then the officers, beginning with the Tiler and ending with the Master. The punishments are, censure or reprimand; fines; pecuniary restitution; suspension from membership of the privileges of Masonry, for a definite or indefinite time; expulsion from the Lodge, and declaration of unworthiness, which is deprivation of all privileges and rights as a Mason. Suspension for an indefinite time can only be terminated by a vote of three-fourths of all the Brethren present at a regular meeting, taken upon a call of names, beginning with the youngest Mason, and after notice given at the preceding regular meeting. Three Brethren may demand a Committee of Inquiry before the ballot. Suspension for a definite period will terminate at the end of the period, unless it is continued by vote of three-fourths of the Brethren present, taken in the same manner, at a regular meeting, after notice by a Brother, and demand for it, at the preceding regular meeting. The notice and demand will continue the suspension until the ballot. Three Brethren may demand a Committee of Inquiry; and the suspension should be continued, if the suspended party have not reformed or made reparation. If continued, it becomes indefinite. A majority of three-fourths is necessary to expel; a simple majority of votes will suspend.

2d. A Lodge can never close until the box of fraternal assistance is sent around, and every Brother must contribute *something*. And no Brother can withdraw from the Lodge before it closes, without depositing his contribution. The sum contributed will be handed to the Almoner, to be used in relieving distress. It may be directed to be applied to a particular case, of a party named or unnamed, on motion of any Brother. However applied, the party relieved is never to be informed from what source the relief comes.

3d. A Lodge cannot be *called off* until another day or evening. When at refreshment, the members remain in presence of the Junior Warden, at whose table the small gilt column of HAR-MONY is placed upright.

4th. The Lodge must *always* be opened and closed in due and proper form. No openings "*without form*," or "*in short*," are allowable.

5th. No Brother can leave the Lodge before it closes, without permission from the Senior Warden, which will only be given for good cause. Any Brother may object to another leaving, and demand a vote of the Lodge; which ought not to permit

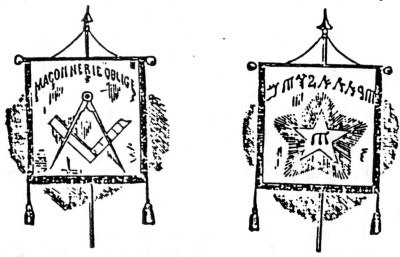

withdrawal, except for good cause, since thereby the most important business is often transacted by a few, or neglected.

6th. The Brethren will *always* be called to order *precisely* at the hour and moment fixed. Brethren arriving afterward must render good excuse, or be liable to censure and even to fine.

7th. The Banner of the Lodge is to be of white silk, edged and fringed with blue. On one side, embroidered or painted in blue and gold, the Square and Compass, emitting golden rays; and on the other the Blazing Star of five points, with the letter ℳ in the centre. Over the Square and Compass, the motto MAÇONNE-RIE OBLIGE, and *over* the Blazing Star the words, in Hebrew, Ⅎℿ⳨2⼂ ⼂⼂ℚℿ [YARAT ALOUIM], meaning

"REVERENCE FOR THE DEITY." The banner should be square, each side measuring about 30 inches; and it should be attached to a light staff, with a spear-head above.

8th. There are no assemblies of Masons, in the Ancient and Accepted Rite, "working after the manner of a Lodge." Masons can only be made in "just and regularly constituted Lodges of such." In a State where there is a Grand Consistory, Letters of Constitution for Lodges will be granted by that body. The Commander-in-Chief may grant temporary Letters, to be confirmed or revoked by the Grand Consistory. If these are confirmed, Letters of Constitution issue, confirming and making perpetual the temporary Letters. Where there is no Grand Consistory, Letters of Constitution are granted by an Inspector General, or Deputy Inspector General. These are perpetual without confirmation. In every case the officers must, at the beginning, be elected and duly installed, to hold their offices until the next Winter Solstice.

9th. If the Master be absent at any meeting, a Past Worshipful Master, or a Prince of the Royal Secret or Inspector General must be called on to preside. The Senior Warden does not take the Master's place of right, or by succession, and will preside only when no Past Master, Prince of the Royal Secret, or Inspector General is present. In the absence of these and of the Senior Warden, the Junior Warden will preside. If none of these are present, a Knight Rose Croix may preside, if he have received also the 20th Degree. In the absence of all these, no Lodge can be held.

10th. No Profane can be initiated who has lost a limb, or is paralyzed, mutilated, or deformed, not having his limbs whole, as a man ought to have; or if blind, even of one eye, or deaf: but slight defects, such as the loss of a finger, or lameness, are not fatal objections.

11th. No appeal to the Lodge can be taken from any decision of the Master, except on questions of order; and not even in such case, when the question whether a Brother is in order, depends for its solution on some landmark or essential principle of Freemasonry.

12th. The Master may, at any moment, close a debate by rising to his feet and rapping once.

13th. Masons of the Ancient and Accepted Rite will use, after initials and abbreviations, three dots, forming an equilateral triangle, thus: "Ven∴"—"A∴ M∴", instead of the single period.

14th. Official letters and documents will be dated as follows: "Or∴ of ...., the .... day of the Hebrew month ...., A∴ M∴....., answering to the .... day of ....18....V∴ E∴"

The initials Or∴ stand for Orient. The name of the Hebrew month may be written in Hebrew or English. The initials V∴ E∴ mean "vulgar or ordinary era," and are to be used instead of A∴ D∴ Each Secretary must annually procure, and keep in his office, a calendar of the Hebrew months for the year.

The Hebrew year begins with the month תשרי, Tisri, which commences on some day in September. Each month begins with the new moon. To find the Hebrew year before that day in September add 3,760 to the current year. After that day add 3,761.

15th. All banquets or refections are held in the degree of Entered Apprentice.

16th. Every Brother entering the Lodge, after it is opened, will salute ☉, ⊕, and ○ in succession, with the sign, beginning with the Master.

DEBATE AND DECISION.

There can be no debate without permission of the Master.

When all except the Orator have been heard on any question of interest or importance, ☉ will say:

☉∴ Brother Orator, make known your conclusions.

Whereupon ☿ rises, and offers such remarks as he thinks proper, after which he pauses a little to see whether what he has said will elicit any reply, in which case he will listen to what is said, and rejoin.

If there are no remarks, or when the matter is sufficiently debated, he will *conclude*, i. e., will state as propositions what, in his opinion, the Lodge ought to determine.

Then ☉ will put the question thus:

☉∴ Brethren of the Lodge, is it your pleasure to adopt or reject the conclusions of the Brother Orator? Those of you who think they should be adopted will give me the sign.

The sign is to raise the right hand above the head.

☉∴ Those of you who think they should be rejected will give me the same sign.

After which ☉ announces, through the Wardens, the result.

If there be doubt as to the result, the vote will be taken again, and a count be had.

Five Brethren, rising, may demand the ayes and noes. In that case the roll is called, beginning with the youngest member, not an officer, and ending with the officers in the inverse order of rank.

f

———

ᎦᏣᏍᎦᎢ

ENTERED APPRENTICE.

———

APPRENTI.

FIRST DEGREE.

ENTERED APPRENTICE.

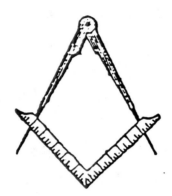

X. OPENING.

The moment the hour for opening arrives, fixed by Regulation or Special Order, ⊙, clothed, and wearing his jewel, will take the East, rap o, and say, standing:

⊙∴ ♪ My Brethren, I am about to open in this place the respectable Lodge, ..., No. ...., of Apprentice Masons, for the dispatch of business. Be pleased to assist me. The officers and Brethren will clothe themselves, and the Dignitaries and officers will repair to their respective stations and places.

Upon this order being given ♄ will spread the tracing-board [*tableau*] on the floor, and ♂ will carry the register of visitors to the ante-room, and place it on the desk open, and the page dated.

When all are clothed, and in their places and stations, ⊙, seating himself, in which all the Brethren imitate him, raps o, and says:

⊙∴ ♪ Very dear Brother Senior Warden, what is the first duty of a Warden in a Lodge?

⊕∴ To assure himself that the Temple is duly tiled, Venerable Master.

⊙∴ Be pleased to assure yourself of that, my Brother, and cause the Tiler to be informed that we are about to open this Lodge of Apprentice Masons for the dispatch of business, that he may tile accordingly.

⊕∴ ♪ Brother Junior Warden, be pleased to ascertain if the Temple is duly tiled, and cause the Tiler to be informed, etc.

⊙∴ ♪ Brother Assistant Expert, ascertain if the Lodge is duly tiled, and inform the Tiler, etc.

♂ draws his sword, examines whether the key of the door is right, places it on the altar, opens the door, communicates the order to the Tiler on the outside, closes the door, raps on it н times at equal intervals, † answering with the same, and then o, to which the Tiler replies by one rap. Then, returning to his place and sheathing his sword, ♂ says to ○:

♂∴ Brother Junior Warden, the Temple is duly tiled.

○∴ ♪ Brother Senior Warden, the Temple is duly tiled.

⊕∴ ♪ Venerable Master, the Temple is duly tiled.

⊙∴ ♪ How tiled, my Brother?

⊕∴ With secrecy and brotherly love, by a worthy Brother Master Mason, without the door, with a drawn sword.

⊙∴ His duty there?

⊕∴ To guard against the approach of all cowans and eaves-droppers, on the hills or in the vales, and to see that none enter here, except such as are duly entitled, and have the permission of the Venerable Master.

⊙∴ It is well, my Brother. What is the second duty of the Senior Warden in the Lodge?

⊕∴ To know, with certainty, that all present are Masons.

⊙∴ Be pleased, my Brother, to satisfy yourself that all present are so.

O. 3.　　＊　　　＊　　　＊　　　＊　　　＊　　　＊

The Brethren and Officers, except the Dignitaries, place themselves under the sign of order, seated. ♄ passes along the column of the North, and ♂ along that of the South, each from East to West, to see if they know all as Masons. If either of them does not recognize a particular person as such, he directs him, by a gesture, to rise. If any Brother *knows* the person rising to be a Mason *in good standing*, he will rise and so declare. It is not enough to have sitten in a Lodge with him. If no one vouches for the party, he will be required to withdraw to the Preparation-room for examination. When none remain but Masons, and the Expert and Assistant Expert are satisfied, they will return to their places, and, standing, ♂ will say:

♂∴ Brother Senior Deacon, all on the column of the South are Masons.

♄∴ Brother Junior Warden, all on both columns are Masons.

☉∴ ♪ Brother Senior Warden, all present are Masons.

⊕∴ ♪ Venerable Master, I have satisfied myself that all present are Masons.

O. 4.   *   *   *   *   *   *

☉∴ How many compose a Lodge of Apprentice Masons?

⊕∴ Three, five, seven.

☉∴ When composed of seven, of whom does it consist?

⊕∴ The Venerable Master, the Senior and Junior Wardens, the Treasurer and Secretary, and the Senior and Junior Deacons.

☉∴ What is the Junior Deacon's [or Assistant Expert's, as it may be] place in the Lodge?

⊕∴ In front of the Senior Warden, to the right, if he is pleased to permit it.

O. 5.   *   *   *   *   *   *

☉∴ Why there, Brother Junior Deacon?

♂∴ To bear his orders to the Junior Warden, and to see that the Brethren conduct with propriety on the columns.

☉∴ What is the Senior Deacon's [or Expert's, as it may be] place in the Lodge?

♂∴ In front of the Venerable Master, to his right, if he is pleased to permit it.

☉∴ Why there, Brother Senior Deacon?

♄∴ To bear your orders to the Senior Warden and other officers, that the work of the Lodge may be the more promptly done.

☉∴ What is the Secretary's place in the Lodge ?

♄∴ To your left, Venerable Master, in the East.

☉∴ Brother Secretary, why are you to my left, in the East ?

△∴ To take note of the materials and works ; to engrave the proceedings of the Lodge ; to receive all moneys, and pay them over to the Treasurer ; to conduct the correspondence with the workshops and workmen ; and to announce the days of labor, and what is to be done thereon.

☉∴ What is the Treasurer's place in the Lodge ?

△∴ To your right, Venerable Master, in the East.

☉∴ Brother Treasurer, why are you to my right, in the East ?

□∴ To receive the moneys of the workshop from the Brother Secretary, and to pay all such accounts as the Venerable Master approves and the Lodge allows, keeping just and full accounts of the same.

☉∴ What is the Junior Warden's station in the Lodge ?

□∴ In the South, Venerable Master.

☉∴ ♫ Why do you occupy the South, very dear Brother Junior Warden ?

◯∴ [*He and* ⊕ *rising*] : The better to observe the Sun at his meridian height ; to send the workmen to their labors and recall them from work to refreshment, that the Venerable Master may have honor and glory thereby.

⊙∴ What is the Senior Warden's station in the Lodge?

○∴ In the West, Venerable Master.

⊙∴ Why in the West, very dear Brother Senior Warden?

⊕∴ As the Sun sets in the West to close the day, so is the Senior Warden in the West to assist in opening and closing the Lodge, to pay the workmen, and send them away content and satisfied.

⊙∴ What is the Master's station in the Lodge?

⊕∴ In the East, Venerable Master.

⊙∴ Why in the East, my Brother?

⊕∴ As the Sun rises in the East to begin his course and open the day, so is the Venerable Master in the East to open the Lodge, to direct it in its work, and to enlighten it with his knowledge.

⊙∴ At what hour are Apprentice Masons used to to open their labors?

⊕∴ At mid-day, Venerable Master.

⊙∴ What is the hour, Brother Junior Warden?

○∴ High Noon, Venerable Master.

O. 6.   *   *   *   *   *   *

○∴ ♪ Venerable Master, all is just and perfect.

⊙∴ ♪ It being high noon, and all being just and perfect, be pleased, Brethren Senior and Junior

Wardens, to proclaim, on your respective columns, that I am about to open the labors of the Respectable Lodge ...., No. ...., in the first degree.

⊕∴ ♪ Brother Junior Warden. Brethren who grace the column of the North, the Venerable Master announces to you that he is about to open the labors of the Respectable Lodge ...., No. ...., in the first degree.

O∴ ♪ Brethren who grace the column of the South, the Venerable Master announces to you, etc.

. . . ♪ It is proclaimed on the column of the South, Brother Senior Warden.

⊕∴ ♪ Venerable Master, it is proclaimed on both columns.

⊙ raps ʜ, rises, and says :

⊙∴ To order, my Brethren.

Then he takes off his hat, and says:

⊙∴ In the name of God and of Saint John of Scotland, and under the auspices of the Supreme Council (Mother-Council of the World), of the Sovereigns The Grand Inspectors-General, Grand Elect Knights of the Holy House of the Temple, Grand Commanders of the Holy Empire, of the 33d and last degree of the Ancient and Accepted Scottish Rite of Free-Masonry, for the Southern Jurisdiction of the United States, whose See is at Charleston, in the

State of South Carolina   .   .   .   [or, if there be a
Grand Consistory in the State]   .   .   .   of the
Grand Consistory of Sublime Princes of the Royal
Secret, 32d degree of the Ancient and Accepted Scottish Rite of Free-Masonry, for the State of ....,
and by virtue of the authority in me vested as Venerable Master of this Lodge of Apprentice Masons, I
declare it to be duly opened, and its labors in full
force.   No Brother may speak aloud, or pass from
one column to the other, without first obtaining permission, or may engage in political questions or controversy, under the penalties prescribed by the
General Statutes of the Order.

O. 7.   *   *   *   *   *   *

⊙∴ ♪ Be seated, my Brethren.   .   .   .   Very
dear Brother Secretary, be pleased to read to us the
engraved plate of the works of the last communication.   .   .   .   ♪ Attention, my brethren.

While △ reads the record, ☿ has before him the original
minutes, to see if anything is altered, added, or omitted. If so,
he makes it known when the reading is finished. If all is correct, he says:

☿∴ Venerable Master, the engraved plate con-
forms to the rough sketch.

Then ⊙ raps o, and the Wardens in succession repeat the
rap.

⊙∴ ♪ Brethren Senior and Junior Wardens, announce on your columns that if any of the Brethren have any remarks to offer, they may, if they please, be heard.

⊕∴ ♪ Brother Junior Warden, Brethren who grace the column of the North, the Venerable Master announces that, etc.

○∴ ♪ Brethren who grace the column of the South, the Venerable Master announces, etc.

Nothing can be discussed, except whether the record is correct. If any discussion occurs, ☿ will conclude, and ☉ determines. When all is settled, or if no one speaks,

○∴ ♪ Brother Senior Warden, silence prevails on my column.

⊕∴ ♪ Venerable Master, silence prevails on both columns.

☉∴ ♪ Brethren Senior and Junior Wardens, invite the Brethren on each column to join me in giving due sanction to the plate of our last labors.

The Wardens announce this in succession:

☉∴ Join me, my Brethren.

All give the plaudit in the usual manner.

XI.

INTRODUCTION OF VISITORS.

WHEN the minutes have been approved, ☉ says:

☉∴ ♪ Brother Master of Ceremonies, be pleased to repair to the Outer Court of the Temple, and ascertain if any Visiting Brethren are in attendance.

♃ goes out, and returns, bringing with him the Register of Visitors. He reports, between the Wardens, the number and rank of the Visitors present, hands the Register to the Secretary, and the certificates, briefs, or patents of the Visitors, if they have produced such, to ☉. He then returns and remains with the Visitors.

Then ☉ directs ♄ to tile [examine] the Visitors without certificates, briefs, or patents, and ♂ to take the signatures of those who have them, that these may be compared with their signatures on the certificates, etc.

If the Visitors are only Master Masons, or only registered as such, ☉ will say, after ♄ and ♂ have performed their duty and reported:

☉∴ ♪ Brother Junior Deacon, inform the Brother Master of Ceremonies that he may present the Visiting Brethren.

If there are also Visitors entitled to honors, he will say:

☉∴ ♪ Brother Junior Deacon, inform the Master of Ceremonies that he will divide the Visitors properly into classes, and introduce first the Apprentices,

Fellow-Crafts, and Master Masons, whom we are now ready to receive.

♃ *being so directed, brings the Visitors, registered as Apprentices, Fellow-Crafts, and Master Masons, to the door of entrance, and gives the Apprentice's alarm. If there be a Pursuivant, he says:*

♐∴ Brother Junior Deacon, some one raps as an Apprentice at the door of the Temple.

♂∴ Brother Senior Warden, some one raps as an Apprentice at the door of the Temple.

⊕∴ Brother Junior Deacon, learn who it is that knocks.

♂∴ Brother Pursuivant, learn who it is that knocks.

♐, *or if there be none,* ♂ *partly opens the door, and asks:*

♂∴ Who knocks?

♃∴ The Master of Ceremonies, accompanying the Visiting Brother Apprentice ["*Fellow-Craft,*" or "*Master*"] Mason [or "the Visiting Brethren, Apprentices, Fellow-Crafts, and Master Masons:" . . . varying the phrase according to the number and character of the Visitors.]

♂∴ [*Closing the door*] Brother Senior Warden, it is the Brother Master of Ceremonies accompanying, etc.

⊕∴ ♪ Venerable Master, the Brother Master of Ceremonies, accompanying, etc., requests admission.

⊙∴ Throw open the doors of the Temple ! . . .
♫ To order, my Brethren !

All rise, and stand under the Sign of Order.

⊕∴ Brother Junior Deacon, throw open the doors
of the Temple !

The door is opened. ♃ enters with the Visitors, and advances with them to the Altar. They stand under the Sign of Order.

O. 8.   *   · *   *   *   *   *

If other Visitors are to be introduced, ⊙ will now direct ♃ to conduct the Visitors to seats, reserving his compliments until all shall have entered. If there are no others, he will say:

⊙∴ Brethren, we congratulate ourselves on our good fortune in being visited by you, and cordially offer you the poor hospitalities of our Temple. We fully appreciate the value of your presence among us, and especially on the present occasion [*giving the reasons*]. With our numbers thus enlarged, we may labor more effectually and impressively, and shall be assisted and strengthened in inculcating and propagating the principles of Virtue and Fraternity, which the Ancient and Accepted Scottish Rite professes. Be seated among us, Brethren. Brother Master of Ceremonies, conduct our worthy and well-beloved Brethren to appropriate seats.

♃ conducts to the East the Masters of Lodges, Kts∴ Rose

Croix, and Visitors of higher rank, though they may have inscribed themselves as simple Masons; and the *Masters* of Lodges, though they enter without insignia. But Knights Rose Croix, etc., are not entitled to any distinction without their insignia, or, at least, their jewels.

If there are other visitors, they are introduced in classes, and in due succession, by the following formula, varying only as to the number of Stars and Swords, and the description of the Visitors. For example:

⊙∴ ♪ Brother Master of Ceremonies, return to the ante-room, and introduce the Knights Kadosh, who do us the honor to visit us . . . [or " the Knight Templar, Sir E . . . W . . . ., who does us the honor to visit us."]

♃ salutes and goes out, and ⊙ then says:

⊙∴ Brother Senior Deacon, take with you five Stars and five Swords, repair to the ante-room, and precede the Knights Kadosh, who do us the honor to visit us, on their entrance into the Temple.

If the Visitors to be introduced are entitled to the Arch of Steel, ⊙ will say, after ♄ has gone out with the Stars and Swords:

⊙∴ Brother Junior Deacon, take —— swords, and place them in due position to form the Arch of Steel.

When such arch is not to be formed, the Stars and Swords, entering by two, ♄ at their head, ♃ after them, preceding the Visitors, will diverge on entering, halt between the door and Altar, and present swords, after facing inwards.

If the Arch is to be formed, ♂ will take as many swords as

have gone out, and place them in a single line, between the door
and the Altar, facing the South, himself on the left. The
Swords, from without, entering by twos, will advance, ♄ at
their head, until that officer is abreast of ♂. Then they will
halt, the left of each two step backwards behind the right, and
all face to the North. The two ranks will then raise their
swords and cross the points above, between them, at the same
time holding the stars above their heads.

When ♂ has formed his rank, ☉ will give notice if the swords
are to be clashed, and the Wardens to beat with their mallets.
If the Brethren are seated he will call them up, order swords
drawn, and that they be presented when the Visitors enter.
He will then say, standing in the East:

☉∴ Throw open the doors of the Temple, and let
our valiant [if Kts∴ Rose Croix or Kadosh] or " *sublime* " [if Princes of the Royal Secret], or " *illustrious* " [if Inspectors-General] Visitors enter!

As the first Visitor crosses the threshold he will say:

☉∴ Present swords!

And when the ranks are finally formed:

☉∴ Salute!

Swords are presented and the salute given, as in the military
manual for small-arms. The Visitors, preceded by ♃, pass in
front of the single rank, it standing, at a salute, or between the
ranks, under the Arch, as the case may be, to the Altar, and
stand in one line, on the West side of it, facing the Master,
where each will give the sign of the degree. ☉, recovering and
carrying his sword, will sheathe it, and return the sign. If
others are to be introduced he will say:

☉∴ Recover swords! Carry swords! Return

swords! Valiant, etc., Brethren, you are welcome.
Brother Master of Ceremonies, conduct our Valiant,
etc., Brethren to appropriate seats!

When all are admitted, and while they yet stand at the Altar,
if none have entered before and been seated, or if one of those
last admitted is entitled to the Mallet, but otherwise, after all
are seated, ⊙ will welcome them in a brief address. The following may be used:

⊙∴ Brethren, we hail with joy, and welcome your
entrance into this Temple of Harmony and Virtue, to
participate in our labors. We thank you for the
encouragement thus given by you to the workmen of
this Lodge, and especially to the young and the
Apprentices of the Craft, whose zeal and ardor in
Masonry will naturally be stimulated by this proof
that our labors are not uninteresting to others, even
to the most distinguished and illustrious of the great
Fraternity; and in whom a praiseworthy ambition
will also be aroused at sight of the due honors paid
to high rank and long service in the Royal Art. Be
indulgent, Brethren, in respect to aught you may see
amiss or imperfect in our work! Aid us with your
wise counsel and advice, since it is the duty of every
Mason of intelligence to dispense light and knowledge among the uninformed Brethren. You are
welcome, Brethren. My Brethren of the Lodge, aid
me in welcoming these Brethren more appropriately,

in the universal language of Masonry. With me, my Brethren!

All give the sign (in which alone the Visitors join), then the battery with the hands, and then the sign three times, each time crying "Huzza." This is the "*Plaudit.*"

The Visitors, all standing during the address, will bow in reply to the compliment. Then, if the Visitor, or one of the Visitors, is entitled to the Mallet, the Venerable Master will descend, walk to the Altar, and offer it to the single Visitor entitled, or to the one highest in rank. Only Inspectors-General are now entitled to it, or the Commander-in-Chief of the Grand Consistory of the State, and these only when the Venerable is not an Inspector-General.

To a deputation from another Lodge, the same honors are paid as to the Master of a Lodge.

When there is an initiation, no honors are paid to *any* one after the candidate is at the door.

After the plaudit, if the Mallet is not offered to any one, and any Visitors are at the Altar, ⊙ directs ♃ to conduct them to appropriate seats. Until they reach them all remain standing. Then all are seated by one rap, ⊙ saying:

⊙∴ ♪ Be seated, my Brethren!

If the Mallet is offered, ⊙ accompanies the Visitor to whom it is offered, to the East, and seats him in the Chair, if he has received it. If he has declined, ⊙ precedes him to the East, and places him on his right. ♃ at the same time conducts the others to seats, and returns to his place. All are then seated.

XII.

EXAMINATION OF VISITORS.

A KNIGHT ROSE CROIX, and of course a Mason of higher degree, is not "*tiled*," that is, examined by the Catechism, but is admitted on his brief or patent, and verification of his signature. Nevertheless, should he be unable to give the Word at the opening of a Fellow-Craft's or Master's Lodge, or otherwise be reasonably suspected of not being what he seems, he may be strictly tiled.

When one is sent out to be examined, or a Visitor in the ante-room is to be so, this will be done by a Committee of three Brethren, of whom, ordinarily, the Orator or Almoner is one.

The Committee will take with them a Bible, a Hebrew Pentateuch (or. Coscher Saphet Thora), and the Letters-Patent of Constitution of the Lodge. They will first require the Visitor to submit to the test of the Oath. To this he *may* reply by demanding to inspect the Letters of Constitution, or Charter, of the Lodge. After, or without doing this, if he be a true Mason, he will say that he is ready to take the usual oath, always provided that they who examine him will take the same at the same time with him, on the Bible or the Pentateuch, on the Sword, or upon honor. The Oath is in these words:

"I, A......... B........, of my own free will and accord, in the presence of God and of these witnesses, do hereby and hereon solemnly and sincerely swear that I have been regularly initiated an Apprentice Mason, passed to the degree of Fellow-Craft, and raised to the sublime degree of Master Mason [with the proper omission, if only the first degree, or the first and second have been received], in just and regularly-constituted Lodges of such, and that I am not expelled or suspended. So help me God!"

He will then be examined in the sign, word, and token of the degree, and then in the proper Catechism or instruction of one or more of the degrees. If found correct, the Committee will so

report to the Lodge, and he will be received in due form as a
Visitor. If he cannot prove himself a Mason, he is sent away.
If he be a York Mason, or of the Rit Moderne, he should be
examined in the formulas of his own Rite.

———

XIII.

RECEPTION.

WHEN a candidate is to be initiated, the Brother who proposed
him will bring him at least half an hour before the time for
opening the Lodge, to the building in which the Hall is, and to
some other than the door of usual entrance to the Lodge, if
there be such other. Here he will take leave of him, as if not
meaning to return.

There a Brother unknown to him, if there be one, will take
him in charge, and conduct him to some retired room, where
they will remain alone. If it can be avoided in any manner, he
must not be taken to the Ante-room or the Preparation-room.
He must neither see nor hear any one except his single companion, and the latter, without being rude, will be grave and
silent, so replying, briefly and unsatisfactorily, or mysteriously,
to any questions the candidate may put to him, or to any remarks he may make, as to disincline him to further attempt at
conversation.

About a quarter of an hour before the Lodge is to open, a
Brother, selected beforehand as Preparer for Initiation, and who
ought to be wholly unknown to the Candidate, will communicate,
by some agreed signal, with the Brother having him in charge.

O. 9.   *   *   *   *   *   *

You have asked to be advanced to the Temple of Free-
masonry. To attain what you desire, you must submit to its
Laws, and undergo the tests of initiation into the Ancient
Mysteries, the tests of the four ancient elements. The first is
of the EARTH. You will undergo it here, in the bowels of the

earth, under-ground, seated on that to which the bodies of men are sooner or later committed. "The way of life is above to the wise, that he may depart from the hell beneath." The loathsome inmates of the dungeon and cavern will keep you company : they, and the dead in his coffin, and the bones of the perjured traitor rotting unburied. When I leave you, carefully survey and explore the place in which you are! Read what is written on its walls! Reflect! Pause! Debate with yourself! If your life has been innocent, or when not so, its faults repented of; if your heart is pure, and your motives laudable, and your courage firm, *Proceed!* otherwise, DEPART! and seek to know no more. "He who comes in with vanity departs in darkness, and his name shall be covered with darkness."

If you resolve to proceed, answer in writing the questions which lie upon the table, and do what is required at the end of those questions. Answer the questions according to your true opinions and sincere convictions! Do all precisely as you would if it were certain that you were never to emerge from this silent darkness into the light of the upper world! When you have finished, ring the bell.

O. 10.　　*　　*　　*　　*　　*　　*

The questions are written on a sheet of paper, with sufficient spaces between them for answers of some length. They are as follows :

"*Profane, buried in the bowels of the Earth, and beyond the reach of mortal aid, except at our will, answer as you would answer to God.*"

"*1st. Man, compounded of a body and a soul, owes duties to himself as each. What are those duties?*"

"*2d. What duties does man owe to his fellow-creatures?*"

"*3d. What duties does man owe to his country, and what is he bound, in her distress, or to defend her honor, to sacrifice upon the Altar of the Commonwealth?*"

"*4th. What duties does man owe to his Creator?*"

When you have answered these questions, write your last will and testament, precisely as you would if on the eve of engaging in battle, or immured here, without hope of a release, for life.

" The lip of Truth shall be established forever: a lying tongue is but for a moment. BEWARE!"

When the candidate has had time to examine the room and read the inscriptions and the questions, to reflect, and to be ready to write his answers,

O. 11.   *   *   *   *   *   *

and so remain until the Candidate rings the bell. He will then hear the steps of the Preparer approaching, who, unlocking the door, and opening it a little, will ask:

P∴ What do you desire?

If the candidate wishes to depart without initiation, he will conduct him to a room, and send to him the Brother who proposed him. If he says that he has finished, the Preparer will ask:

P∴ Have you answered the Questions?

C∴ I have.

P∴ Have you made your last Will and Testament?

C∴ I have.

P∴ Your probation is not yet over. We are not sure of your sincerity. Eat of the bread and drink of the water before you. They are the food of the victims of temporal and spiritual tyranny. Before you, also, are salt, sulphur, and mercury, the three principles of our Brothers the Alchemists, with which to perform the great work. To separate and unite are the great processes of the Universe. Man is threefold, of body, mind, and spirit conjoined. The salt, sulphur, and mercury are their symbols. Taste of the salt. The bodies of the dead dissolving, their particles become parts of the bodies of the living. Burn a little of the sulphur! Its flame and smoke are symbols of your good and evil thoughts. Take of the mercury in your hand, and seek to divide it into portions, these remaining near each other! The spirit is simple and indivisible. Reflect, and learn!

He again closes the door; but soon re-opens it, and asks:

P∴ Hast thou done as thou wast bidden?

If he answers in the affirmative, the Preparer will advance to the table, blindfold him again, and, taking the questions and answers and the will, conduct him by the way he came, to the Preparation-room.

Arrived there, he raps once, lightly, at the door opening into the Lodge, and in a whisper informs ♄, who opens it, that the candidate is there, having done what he was required in the Chamber of Reflection. ♄, returning, so informs ☉, in a low voice. Meanwhile, the bandage is removed from the candidate's eyes.

☉ raps once, and ⊕ and ○ repeat it.

☉∴ My Brethren, the Profane, A...... B......, having been duly elected to receive the first degree of Freemasonry, it is now in the order of the work to proceed with his reception. If you are disposed to do so, give me the sign!

All do so, by extending the right arm and hand.

☉∴ The Profane, having passed through the Chamber of Reflection, is in waiting, in the hands of the Brother E......, his Preparer. Brother Senior

Deacon, repair to the Chamber of Preparation, receive what the Brother Preparer may hand to you, and bring the same hither.

℞ goes to the Preparation-room, receives from the Preparer the questions, answers, and will, inquires in a whisper as to the conduct of the candidate, returns to the Lodge, and, standing in his place, gives the sign, and reports what he has been informed by the Preparer.

⊙∴ Has he been duly tested by salt, sulphur, and mercury, which are of the earth?

♄∴ He has.

⊙∴ Bring to the East his answers to the customary questions, and his last will and testament!

This is done, and ⊙ reads the answers aloud, and says:

⊙∴ ♪ Brethren Senior and Junior Wardens, invite the Brethren on your columns to offer such remarks as they think proper in regard to these replies, and whether he who makes them is a fit person to be initiated.

⊕∴ ♪ Brother Junior Warden, Brethren who grace the column of the North, the Venerable Master invites you, etc.

○∴ ♪ Brethren, who grace the column of the South, etc.

[This form of announcement, being always followed, will not need to be repeated hereafter. It will only be said, " *The Wardens repeat.*"]

After debate, or if there is none, ☿ will conclude. If he advises reception, ☉ will read aloud the last will and testament. If he advises against it, a ballot will be taken in the manner already prescribed. If a majority of votes be for reception, then the last will and testament will be read. If a majority be against it, the candidate will be sent away. If his replies show great lack of intelligence, Atheism, or want of moral principle, he should not be received. This is what ☿ will have discussed.

When the will has been read, ☉ will again direct that the Brethren be invited to offer their remarks. The Wardens invite them. ☿ concludes; and whatsoever he may advise, the ballot is taken again. If a majority are still in favor of reception, it proceeds. The questions and answers and will are passed to the Secretary, and placed in the Archives. Then ☉ says:

☉∴ Brother Secretary, are you satisfied that we should proceed ?

If he says *Yes*, the ceremony proceeds. If the fee has not been actually paid him, he says *No*, and ☉ says:

☉∴ Then, my Brother, go and do your duty !

In that case △ goes out, and demands and receives the fee; but it *should* always be paid him before ✠ enters the Chamber of Reflection. If he declines to proceed, or is sent away, it will be returned; but his answers and the will must always be retained. When △ returns, having the fee, he says:

△∴ Venerable Master, I am now satisfied.

☉∴ Brother Senior Deacon, you will now return to this Profane. Duly prepare him ! Bring him to the door of the Temple, and give him in charge to the Brother Master of Ceremonies !

♄ obeys, taking assistance with him, if he desires. He first requires the candidate to read over, aloud, the sentences painted on the wall, or printed and suspended there.   Then he proceeds duly and truly to prepare him.

O. 12.   *   *   *   *   *   *

Thus prepared, he is led to the door.   ♃ receives him, and ♄ returns into the Lodge.

-Then ♃ gives one loud rap on the door.   ☉ repeats it, and then ⊕, and ⊕ says, with a loud voice:

⊕∴ ♪ Venerable Master, some one knocks at the door of the Temple, as a Profane.

☉∴ ♪ See who it is, my Brother!   See who is the rash man that dares disturb our labors!

⊕∴ ♪ Brother Junior Warden, see who knocks, and who is the rash man that dares disturb our labors!

☉∴ Brother Junior Deacon, see, etc.

[If there is a Pursuivant, ♂ will pass this and future orders to him, and he will reply *to* ♂, what is set down *for* the latter, *he then replying to* ☉. This will be continually understood hereafter in all the degrees.]

♂ or ♐ will entirely open one leaf of the door, if it have two.

O. 13.   *   *   *   *   *   *

♃∴ It is the Brother Master of Ceremonies, who presents a Profane, desiring to be admitted to our Respectable Lodge, dedicated to Saint John of Scotland.

♂∴ Brother Junior Warden, it is the Brother Master of Ceremonies, who presents a Profane desiring to be admitted to our Respectable Lodge, dedicated to Saint John of Scotland.

☉∴ ♪ Brother Senior Warden, it is, etc.

⊕∴ ♪ Venerable Master, it is our Brother, the Master of Ceremonies, who rashly dares to present a Profane desiring to be admitted to our Respectable Lodge, dedicated, etc.

⊙∴ [In a loud and excited tone] : My Brethren, arm! Seize your swords! Brother Master of Ceremonies, how dare you seek to bring a Profane into the Temple? Was not the ancient warning given? *"Remain afar, ye Profane!"* What is it you mean? What is it you seek?

♃∴ That this Profane be admitted one of ourselves.

⊙∴ By what right does he dare to hope for that?

♃∴ By being a MAN—free-born, and of good repute.

⊙∴ Since he is a man, free-born, and of good repute, demand of him his name, the place of his birth, his age, his religion, his profession, office or occupation, and the place of his present residence.

♃∴ [To the candidate, who will be hereafter designated, for brevity, by the character ✠∴] : The Venerable Master demands your name. What is it?

✠∴ A...... B......

♃ stands on the outside, and asks the questions. ♂, standing within, reports the answers to ○, he to ⊕, and he to ⊙, thus:

♃∴ Brother Junior Deacon, his name is A...... B......

♂∴ Brother Junior Warden, his name is A......
B......

○∴ Brother Senior Warden, his name is A......
B......

⊕∴ Venerable Master, his name is A......
B......

♃∴ Where were you born?

The questions directed are thus all separately asked and answered. As the answers are given, the Secretary notes them in his minutes. When all are answered:

☉∴ Let the Profane enter!

As this order is given, a mournful strain of

MUSIC

is played in the East.

O. 14.   *   *   *   *   *   *

✠∴ It is.

☉∴ Consider well, sir, what it is you ask. You do not know the dogma or the objects of the Ancient Order to which you seek to surrender yourself. It is not merely a society for mutual relief, and to dispense charities within a limited outer circle. When any society has the strength of numbers, it necessarily owes duties to *the* COUNTRY, as a *Society*, far higher than those which the members owe to each other. To fail to perform these duties is to abdicate, and the non-performance being continued, becomes chronic impotence. For a long time not only most societies, but most individuals, have failed to perform their highest duties to their country, exclusively engaged, as they have been, in selfishly caring for their own interest and welfare.

The Order into which you now ask to enter acknowledges its responsibilities, its duties to the country, its duties to humanity, the necessity for progress. Thus it has the right of demanding the performance of grave duties, and stern sacrifices, of its Initiates. It has foreshadowed to thee what these duties may be; what the extent of these sacrifices. Thy descent into the bowels of the earth, thy confinement in the dungeon, are typical of, and shadow forth, both. The sword near thy heart indicates also one sacrifice that may become necessary, as well as the punishment of those who refuse to follow out the inexorable rectilinear logic of duty, and to obey the mandates of a despotic patriotism. Death, or a grave in exile, is an acceptable alternative for dishonor, and the true name of Devotion is Disinterestedness. We are but atoms of the great aggregate which constitutes that fraction of the unit of humanity, our country. We are the leaves on the great tree. What though the leaves fall upon the roots! will not the tree still continue to grow? The calamities of the present are the terrible price of the future. From the pressure of all desolation faith gushes forth. Sufferings bring their agony, and ideas their immortality. These mingle, and compose death. He who dies in the performance of duty, dies in the radiance of the future, and enters a grave illuminated by the dawn.

It is always for the ideal, and for the ideal alone, that those devote themselves who do devote themselves. Men sacrifice themselves for visions, which, to the sacrificed, are almost always illusions, but illusions with which, upon the whole, all human certainties are mingled.

The preparation by Abraham to sacrifice his only legitimate son, is a grand and sublime allegory. So a country or a society must place its children on the altar when the coming generation demands it.

We have spoken to you of an obligation. The Order will demand one of you—solemn, exacting, terrible. It has been taken by many of the best and greatest men that ever lived. By the lives and deeds of these men you may know to what the Ancient and Accepted Scottish Rite prompts and stimulates its initiates. Nor is that obligation all. The Roman youth, in the days before Octavius, saw daily in the atrium of his habitation the marble statues of his ancestors, and was thereby daily taught and obligated to imitate their virtues, and emulate their heroic deeds. He is a traitor to a heroic ancestry who is not himself heroic. The old French said, " *Noblesse oblige.*" With us, "*Maçonnerie oblige.*" It is our motto: MASONRY IS OBLIGATION. He is a traitor to Masonry who does not do the duties of a Mason, into whatever calamity that may lead him. He might justly be dealt with by the sword or the cable-tow; and of this, the sword at your heart, and the rope around your neck, remind you. Let the feeling of each be never effaced from your memory.

Sightless and helpless, you know your rights as a man, since, by being such, you assert a claim to enter here. Yet you are at the mercy of you know not whom. Sad type of a people, blind, bound, and defenceless, with the threefold cord of oppression around its neck!

This Order had its birth in that Mysterious Orient, which is yet an enigma to the Profane; and its roots reach back to the remote past. It is the growth or ruin of centuries. It is a sphinx. The Oidipos who attempts to solve the enigma and fails, or half succeeds, dies the victim of inexorable Fate. You have passed through the first test of the ancient initiations, that of the EARTH. Its pitiless rigor has been softened, so that it remains but a symbol of what it was. Others are to follow, to bear which, without faltering, will require all your courage. Are you resolved to submit to them? Have you the courage to brave all the possible dangers to which that resolution may expose you?

✠∴ I have.

☉∴ Once again, I warn you to reflect. If you

become a Freemason, of the Ancient and Accepted Scottish Rite, you will find the stern realities of duty behind its symbols. You must not only war against and subdue your own passions, but you must, in earnest, strive and strike to overcome other foes of Humanity ; the hypocrites, who deceive it ; the faithless, who defraud ; the fanatics, who oppress it ; the ambitious, who usurp upon it ; and the corrupt and unprincipled, who make profit of the confidence of the masses. One does not war against these without personal danger. Have you the energy, the resolution, the devotion, to engage in that life-long warfare against Darkness, Perfidy, and Error ?

☩∴ I have.

☉∴ Since you are resolute, proceed ! I am acquit of all responsibility. Terrible Brother, take this Profane beyond the precincts of the Temple, and let him pass through that which every mortal must pass through, who is resolved, rashly, to enter into this Holy place !

The Terrible Brother takes the candidate by the arm, leads him out, through the Preparation-room, and round by different circuits and passages, to the principal entrance to the Lodge. Meanwhile this door will have been opened, and the Cave placed close to the door on the inside.

O. 15.   *   *   *   *   *   *

☉∴ Whom have you there, Brother Senior Warden ?

⊕∴ The Terrible Brother, Venerable Master, our Minister of Justice, with the Profane, who asks initiation.

☉∴ Has he brought the Profane hither again in safety?

⊕∴ Brother Junior Warden, has the Terrible Brother brought the Profane hither in safety?

○∴ Terrible Brother, hast thou brought the Profane hither in safety?

Terr∴ He is here, unhurt. The Brothers of the Light dragged him from me as a spy, into the Cave of Death, from which I rescued him for further trial.

○∴ He is here, Brother Senior Warden, unhurt. The Brothers of the Light dragged him from the Terrible Brother, as a spy, into the Cave of Death, from which the Terrible Brother rescued him for further trial.

⊕∴ Venerable Master, he is here unhurt, etc.

☉∴ It is thus, my friend, through dangers and difficulties that men attain initiation. So do false philosophies and specious plausible creeds, pretending to be Brethren of the Light, drag down the soul that listens to them into the Pit of Error. Though Masonry, sir, is not a Religion, and proclaims absolute freedom of conscience, still it has a creed, and Masons agree that one ought not to engage in any important undertaking, without first invoking the assistance of the Grand Architect of the Universe.

Conduct the candidate near to the Junior Warden.
and let him kneel for the benefit of prayer. If he is
worthy to become a Mason, he will join us in the
prayer we are about to offer up in his behalf.
Brother Junior Warden, place him in charge of the
Senior Deacon !

Then, calling up the Brethren, he will say :

⊙∴ My Brethren, join me in the orisons I am
about to offer up to the Author of all created things,
for this our friend !

If there be a musical instrument, and Brethren who can sing,
the Prayer may be sung or chanted, as follows :

HYMN.

GRAND ARCHITECT of all that hath a place
In the illimitable realms of space,
To whom Humanity its being owes !
THE ONE, from whom the manifold outflows !

Benignly bear our earnest, humble prayer,
And over us extend Thy watchful care !
Help us, Thy faithful workmen, to fulfill,
In this our workshop, Thy majestic will !

In this great warfare which we here maintain,
Let us the victory o'er our passions gain !
And let the world behold us, evermore,
Bow reverently the God-like Truth before.

Be Thou, Oh Father! guardian and guide
To this Profane, blind, feeble, and untried!
Fraud, malice, evil, help him overcome,
And let him find the Lodge a happy home!

If there be no instrument or no singers, ☉ will repeat, instead of the Hymn, all kneeling, the following

PRAYER.

OUR Father who art in Heaven! we humble ourselves before Thee, the Sovereign Arbiter of all the worlds. We recognize Thy infinite Power and our infinite feebleness. Help us to contain our hearts and souls within the limits of righteousness, and enable us, journeying by safe ways, to elevate ourselves towards Thee, the Grand Architect and Lord of the Universe! Thou art One, and Self-existent; to Thee every. created thing owes its being. Thy energy acts in everything and through everything; and, invisible to every creature, Thou seest all things. Thee alone we invoke, and to Thee alone we address our prayers.

Deign, oh Grand Architect, to protect the peaceful workmen whom Thou seest here assembled! Make more ardent their zeal and devotion! Strengthen their souls in the arduous struggle against their passions; fill their hearts with the love of Virtue, and enable them to overcome! So also enable this aspirant, who desires to partake of our august mysterics.   Lend him Thy aid, and uphold him now and always, in all trials and perplexities, in all dangers and difficulties, with Thy Omnipotent arm!   AMEN!

All. SO MOTE IT BE!   AMEN!

When the hymn or prayer is ended, the Brethren will rise; ⊙ will rap o, and all will be seated, the candidate continuing to kneel.   Then ⊙ will say :

⊙∴ My friend, in whom do you put your trust?

☩∴ In God.

⊙∴ Since your trust is in God, arise! follow boldly your leader, and fear no danger.

♄ causes him to rise, places him between the columns, and profound silence ensues.

⊙ raps once : ⊕ and ◯ repeat it.   Then the following questions are put to ☩, ♄ first giving him a seat.

XIV.

THE INTERROGATION.

⊙∴ SIR, before the august association, whose organ I am, permits you to be tried by the other material and corporeal tests, it seeks to fathom the depths of your heart; and it requires you to respond with entire freedom and frankness.

What thoughts occurred to you when you were buried in the bosom of the earth, and required to

write your will? Answer frankly! Your answer
will not offend us.

✠ must answer each question without prompting. The remarks of ☉, following his answers, will be varied, if the answers
should require it; or they may, if necessary, be added to.

When the first question is answered, ☉ says:

☉∴ We have already in part indicated to you
for what purpose you were submitted to the first
test—that of the EARTH. The Ancients held that
there were four elements, EARTH, AIR, WATER, and
FIRE. That they were mistaken in these being elements, or the Simple Principles of things, in no way
interferes with the Symbolism which connected itself
with them, and has come down to us; since the
Truths embodied in that symbolism are genuine and
immortal. The Kabalah of the Hebrews, and our
Brethren the Alchemists and Hermetic philosophers,
also recognized these as the four elements; and
aspirants to Initiation have in all ages been tested by
each.

You were immersed, alone, in the darkness and
silence of a subterranean vault or dungeon, as a
prisoner, and surrounded by emblems of mortality
and the written utterances of wisdom: firstly, to
compel serious and solemn reflection, the proper preparation of a step so momentous as initiation into the
Mysteries. It was hoped that you would remember
that the Dungeon has ever been one of the chief in-

struments of Tyranny, whether of the Despot or the
Prelate: that in the Middle Ages, the castles of the
nobles were reared on the arches of dungeons: that
the Inquisition had its dark cells for its victims: and
that the Bastille was but one among hundreds of
prisons, built by Kings, or Tyrants like those of
Venice, and tenanted by those who were deemed
dangerous or suspicious, who were in the way of a
royal or noble amour, or who had in their keeping a
perilous secret.

And we hoped that you, remembering this, would
be inspired with a pious anger against all Despotism,
over the body or the conscience: and with a more
fervent love for such free institutions of Government
as forbid the imprisonment of a Galileo for announcing a physical fact, and that of a Hampden or a
Sydney for proclaiming political truths so rudimental
that they are now taught as axioms to children.

The first act of an oppressed people, asserting its
right, under God's patent, to freedom, is to destroy
the Bastilles which were the pride and safety of
their imperious Masters. We hoped that you would
reflect that it could not but be the duty of a Society
of intelligent men not only to do its utmost to release
the prisoners unjustly confined in dungeons of stone
and iron ; but also to demolish the Bastilles, stronger
than those material ones, in which Ignorance and
Error, Superstitions and Prejudices, keep manacled

the spirits, the intellects, and the consciences of so vast a majority of the great human family.

Remembering, too, how the dungeon had often been more ennobled than the throne and the altar, by the presence and immolation there of the noble victims of Tyranny; how great works of intellect had been written there; how often their doors, turning on the harsh hinges, had opened only to send the wise, the great, and the good to the pyre or the scaffold, we had the right to hope that you too would resolve to maintain the sacred cause of freedom and toleration, even at the risk of incarceration, and of a lifetime spent in solitude and darkness. The cell of the Martyr of Liberty is irradiated with a holy light; the dungeon of the Victim of Spiritual Despotism retains the traces of the consoling presence of the Holy Spirit of God.

The emblems of mortality around you could not but teach you to reflect on the instability and brevity of human life. But that, by itself alone, is a trite lesson, daily taught and ever disregarded. You should also have reflected of how little value is that which is so short and held by so uncertain a tenure, when weighed in the scales against Duty and Honor; and how infinitely mean is an ignoble, useless, idle life, in comparison with a glorious death, or with benefits conferred on one's country or one's fellows, at the risk of life.

Orpheus, the Grecian allegory said, descended into the gloomy shades of the Infernal regions; and Virgil makes Æneas to do the same. The Candidate in the Ancient Initiations did so, and saw represented many of the Tartarean horrors. Initiation was constantly termed '*a new birth,*' '*regeneration*;' and to be born again, it was deemed that one must first descend into the grave. Of that the Cave into which you were dragged is symbolical. If you desire to become a true Mason, you must first die to vice, errors, and vulgar prejudices, and be born again, ascending through the Seven Spheres over which the Seven Archangels preside, to Virtue, Honor, and Wisdom—to *manliness,* in short—the synonym of the Roman word for virtue.

In whatever you see or hear in Masonry you will find a meaning. If it is hidden from you, search and you shall find it. Every symbol and all the ceremonial are replete with significance, and have a reason for being found here. Let those who deem our ceremonies idle and ridiculous, still think so. "*Cast not your pearls before swine,*" the MASTER said, "*lest they trample them under their feet, and turn again and rend you.*" The Mason to whom Freemasonry is not a grave and serious affair, is a *false* Mason; and if anything in the ceremonial seems absurd or trivial, it seems so only to ignorance, which we are glad to enlighten, or to self-conceit, which is not worth enlightening.

Let me also caution you against imagining that we scoff at religious creeds. You will learn the creed of Masonry hereafter. Know, meanwhile, that although we deem no homage more worthy of God than Candor, Science, and Virtue; and although we admit into the bosom of our Order all men possessed of those gifts, whatever their religion; though the Christian, the Hebrew, the Mahometan, the Hindū, and Pagans, like Socrates, and Cicero, and Plato, may meet around our altars as brethren; and the Holy Bible is of the furniture of a Christian Lodge alone; still we are neither hostile nor indifferent to religion, nor seek to set Masonry in its place. There is no antagonism or rivalry between the altars of the two. They may well and fitly stand side by side, if Intolerance do not minister at those of Religion.

Nor are you to imagine that we are the enemies of Government or of the constituted authorities, if that be just, and these worthy of honor. We censure and impeach only that which is wrong and hurtful; that, in government, which degrades man and abases the dignity of human nature. But woe to the Mason who permits himself to become the instrument of tyranny, the supporter of usurpation, and the apologist for injustice and contempt for the laws and constitutions which contain the eternal guarantees of Liberty.

II. . . . *Do you believe in one Supreme Being?*

* * * * * *

This belief, creditable as it is to your heart, is not the exclusive patrimony of the philosopher, but is also possessed by the savage. Yet this is true in only a limited sense. For though the Barbarian feels that he is not self-existent, and seeks in nature the cause and Author of existence, his God is always in nature, his idol is this God, and his ideas of the Deity being wholly confused and false, he does not really believe in God, but in a *something* above him, which is *not* God, but an idol of the mind. Little more correct are the ideas of a large proportion of the civilized world. Only a few really believe and feel assured that there is a Deity, without form or local habitation, to Whom everywhere is Here, and everywhen is Now; beneficent, tender, merciful, loving, pitiful: an Infinite Wisdom as well as Infinite Power; Whose laws are not the mandates of His will, but the expression of His nature; not right *because* He enacts them, but which His will enacts because they are right, and could not *not* be His laws. Of the existence of the Supreme Deity we have the same evidence as we have of that which exists and thinks in other men and in ourselves. We know the *Soul* when we know its utterances, its action, its effects. In the same manner we know there is a GOD. The Universe is His manifestation. IT, we are sure, does not reflect and think. Thought and speech prove the existence of the soul. The universe

is the Book of God, in which His Thoughts are registered; and by it we know Him and His nature. He
speaks to the soul by its spheres, phenomena, and
events, its greatnesses and its littlenesses, and within
our souls as well as without. Nature is the primitive revelation. Science enlarges our knowledge of
God, because it translates for us more of His language,
and translates it more truly. Philosophy is the Interpreter of Nature, the REVEALER; and Masonry
consists in Morality, Science, Philosophy, and Political and Religious TRUTH.

III. . . . *What do you understand by the word*
VIRTUE?

*   *   *   *   *   *

VIRTUE is an attribute and disposition of the mind,
from which flows effort to overcome or govern the
appetites and passions. It is, we have already said,
in its primitive meaning, *Manliness*. For the word *Vir*,
in the Latin, means a *man*, not merely one fraction
of humanity, which was expressed in the word *homo*,
a human creature, but a true, real, genuine MAN.
The man is VIR*tuous*, who is not *without* desires, appetites, instincts, and passions; but who is master of,
and controls them. For virtue to exist, there must
be a struggle and a warfare. The tame, spiritless,
passionless, negative being is not virtuous. Virtue,
therefore, is not to be confounded with honesty,
benevolence, or even charity, or, calling this by its

better name, Loving-kindness. For honesty belongs
often to the merely apathetic and untempted ; benevolence to negativeness, weakness, and imbecility ; and
kindliness to those who are in many other respects vicious. Virtue is strong, vigorous, active, impassioned,
more sublime in proportion to the energy of the passion
it overcomes. To deprive ourselves of that which
we value, or need, in order to make the unfortunate
happy ; to incur personal danger or discomfort in
order to defend the weak against the powerful, the
unpopular against the popular, the losing cause
against the winning ; to toil for others or the country
without the hope of fee or reward, is virtue ; and to
sacrifice one's self for the country or Humanity, is to
obtain the highest eminence of virtue ; an eminence
which the poorest citizen or private soldier may
reach. Nor is there any pleasure so great and true
as that which attends and follows a victory over our
own instincts, appetites, or passions. To be virtuous is to be happy ; and if it were not, happiness is
not the chief end of man's existence. To be happy
and contented is a privilege bestowed on the animals.
To be satisfied with one's self, even in misery, is the
privilege of a nature in which the human and divine
are intermingled.

IV. . . .   *What do you understand by the word*
" VICE ?"

*   *   *   *   *   *

VICE is the absence or opposite of Virtue; as Darkness, its Symbol, is the absence or opposite of Light, the Symbol of Virtue. It is that disposition and attribute of the soul, which produces the habit of satisfying our desires, and by means of which our appetites and animal instincts and passions continually gain strength, and at last become irresistible. As the habit of the virtuous man is to obey the dictates of Conscience, of that universal Conscience which is the Very Truth, because it is an Emanation from the Eternal Wisdom, so the vicious man offends against the dictates of that Conscience, repents, and again offends, until he at last comes to disregard them altogether, and defy them. It is to impose salutary restraints on the impetuous rush of the appetites, to rise above the vile interests that trouble the Profane, to calm the feverish ardor of the passions, to learn the lofty truths of a sublime philosophy, and teach those truths to one another, and to unfold the wings of the soul to the pure and noble affections only, that we meet in our Masonic Temples. We work indefatigably here, to attain unto sound and solid ideas of glory and virtue; and regulating our conduct by the eternal principles of rational morality, and those rules of Duty and Right which an enlightened conscience prescribes, we educate our souls to attain that just equilibrium of force and sensibility which constitutes the Wisdom and Perfection of Humanity.

But this is no easy task, to be accomplished without laborious effort, in a week or a month. It is to create a *habit*, that shall be a second nature. But it is this task to which you must devote yourself incessantly, until success crowns the work, if you persist in your determination to be received as a Mason.

Perhaps you have come here, a captive to very different ideas, possibly a slave to the false and gross notions of depraved and illy-educated intellects. If to toil earnestly and incessantly in order to attain moral perfection, seems to you an undertaking beyond your strength, you are yet at liberty to return the way you came. If, on the other hand, you feel yourself equal to what Masonry will demand of you, say so! In either case be frank and true, as becomes an honorable man! Do you still persist in your intention to become a Mason?

✠∴ I do.

⊙∴ Every association, sir, has its peculiar laws, and every member has duties to perform: and, as it would be neither just nor wise to impose on any one obligations of whose nature he was not previously informed, I shall now explain to you what will be your primary engagements.

Your first engagement will be absolute secrecy in regard to everything you may have already heard, understood, or discovered among us, and as to everything you may see or that may come to your knowledge hereafter. It would be enough for us to say that we regard this secrecy as an indispensable condition of your initiation, whether it were reasonable or unreasonable. But it is our pleasure to add, that it has always been required, has generally been kept inviolably, and has enabled the Order to render important services to the cause of Human Liberty, at times and in countries when and where Masonry, its objects known, would have been, as indeed it often was, persecuted as heretical or revolutionary.

The second, which would of itself make Masonry the most sacred of all the bonds that unite humanity, if even it did not make it the most noble, imposing, and respectable of associations, expresses a duty that is imbedded as one of the constituent principles of Masonry in its very substance, and belongs to its essence. It is, as I have informed you, the duty of warring against those passions, to be subjugated by which dishonors man, and at last makes him miserable, an object of hatred, or of contempt and pity; of practising the kindly, generous, and beneficent virtues; of giving aid and comfort, physically, morally, and spiritually, to the Brethren, foreseeing, and with kind forethought providing for, their necessities, or relieving these as they arise; giving them good advice and wise counsel, and dispensing among them light and knowledge. All this, regarded as a rare excellence in a Profane, will be, for you as a Freemason, the simple performance of ordinary acts of justice.

Every opportunity to do a kindness, confer a benefit, or render a service to a Brother, of which a Mason does not avail himself, when he can do so without grave and serious injury and injustice to himself and those near to him by the ties of blood-relationship, makes him guilty of an act of faithlessness, and dishonors him : to refuse to assist a Brother is perjury : and true friendship, tender and consoling, is worshipped in our Temples, less because it is a sentiment, than because, being a duty, it may become and be made a virtue.

The third obligation, which you will not contract until after your initiation, will be to conform at all points to the ancient landmarks and general statutes of the Order, and to the particular Laws of your Lodge ; submitting yourself to whatsoever shall, in its name, be legally demanded of you ; and to obey the constitutional and legal mandates and edicts of your lawful chiefs in Masonry.

Now, sir, you know what are the principal duties of a Mason. You may say that Masons too generally do not perform those duties : that their charities are small and rarely bestowed : that their moneys, received for initiations and by contributions, are spent in show and parade : that they rarely assist or advise each other : that they defame and malign one an-

other : that rival rites and rival bodies quarrel : that
Masons prove to be no better and no wiser than
other men : and that a Mason is often the last man
to whom a Mason will apply for assistance in distress,
or for encouragement and support when maligned or
persecuted. You may therefore say to yourself, that
the obligations of the Order are unreal, and its pre-
tensions unfounded ; and that you, too, may safely
take those obligations, because you may, with the
same impunity as others, *neglect* or *violate* them.

However it may be elsewhere, it cannot be justly
charged that such is the condition of the Ancient and
Accepted Scottish Rite. There is no Order or Church
that has not Members who do not practise what they
profess. The authorities of the Ancient and Accepted
Scottish Rite have resolved to form select bodies of
Masons by initiation according to their own forms,
and by selection of the best from among Master
Masons, already made such in the other Rite ; and
within this limited circle to *insist* on the *full* performance of *all* Masonic duty ; to lop off, without mercy,
all dead and decayed branches, and no longer to permit the presence of the faithless, the lukewarm, or
the apathetic in their Temples. *Here* Masonic obligations are serious, solemn, and real. Imagine not
that they can be lightly taken, and as lightly disregarded, with impunity. It would be a fatal mistake.

Before proceeding further, we require your oath

of Honor. You must give it, drinking of a Consecrated Cup. If you are sincere, you may drink with confidence; but if falsehood and dissimulation must accompany your promise, swear not at all! Rather put away the Cup, the same as that which, among the ancient Hebrews, drunk by the guilty, caused the curse. Are you prepared to swear?

✠∴ I am.

☉∴ ♪ Let this aspirant arise, and conduct him to the altar!

♃ conducts him to the altar, where he stands on the West side of it, facing the East.

☉∴ Brother Sacrificer, present to this aspirant the Consecrated Cup, deadly as aconite to the forsworn!

SOFT, SLOW MUSIC.

O. 14.   *   *   *

He is reconducted between the Wardens, and seated.

MUSIC CEASES.

☉∴ I will not believe, sir, that you are deceiving either us or yourself. Still, it is well for you to interrogate yourself, since self-deception is the most common and dangerous of errors. It is still permissible for you to decline advancing. And it would be far better to do so, while you may, with honor, than, governed by a false pride, to persist in what, at first

a venial error, would, if continued after repeated
warning, become a crime.

All men drink of the cup of good and evil fortune.
It is the cup of human life. We have permitted you
to do little more than taste the sweet, while you have
been required to drain the bitter to the dregs. Let
this remind you that the wise and just man enjoys
the pleasures of life in moderation, and is not osten-
tatious of the good that he enjoys, since by that
ostentation he would insult misfortune ; and that as
suffering enters more largely into the lot of most men
than happiness and enjoyment, we should be patiently
resigned to suffer when our Father in Heaven sends
us calamities and afflictions. We should be unworthy
to share the benefits which society and association
afford, if we were not also ready to share the evils
which our Brethren and fellows suffer. Woe unto
him who despairs, when he has to drain the Cup of
suffering to the bottom! He is unworthy to be called
a man! Wherefore, if unfortunately thou becomest
a victim, consult thy Conscience! If it accuse thee,
humble thyself, without abjectness, and reform! If,
on the contrary, it do not denounce thee, lift up thy
forehead! for God has made thee in His image and
likeness ; and let reflection enable thee to draw
strength from weakness. Fall not in the struggle,
like a Coward ; but resist like a Hero!

*   *   LITURGY A.   *   *

Our tests are symbolic, and not terrible or dangerous. Still they will try your firmness and resolution.
They foreshadow what you may have to endure, or
violate your obligation as a Mason; and they remind you anew that your resolution must not falter,
nor you purchase liberty or life by dishonor; even
if, like our Masonic fathers, you should some day
find yourself in the cruel and pitiless embrace of a
political or religious Inquisition, that imprisons, and
in the depths of its dungeons, or on its scaffolds, im-
molates those who defend Freedom, or teach her Holy
Doctrines. The Inquisition never found a coward or
informer among Masons. It only sleeps, and may
awake again. The kings imitate each other. You
may not always live in a country where the incontro-
vertible rights of Human Nature are respected. If
they now are so in your own, you may unexpectedly
see a Usurper declare his will to be the only law, and
be suddenly required, at any hazard, to assert the
rights of the People and the majesty of the law
against him. The nation that is free to-day may be
enslaved to-morrow; the too free soonest submitting,
subservient to the Despot's ancient plea, Necessity.
Republic yesterday, Kingdom to-day, Empire to-
morrow—such are the fantastic scene-shiftings of
Nations. Therefore reflect well before you further

commit yourself! When you shall have taken a step further in advance, it will be too late to draw back. Your destiny will then have been determined.

O. 17.   *   *   *   *   *

XV.

THE JOURNEYS.

⊙∴ HAVE you well reflected, sir, on the grave issues involved in that which has engaged your consideration? I ask you for the last time. Will you return to the outer world, or do you still resolve to become a Mason?

✠∴ ——— ——— ——— ———

The candidate replying that he will advance, ⊙ raps once, ⊕ and ○ repeat it, and ⊙ says, in a loud voice:

⊙∴ Terrible Brother, take possession of this Profane, and cause him to make his first journey! Use your best efforts to bring him back in safety!

O. 18.   *   *   *   *   *   *

⊙∴ I congratulate you, sir, on your safe return. You have already been informed that the tests of Masonry are symbolical. What have you chiefly remarked in your journey? What ideas has it sug-

gested, to what reflections given birth? Of what
does it seem to you symbolical?

✠ answers, and is then seated.

☉∴ This first journey, with its roarings, its thun-
ders, its electric shocks, represents the second element, the Air, which, with its meteors, miasms,
lightnings, and continual fluctuations, incessantly
menaces us with death. It was anciently considered
one of the means by which the souls of the dead were
purified. "As physical bodies," the old sages said,
"are exalted from earth to water, from water to air,
from air to fire, so the man may rise into the Hero,
the Hero into the God." In the course of nature the
soul, to recover its lost estate, must pass through a
series of trials and migrations. The scene of those
trials is the Grand Sanctuary of Initiation, the universe: their primary agents are the elements, and
Dionusos is official arbiter of the Mysteries, guide of
the Soul, the Sun, the Liberator of the elements,
Creator of the world, Guardian, Liberator and Saviour of the Soul, ushered into the world amidst
lightnings and thunder.

Again, the Air is a symbol of *Vitality* or life.
When Yehûah-Alohim, says the Ancient Hebrew
Cosmogony, had formed man of the dust of the
ground, He breathed into his nostrils the breath of
life, and man became a living Soul. The Air, to the

Hebrews, symbolized *Nephesch,* or Vitality, the lowest portion of the immaterial part of man, of the Trinity of LIFE, SPIRIT, and MIND. The Air, therefore, is a natural and apt emblem of human life, with its cross-currents, its agitations, its stagnations, its lassitudes and energies, its storms and calms, its electrical disturbances and equilibria. So also the comparison of the life of man to a journey, has always been familiar to moralists and philosophers: and thus the journey you have taken is a fit emblem of that life, with its tumult of the passions, its shocks of conflicting interests, its difficult undertakings, its successes and reverses, its obstacles, multiplying and co-operating to hinder and embarrass.

But this is too trite an interpretation, though true, to be the only one. Your journey also represents the Progress of a People; that Progress, to assist in which is the highest aim of Freemasonry. Progress is the Mode of Man. The general life of the Human Race is called Progress. It is the collective advance of the Human Race. Progress marches; it makes the great human and terrestrial journey toward the Celestial and the Divine, from the Square to the Compass. It meets delays, recoils at and then overcomes its obstacles: it has its halts, where it rallies the belated flock: it has its stations, where it meditates, in sight of some Canaan, suddenly unveiling its horizon. It has its nights when it sleeps: and it is one of the bitter anxieties of the Thinker, to see the shadow upon the Human Soul, and in the darkness to feel Progress asleep, without being able to waken it.

But he who despairs is wrong. Progress infallibly awakens; and even in sleep it advances, for it has grown. When we see it standing again, we find it taller. To be always peaceful belongs to Progress no more than to the air and the river. Each of these meets obstructions; the air-currents flow against and around forests and mountains; the river flows over rocks. These make the air roll and eddy in billows, the water foam, and humanity seethe. Hence storms, hurricanes, cataracts, eddies, and counter-currents, troubles, confusions, revolutions; but after these we find that ground has been gained. The Inquisition imprisons Galileo, but the Earth still moves. Until Order, which is but Universal Peace, be established, until harmony and unity reign, Progress will have Revolutions for stations.

The Nations, moreover, are blind, and the DESTINY that leads them onward is symbolized by your guide, the Terrible Brother. Statesmen are but puppets in the hands of Destiny and Providence; blind instruments of a Higher and Inscrutable will. The ends to which their labors and their virtues or villainies tend, are not those for which they struggle, and toward which they seem to themselves to make the nation march. The few intellects that really and truly foresee, rarely control and govern. They are Cassandras, whose prophecies are wholly unheeded. The individual man, also, is blind, led by the cords of destiny in the hands of those who educate him, and of the circumstances that surround him. The opinions of the mass of men are imposed upon them, not adopted upon reflection and examination. Custom and Prejudice are the blind guides of the blind. Yet the Truth dreads nothing : and he who does not exercise his Reason, even in matters of faith, remains a child, a blind traveller, all his life. To forbid one the use of his reason, and to require him to accept his faith at the dictates of another, is an absurdity ; since, if faith be unreasoning, no man can show in what respect *his* faith deserves the preference over that of any other. Every man has a right to say, *for himself*, like Tertullian, that he will believe a thing because it is a folly, and hold it certain, because it is impossible ; but no man has a right to demand that any other man shall, at his dictation, do the same.

Wherefore, as you have now experienced the helplessness and abdication of manhood which are involved in being blinded and led by a guide, let no one hereafter lead you, blinded, in matters of faith ; but in all things see for yourself, and judge for yourself by the laws of Reason and Analogy.

Finally, as after the storm comes a calm, and after the earthquake repose, so, when the period of tests and trials shall have passed—the age of error and doubt—the tranquillity of Reason will be enjoyed, of that peace of the soul which satisfies the conscience. After the Revolutions of Progress, the stability and repose of Free Institutions! After the storms and conflicts of the individual life, the serenity and quiet of the soul—result of a just equilibrium of the appetites, the passions, the moral energies, and the intellectual powers. To attain this within himself, to aid his country in its progress toward it, is to do the true work of a Mason, and requires, above all things, constancy and courage. Such are the wise lessons of the test by AIR. Are you ready to encounter the hazards of the second journey?

✠∴ I am.

☉∴ Terrible Brother, take this Profane on his second journey!

O. 19.   *   *   *   *   *   *

☉∴ Again I congratulate you, sir, on your safe return. Terrible Brother, permit him to be seated!

You have been subjected to the third test, that of WATER. The brazen laver, containing the Water in which your hand has been three times dipped, represents those placed by King Salamoh in the Temple, and that Brazen Sea in the Temple, which, supported on twelve oxen that looked to the cardinal points of the Compass, was an image of the great ocean that washes the shores of the world. In all the ancient initiations, the symbolical purification of the soul, by the washing of the body, was an indispensable part of the ceremonial.

* * LITURGY B. * *

In all, the symbol of washing or baptism by water meant the same thing—purification of the hand and heart. As such it was used by the Essenes and John the Baptist, and adopted as part of the ceremonial of Christianity. It was peculiarly expressive in the hot, dry Orient, where rivers are blessings flowing from God, and springs in the desert are called diamonds. Naturally, to the dweller on the Nile, the Ganges, the Euphrates, or the Jordan, purification of the body by water became the symbol of purification of the soul.

The Ocean, also, has always been an apt symbol of the People, to whose service every true Mason devotes himself. Inert in calm, and in the tropics almost stagnant, it is agitated and wrinkled by the least movement over it of the winged winds. Tortured by tempest, its huge waves shake its iron-bound shores. Its great icebergs drift through it, like Empires on the Seas of Time. Its instability and fury picture the fickle humors and merciless revenges of an exasperated people. Its great currents are like

those of popular opinion. The huge tidal waves, un-
dulating in a few moments across the expanse of the
wide Atlantic, are like the impulses that flash mysteriously through an awakened nation ; and individual men are but the drops of the vast ocean of
humanity, of which the nations are the waves. As
the mariner must incur the hazards of shipwreck and
engulfment in the waves, so must the Patriot who
would serve the People do so at the risk of becoming
odious to it, and being crushed by it in its blind
rage. Let this remind you that you must have a
higher motive for your public action than office and
honors ; since, if the desire for these alone actuates
you, you will infallibly cease to serve the People when
it the most needs your services, and when to be
its benefactor is most noble, because it is most dangerous and least profitable. Terrible Brother, take
this Profane on his third journey !

O. 20.   *   *   *   *   *   *

⊙∴ In this last journey, sir, you have passed
through the test of FIRE, the last mode of symbolic
purification. "*I, indeed,*" said JOHN the BAPTIST,
"*baptize you with water unto repentance, but He that
cometh after me shall baptize you with the Holy Spirit
and fire.*" Human ceremonies are indeed but imperfect symbols, and the alternate baptisms in fire and
water, intended to purify us unto immortality, are

even in this world interrupted at the moment of their anticipated completion. Life is a mirror, which reflects only to deceive, a tissue perpetually interrupted and broken, an urn forever fed, yet never full.

The Deity Himself was symbolized by all the ancient nations as LIGHT, FIRE, or FLAME. The worship of the SUN was the basis of all the Religions of Antiquity. To the Ancients light and heat were mysteries; and the symbol of purification by fire became, in the worship of the Gods, the actual sacrifice of innocents in the flames. For so the symbol, especially in religions, always tends to usurp the place of that which it symbolizes; the idol comes to be worshipped as the God of which it was originally the symbol, and the ceremony and formulas to be deemed possessed of the virtue and efficiency of saving grace.

Purified by water and fire, you are symbolically free of all stain of vice. It is a solemn pledge on your part that you will continually strive to become so. The fire, moreover, whose flame has always symbolized aspiration, ardor, and zeal, reminds you that you must always aspire toward excellence and true glory, and labor with ardor and zeal in the cause in which you engage, especially if that cause be the cause of the People.

One other test remains. The Masonic Order or

your country may at some time need that you should shed your blood in its defence. A true Mason cannot shrink from the sacrifice. Socrates refused to escape when the prison-doors were opened. Regulus advised Rome not to make peace, and returned to the enemy to be put to death. Undoubtedly the principal Martyrs of Liberty and the Faith, in all ages, might have lived a little longer, and lost immortal glory, if they had but consented to fawn upon tyranny and sacrifice to the Pagan Gods. Before you can be initiated into our mysteries, you must pass through the baptism of blood. This can, by no means, be omitted. If you feel that you are possessed of devotedness and fortitude enough to offer yourself as a sacrifice to serve the Country, the Order, Humanity, your fellows, at the imminent risk of life, you must now seal your profession of faith with your blood. We cannot accept mere words and promises. Are you prepared?

⊬∴ I am.

O. 21. *   *   *   *   *   *

⊙∴ The Baptism of Blood is not a symbol of Purification. It is the Baptism of Heroism and Devotedness, of the Soldier and the Martyr. It is a solemn pledge that you will not falter in the performance of Masonic duty to your fellows, the Order, or your Country, through fear of the Persecutor or the

Tyrant. The duties of life are more than life ; and to lengthen his days is not the most important of all things to a true Man and Mason. Even the wild Indian, condemned to die, and permitted to go to a distance upon his promise to return, presents himself at the day to be slain, rather than save his life by violating his word. The soldier risks his life daily, not for his pay of a shilling, but for his duty to the flag under which he serves. Shall the Mason's love of life weigh more heavily in the scale against Duty and Honor than that of the rude soldier or ruder barbarian ?

It reminds you also of the blood shed in all ages by Intolerance and Persecution, and pledges you to Toleration and the defence of the sacred rights of Conscience. It reminds you of the Martyrs of all creeds, dying for their faith ; of the bloody sacrifices of the Hebrew altar and the Mexican Teocalli ; of the stake and the rack of the Inquisition, and the gallows stretching its arm over the Christian pulpit ; of all the long roll of atrocities and murders sanctioned by religion, and deemed grateful service to a God of Love.

The time has come, sir, for you to perform a simpler and easier act of Masonic duty. We have unfortunate Masons, widows, and orphans, to whom the Lodge gives continual assistance. I shall send a Brother to you, to whom you will make known, in a

whisper, how much you are now willing to contribute
for the relief of these unfortunates. You will not
say it aloud; for you are to know that the charitable
acts of Masons, not being acts of ostentation and
vanity, to minister to the pride of him who gives,
and humiliate him who receives, ought always to be
shrouded in secresy. "When thou doest alms, let
not thy left hand know what thy right hand doeth;
that thine alms may be in secret; and thy Father
which seeth in secret, will reward thee openly."

c goes to the Candidate, ☉ raps o, and says:

☉∴. Hold! Charity ceases to be a virtue when it
prevents the performance of more sacred and more
pressing duties. Civil engagements to be met, a
family to maintain, relations dealt harshly with by
fortune to relieve, children to rear and educate—
these create the foremost duties that nature imposes
on us; these are the creditors of every man whose
conduct is regulated by the principles of Equity.
The maxim of the Law is the maxim of Masonry—
"*Nemo liberalis nisi liberatus.*" No one must be
liberal until liberated of these paramount duties. To
give what is elsewhere pledged and owing, is to give
what is not our own; is to give, without their consent, what belongs to others. Give, therefore, only
what you *can* give, and yet fully perform those same
duties! At the same time, consider not your own

ease, indulgence, comfort, or luxury, as creditors to be preferred to the poor. To give only so much as we could *throw* away without losing a comfort, or mortifying an appetite, or denying ourselves the indulgence of a wish or whim, is an act of no merit, since it *costs* us nothing and *deprives* us of nothing. He who gives shillings to the poor, and squanders pounds in luxuries or gaming, may indeed do good ; but there is no merit or charity in the act. Determine now what thou wilt give the destitute wards of the Lodge out of what is thine own !

If he refuses to give anything, the Lodge will determine, upon the reasons given by him, whether he shall be received.

The Almoner will, in a whisper, inform ⊙ of the amount he proposes to give. If the offer is a generous one, ⊙ will say :

⊙∴ The gift is a generous one, sir. I expected no less after your professions and promises. The Lodge, which is about to receive you as a Member, expresses through me its approbation, and returns you its thanks. And though the needy, whom your gift will relieve, will not know from whom it comes, you will none the less be enriched by their gratitude and benefited by their prayers.

If the gift is small, ⊙ will say :

⊙∴ If, sir, what you have offered to give be all that your paramount obligations will permit, and if to give it deprives you of some luxury or comfort, and truly makes you poorer than before, it is the widow's mite, as acceptable in the sight of heaven as the rich man's costly offering would be. Your gift is received and accepted by the Lodge with grateful thanks.

After either of these, ☉ will say:

☉∴ You are about, sir, to receive that of which your pledges are the consideration. If those pledges are not faithfully kept, you will have obtained initiation under false pretences, and be guilty of an offence equivalent to that which the law punishes. If you should so offend, you will have given *us* the right to punish you. If we should not exact the penalty, remember that the consequences of crime and wrong inevitably flow from them, and are eternal, by the inflexible law of cause and effect. That law is irrepealable. Brother Master of Ceremonies, take this candidate, and conduct him to the Brother Senior Warden in the West, who will teach him how to take the first step on the angle of an oblong square ; and so let him approach the Altar, to take upon himself the obligation of an Entered Apprentice Mason !

XVI.

THE OBLIGATION.

O. 22. *　　*　　*　　*　　*　　*

☉∴ Rіsе, and again follow your guide!

♃ takes him by the arm, and leads him into the Preparation-
room.
The Hall is darkened. At the entrance to the East are placed
two pans, with resin and alcohol, which, burning, will give the
only light.

O. 23. *　　*　　*　　*　　*　　*

All the Brethren are now armed with naked swords, and form
a semi-circle on the east side of the Altar, the Master and Wardens in the centre. During the Scene that ensues, all point
their blades toward the Candidate. He is led in, and placed
on the West of the Altar, facing the East.

☉∴ In your present condition, sir, what is it you
most desire?

✠∴ LIGHT.

O. 24. *　　*　　*　　*　　*　　*

☉∴ The fitful, melancholy gleams of sombre
light enable thee to see that which represents the
bodiless head of the Essenian Preacher, Jоһנ the
Bартіѕт, whose doctrines, many years after his
death, Apollos, coming from Alexandria, in Egypt,
to Ephesus, taught: of whom, also, after his death,

the Chief Priests and Scribes feared to say that he
was not inspired, lest the people, who all believed
him to have been a prophet, should stone them; to
whose counsel and rebukes Herod listened with
reverence, and who, he thought, was risen from the
dead when CHRIST began to preach. JOHN, an Ere-
mite, preaching reform in the desert-country, near
the Jordan, clad in the garments of a penitent, and
living on the food of a Bedouin, boldly rebuked the
ambitious, haughty, and self-righteous Pharisees and
the skeptical and scoffing Sadducees, as a race of
vipers, and preached human equality and the ultimate triumph of good and evil in the Salvation of the
Lord. He inculcated repentance and reformation, a
liberal charity, and a virtuous life. He exhorted
public officers to exact no more from the people than
that which the law required, and the soldiery to do
violence to no one, accuse no one falsely, and be
content with their legal power and pay. He sternly
reproved Herod for his sinful connection with the
wife of his brother. The lewd and revengeful woman
sought his Death; but Herod imprisoned him without
trial, and so kept him confined, until her daughter,
dancing before him, his lords and captains, on his
birthday, obtained his promise that he would grant
her whatever she might ask, and, prompted by her
mother, she demanded the head of the eloquent
Essenian Missionary.

The abuses of arbitrary power in all ages are summed up in this single legend: the baleful influences of the mistresses of Kings and Emperors; imprisonment, without trial, by *lettres de cachet* and other inventions of tyranny, for acts or words that were not offences defined and punishable by any law; the dependence of liberty and life on the word, revengeful or lascivious, of an amorous Tyrant or wanton woman. In the arbitrary imprisonment of JOHN we see the very essence of tyranny and despotism, the power to imprison, without trial, for what is no crime defined by law; the absence or impotence of any impartial judicial power, to set free the prisoner illegally detained. In the execution we see Murder, as committed in all ages and countries, by Kings and the usurpers of civil and military power; and in JOHN, the bold rebuker of the vices of the people, of the arrogance, hypocrisy, ambition, and infidelity of the Priesthood, of the unjust exactions of the agents of Power or the Law, of the license, violence, usurpation, and rapine of the soldiery, and of the vices of the Crown and Court, we have the type of the true and genuine Freemason, Successor of the Ancient Essenes. Him thou art to imitate, even, if necessary, in his fate.

Moreover, if thou shouldst violate thy solemn obligation, these sombre and gloomy lights, these blades, aimed at thy heart, this bodiless head, typify the vengeance which thou hast now made lawful for us, and from which, if we refrain, it will be to deliver thee to the more terrible punishment of universal hatred, contempt, and execration, to an immortality of infamy and ignominy, in comparison with which death would be a blessing.

Brother Master of Ceremonies, remove this Candidate once more! and let him now and always be sure that, should he prove a traitor to us, there will be no corner of the wide earth in which he can take refuge, into which he will not bear with him the stigma of his crime: that everywhere the report of his excommunication will have preceded him, as if borne by the lightning, and that everywhere he will find Masons informed of his guilt, and detesting his perjury.

The Candidate is again blinded and led out. Then all the lights are lit, and the Lodge assumes its most brilliant appearance. The Brethren are all standing in their places, their swords drawn, sword-arm extended to the front, but the sword-points lowered. The Candidate re-enters, and is led up to the Altar. ☉ raps 0, and says:

☉∴ ♪ Brother Orator, thou hast seen this Candidate descend into the bosom of the earth and there read our solemn lessons. Thou hast heard him renounce the Profane world. Thou hast heard his obligation, and his solemn-sacred pledges. Thou hast seen him cast his prejudices and preconceptions to the wind, be tested by the air, purify himself with water, be sublimated in fire. Dost thou now deem him worthy to be received among us?

☿∴ I do, Venerable Master.

☉∴ ♪ Brother Junior Warden, on whom rests one of the Columns of the Temple, thou hast seen this Candidate offer up his blood as a sacrifice and a pledge that he will serve his fellows, his Country, and Humanity at the hazard of his life. Dost thou deem him worthy to be received among us?

○∴ I do, Venerable Master.

☉∴ ♪ Brother Senior Warden, on whom rests one of the Columns of the Temple, thou hast seen and heard all. In thy presence and hearing the Candidate has taken his vow and sealed his solemn obligation. He is pledged, like our glorious exemplar, JOHN the BAPTIST, to rebuke with boldness, Power, Hypocrisy, Ambition, Usurpation, and Vice; to be the Apostle of the Truth, and to speak it boldly, at the risk of Martyrdom. Dost thou deem him worthy to be received among the Brethren of the Truth, the Vindicators of the Rights of Man?

⊕∴ I do, Venerable Master.

☉∴ And I, too, deem him worthy. Brother Orator, what dost thou ask for this Candidate?

☿∴ *Light!*

☉∴ Brother Junior Warden, what dost thou ask for this Candidate?

⊙∴ LIGHT!

⊙∴ Brother Senior Warden, what dost thou ask for this Candidate?

⊕∴ THE GREAT LIGHT!!

O. 25.   *   *   *   *   *   *

XVII.

LIGHT.

⊙∴ IN the array of swords that now surrounds thee, my Brother, there is nothing at which to be alarmed. Now they are not directed against thee. On the contrary, they are drawn to defend thee until the death, because we have thy obligation, which makes thee a Mason, and we believe thee to be a man of honor and good faith. The fortunate day of loyal friendships and loving Brotherhood dawns for thee; and hereafter thou art to see in us not merely friends, but brethren, ready, with thousands upon thousands over the whole surface of the earth, to hasten to thy assistance against any who may assail thy life or honor, though thou art as yet only an Apprentice, and not entitled to the wages of a Craftsman.

On being brought to light, you see before you the Holy Bible [or the Hebrew Pentateuch], the Compass, and the Square, upon the Altar of Masonry—both points of the Square being over the Compass. These are deemed indispensable in every [Christian] Lodge, and they are called the THREE GREAT LIGHTS of the Lodge. You see them by the blaze of the three lesser Lights of the Lodge, on the East, West, and South of the Altar, Symbols, it is ordinarily said, of the Sun, the Moon, and the Master of the Lodge. These latter are termed, also, the SUBLIME LIGHTS in Masonry. The HOLY BIBLE, it is said, is the rule and law of Government of Masons : the SQUARE governs our actions, and the COMPASS keeps us within just bounds as to all men, and more particularly toward our Brethren.

Our Brethren of the English or York Rite say : The BIBLE points out the path that leads to happiness, and is dedicated to GOD. The SQUARE teaches us to regulate our conduct by the principles of Morality and Virtue, and is dedicated to the MASTER; and the COMPASS teaches us to limit our desires in every station, and is dedicated to the CRAFT. The BIBLE is dedicated to the service of GOD, because it is the inestimable gift of God to man : the SQUARE to the MASTER, because it is the proper Masonic emblem of his office, and it is constantly to remind him of the duty he owes to the Lodge over which he is appointed to preside ; and the COMPASS to the CRAFT, because, by a due attention to its use, they are taught to regulate their desires, and keep their passions within due bounds.

And, as to the Lesser Lights, they say that they are thus explained: As the Sun governs the world by day, and the Moon rules it by night, so ought the Master to rule and govern his Lodge with equal regularity.

⊙∴ raps o, and all the Brethren lay aside their swords, and remain standing, and under the Sign of Order.

⊙∴ ♪ Brother Master of Ceremonies, conduct this new Brother to the Throne.

He is conducted to the East.

⊙∴ Kneel again, my friend, on your right knee.

He does so; and ⊙ laying the blade of his sword on his head, says:

⊙∴ To the Glory of the Grand Architect of the Universe, and under the auspices of the Supreme Council (Mother Council of the World), of the Sovereigns the Grand Inspectors-General, Grand Elect Knights of the Holy House of the Temple, Grand Commanders of the Holy Empire, of the 33d and last Degree of the Ancient and Accepted Scottish Rite of Freemasonry for the Southern Jurisdiction of

the United States, whose See is at Charleston, in
the State of South Carolina . . . [or, if there
be a Grand Consistory, under whose jurisdiction the
Lodge is held . . . "of the Grand Consistory
of Sublime Princes of the Royal Secret, of the 32d
Degree of the Ancient and Accepted Scottish Rite
of Freemasonry, for the State of ...."], and by
virtue of the powers in me vested by this Respectable
Lodge, I do receive and constitute you, A........
B........, an Entered Apprentice Mason, of the
Ancient and Accepted Scottish Rite, and a Member
of this Respectable Lodge.

O. 26.　　*　　*　　*　　*　　*　　*

⊙∴ now hands the Neophyte the Apron, saying:

In the *Rit Moderne*, the Candidate here repeats, or rather
confirms, his obligation, kneeling at the Altar, under the Arch
of Steel.

⊙∴ As you are now a Mason, it is necessary for
you to be clothed as such. Receive this Apron of
white lamb-skin, which Apprentices wear with the flap
turned up. It is the distinctive badge of a Mason;
and our Brethren of the York Rite say that it is
more ancient than the Golden Fleece or Roman
Eagle, more honorable than the Star and Garter, or
any other decoration. It is at least as ancient. It is

honorable, because it is an emblem of labor. You ought, the same Brethren say, to wear it with pleasure to yourself and honor to the fraternity. It has, in all ages, been deemed an emblem of innocence; he, therefore, they say, who wears the lamb-skin as a badge of Masonry, is continually reminded of that purity of life and conduct which is so essentially necessary to his gaining admission into the Celestial Lodge above, where the Supreme Architect of the Universe presides.

The APRON is the evidence of your right to sit among us; and you must never be present in any Lodge without it. Its peculiar and real Symbolism will be made known to you hereafter. You have already the surface-symbolism, that of the horn-book — *Innocence* and *Candor*. "We speak wisdom among them that are *perfect;* not the wisdom of this world, or of the Princes of this world, that come to nought: But we speak GOD's wisdom in a mystery— the HIDDEN, which God had in idea before the Universe existed, to be our Glory, and which none of the Princes of this world knew." PAUL, like the York Rite, spoke to the Corinthians as infants, having an animal, and no spiritual nature, and fed them with milk, and not with meat—*the points of the Compass under the Square.*

Then ⊙ hands the Candidate a pair of white GLOVES for himself, and says:

⊙∴ These also are part of the clothing of a Mason. Be it your care to keep them unsullied, never staining them by vice! Let your hands and heart be always pure and undefiled! Walk as a child of Light, and have no fellowship with the unfruitful works of darkness.

Then he hands him a pair of gloves for a lady, saying:

⊙∴ These the Lodge presents to your wife, or to her who, beloved by you, may hereafter become such. They will be a fit symbol of the purity of true affection, and will be to her as a pledge on the part of the Lodge, that if she should ever need its assistance, consolation, or encouragement, an advocate or a defender, she will find all in the Lodge or among the Brethren.

Masonry, my Brother, has its own speech and peculiar language, which forms a bond of union among all the Masons in the world. It consists in *Signs*, *Grips* or *Tokens*, and *Words*.

O. 27.　　*　　*　　*　　*　　*　　*

⊙∴ Whenever you enter the Temple you will give the SACRED WORD to the Brother Junior Deacon or Pursuivant, who is on the inside; lettering it without preliminary.

Masonry, my Brother, is known all over the world. It is divided into many Rites, the three principal of which are the York or English Rite, worked in Great Britain and her Colonies, and in the United States and in Germany, and some other parts of Europe; the Ancient and Accepted Scottish Rite, and the Rit Moderne, sometimes called the French Rite. The Degrees of the Blue Lodge are essentially the same in all. All rest on the same basis, the same principles. We work in the Ancient and Accepted Scottish Rite, because we know it to be, in its groundwork and principles, and the chief points of its ceremonial, the least defiled by innovation.

There are differences in the language of these Rites, of which you are entitled to be informed.

O. 28.　　＊　　　＊　　　＊　　　＊　　　＊　　　＊

When this instruction has been given, ☉ embraces the Neophyte three times, or kisses him three times on the forehead. Then he says:

☉∴ ♪ Brother Master of Ceremonies, conduct the Neophyte to the Brother Senior Deacon! My Brother, be seated!

The Brethren all sit down. The Neophyte is led to ♄.

☉∴ ♪ Brother Senior Deacon, Grand Expert of the Lodge, be pleased to receive from this Neophyte the Word, Signs, and Token.

♄ receives them, and says:

♄∴ Brother Junior Warden, the Word, Signs, and Token are just and perfect.

○∴ Brother Senior Warden, the Word, etc.

⊕∴ Venerable Master, the Word, etc.

☉∴ ♪ Brother Master of Ceremonies, let this Candidate be reconducted to the place whence he came, and be there reinvested with all whereof he was divested, and then return to the East for further instruction.

When he re-enters the Lodge, ♃ causes him to gain admission for himself by giving the proper battery and the Word to ♂. He then goes with him to near the Altar, and causes him to salute the East, West, and South; and then conducts him to the East.

☉∴ My Brother, it is necessary that a Mason should have the proper implements with which to work. The tools or implements with which an Entered Apprentice works are THE TWENTY-FOUR-INCH RULE or GAUGE and COMMON GAVEL.

They are presented to him.

XVIII.

EXPLANATION OF CEREMONIES, ETC.

☉∴ " THE TWENTY-FOUR-INCH GAUGE," our Brethren of the York Rite say, " is an instrument used by operative Masons to measure and lay out their work; but Free and Accepted Masons make use of it for the more noble and glorious purpose of dividing their time. Its being divided into twenty-four equal parts, is emblematical of the twenty-four hours of the day, which we are taught to divide into three equal parts, whereby are found eight hours for the service of God and a worthy distressed Brother, eight for their usual avocations, and eight for refreshment and sleep."

This was Saint Augustine's division of time; and it was perhaps real with him, he being a Bishop. But there is not, nor ever was, any such division of his time by one Mason in ten thousand; nor is it required of a Mason. Wherefore the explanation and application are faulty and incorrect. It is neither appropriate nor philosophical.

The same Brethren say of the GAVEL: "It is an implement made use of by operative Masons to break off the corners of rough stones, the better to fit them for the builder's use; but Free and Accepted Masons are taught to make use of it for the more noble and glorious purpose of divesting their hearts and consciences of the vices and superfluities of life, thereby fitting their bodies, as living stones, for that spiritual building, that house not made with hands, eternal in the Heavens."

We can as little approve this application and attempt at symbolism; because the comparison is strained and artificial; the vices and superfluities of life are *not* divested as with a stone-hammer, and by the knocking off of rough corners.

When those who made our Association what it now is, concealed its true nature by adopting the name and character of a particular body of artificers, in order that they might pursue their great and beneficent purposes in safety, they of course adopted the implements of that trade, and distributed them among the different classes of their members. To the Entered Apprentices they assigned those of the appropriate hard and rudimental labor, the hammering or cutting down to certain lines and dimensions, of the rude, rough blocks of stone. Probably these implements had originally *no* symbolic meaning. It is true that, in the Hieroglyphic language of Egypt, a *hatchet* denoted GOD, and a *cubit*, JUSTICE. But it is not to be imagined that the RULE and GAVEL were adopted as symbols of JUSTICE and GOD, because something resembling each was a symbol in Egypt, any more than that the GAVEL alludes to the hammer of the Norseman's God, THOR.

The RULE is the natural symbol of *accuracy* in workmanship, of strict *definition* and *limitation*, of STATUTES and LAWS, of rigid, unbending JUSTICE. The HAMMER or GAVEL is an emblem of FORCE, and therefore of LABOR, which applies Force to Matter. The peculiar *Masonic* use of this Force and that accurate regard to the lines defined and marked, is to shape the double cube, a symbol of perfection, out of the rough ashlar or block of stone. If Masonry were merely an association for the moral improvement of our individual selves, and if a Mason had no more to do than to hammer off " the vices and superfluities of his own heart and conscience," some exclusively moral application of these implements might be admitted. But it is by no means so. There never was any need of association, secresy, and terrible obligations, for *that.*

The GAVEL symbolizes FORCE: the Force of Numbers, of Intellect, of Passion, Energy, Enthusiasm ; the Force of Truth, Right, and Justice ; the Force of the Principles of Freedom, Equality, and Brotherhood ; the immense Force of Ideas ; the Force, combining all these Forces, of the Order of Freemasons, and of a People resolved to be free.

In the printed volume of the Morals and Dogma of the Symbolic Degrees with which you will be furnished, and which you must carefully study before you can advance, you will find a full explanation of what we understand to be symbolized by the RULE and the GAVEL. To that volume you will hereafter be frequently referred, and it will perhaps furnish you, as it is intended to do, with food for sober, serious, and profound reflection.

*　　*　　*　　*　　*　　*

I shall now proceed, my Brother, to give you such further instruction as in this Degree you are entitled to receive. You are taught in Masonry by Symbols. These were the almost universal language of the ancient theologies. They were the most obvious method of instruction; for, like Nature herself, they addressed the understanding through the eye; and the most ancient expressions, denoting communication of religious knowledge, signify ocular exhibition. These lessons were the enigmas of the Sphynx. "The Gods themselves," it was said, "disclose their intentions to the wise, but to fools their teaching is unintelligible." The King of the Delphic Oracle was said not to *declare*, nor, on the other hand, to *conceal*, but to *intimate* or *signify*. The mysteries were a series of symbols, and symbolical instruction is recommended by the constant and uniform usage of antiquity. The mysterious knowledge of the Druids was embodied in signs and symbols; and Taliesin, describing his initiation, says, "The secrets were imparted to me by the old Giantess" (CERIDWEN, the same as ISIS), "without the use of audible language. I am a *silent* proficient."

The method of indirect suggestion, by allegory or symbol, is a more efficacious instrument of instruction than plain, didactic language, since we are habitually indifferent to that which is acquired without effort. "*The* INITIATED *are few; though many bear the Thyrsus.*"

Symbols were used, to a great extent, to *conceal* particular truths from all except a favored few, who had the key to their meaning. To the mass of the Initiated only some trite and obvious explanation was given; the primary among many readings. The meaning of the Symbols of Masonry is not unfolded at once. We give you hints only, in general. You must study out the recondite and mysterious meanings for yourself. A single symbol often has several meanings. There are, indeed, to almost every one of the ancient among these symbols, *four* distinct meanings—one, as it were, *within* the other: the *moral*, *political*, *philosophical*, and *spiritual* meanings. The Apprentice and Fellow-Craft are taught only the two first.

The symbols of these degrees are partly ancient and partly modern. The ancient have come down to us from the old Mysteries, of which we have already spoken, but of which we shall not fully speak in this degree.

The first scene in the Greater Mysteries of Eleusis, was in the Outer Court of the inclosure ; as this place, where you have been received, signifies the outer court or ground-floor, the Pronaos, of King Solomon's Temple. The Candidates were awed with terrific sights and sounds, while they painfully groped their way as in the gloomy caverns of the soul's sublunar migration. For by the immutable law, exemplified in the trials of Psūché, man must pass through the terrors of the under-world, as you have done in the dungeon and cave, before he can reach the height of Heaven. The material horrors of Tartarus, as depicted by Virgil, were represented to the Candidate. Successive scenes of darkness and Light passed before his eyes, and many mystic representations of wondrous magnitude and beauty. Astonishment and terror took his soul captive : in the Mysteries of Isis he passed through the dark valley of the shadow of Death, and then into a place representing the elements, where the two principles, Darkness and Light, symbols of Good and Evil, clashed and contended. In the Dionusiac Mysteries, the Candidate was kept in darkness and terror, three days and three nights. If you thought that we kept you too long blindfolded, learn that in this, also, Masonry has softened down the tests of the ancient

Mysteries! In the Ceremonies of Eleusis, there were frightful scenes, alternations of fear and joy, darkness and light, glittering lightning and the crash of thunder, the apparition of spectres, or magical illusions, impressing at once the eyes and ears.

In explaining the ceremonies through which you have passed, if we speak to you in enigmas and hints, as it were in initials and hieroglyphs, remember them. They will be your guide in future studies.

There are Catechisms in this degree, called in the York Rite "*Lectures*," parts of which you must learn. To commit them to memory is indispensable. The first repeats the mode of your initiation, step by step; the second gives the explanation of, and reasons for, that ceremonial; the third describes the Lodge and its furniture, and gives the primary meaning of these as symbols. You will receive these in full from the Brethren Senior and Junior Deacons.

We need say no more in regard to the *dungeon* and the *cave*. "Masons," our French Brethren say, "build Temples to the Virtues and dig Dungeons for the Vices." The Donjon or Dungeon is a symbol of Royal and Feudal Power; of the rule of the Inquisition, the Monastery, and the Cloister. There are dungeons for States and Nations also, in which these sit and crouch and shiver, and decay into their dotage, loaded with fetters; the bones of their good and brave flung into the corners, that they may weep bitter tears over them ; Liberty lying in her Coffin ; the skeleton of their old glories against the wall, the lamp of Superstition, instead of the sunlight of Truth and Reason, enabling them to read the sad record of their woes and shame ; the bread and water of the pining prisoner; the skull, holding the sepulchral lamp, teaching that their feeble light will soon be quenched in darkness, and they go down to join the old dead Despotisms. Slaves to the dogmas of Divine Right, of time-honored authority, legitimacy, and sacred tradition, or of the Centralism that begets Anarchy, that it may have the right to crush it out by the Consulate and the Empire, the *Salt*, the *Sulphur* and the *Mercury* fail to remind them that nations, like individuals, have not only bodies of the earth, earthy ; but souls, that should respond to the calls and inspirations of Honor and Pride, and to the sentiments of Liberty, Equality, and Fraternity ; spirits that should irradiate the world with the Light of Philosophy, Thought, and Intellect.

And before we pass finally from the Dungeon and the Cave, let us return to the first and simplest lesson they teach. A perpetual remembrance of the tomb is proper for the living. All must die. To mingle with our life a certain presence of the Sepulchre, is not only the law of the ascetic, but of the wise man. In this relation they tend toward a common centre.

*   *   *   *   *   *

Your *Preparation* was at all points Symbolic. You were, in the language of Masonry, ...

O. 29.   *   *   *   *   *   *

The Candidate in Masonry is in search of LIGHT. He represents both an individual man and a People. As one and the other, he comes from the darkness, and he wanders in the darkness, until, guided first by the *Terrible Brother*, EXPERIENCE, in which are involved Suffering, Calamity, and Distress; and afterward by REASON, as the *Master of Ceremonies;* FAITH and LOVE, the two *Deacons*, unseal his eyes to the LIGHT of KNOWLEDGE and LIBERTY. The darkness and the Preparation represent the condition of the Individual—slave and prey of Ignorance, Superstition, and Tyranny, of Error and Vice : of the People, at once the blind instrument and bound victim of Power that oppresses, Craft that enslaves, and Policy that brutalizes. He is emphatically a Pro-fano, enveloped in mental darkness, poor and destitute of rights and knowledge, naked, to show that he is defenceless, deprived of everything of value, because he holds even what he earns by the frail and uncertain tenure of the will and pleasure of his Tyrants and Masters; and round his neck is the threefold Cord of servitude and bondage, to *Royalty,* the *Church,* and the *Nobility.*

Decency forbids his being made entirely naked, and therefore he is so only symbolically. Nakedness and bare feet were symbols, with the Orientals, of degradation, subjugation, affliction, humility, and sorrow. He has already "*eaten the bread of adversity, and drunken the waters of affliction.*" The heart is on the left side, and to "bare" it is symbolically to *open* the heart, by which are denoted frankness, and entire absence of fraud, deceit, and concealment. The heart, to the ancients, was the seat of the passions, emotions, and affections, and although its functions are now well known to be merely mechanical, the word is still used by all men in the same metaphorical sense.

To "bow the knee" is an expression used to indicate an act of worship and adoration. "ABRECH! *Bow the knee!*" was cried before JOSEPH, when, after he had interpreted Pharaoh's dream, that monarch freed him from prison, made him his Prime Minister, arrayed him like a Prince, and caused him to ride in triumph in his second chariot. "*I will leave seven thousand in Israel, all the* KNEES *which have not bowed unto Baal,*" said the Lord to the Prophet ELIJAH. "*Strengthen ye the weak hands, and make strong the feeble* KNEES! *Say to them that are of a fearful heart, be strong! fear not!*" says the Prophet ISAIAH. The *right* side of the body, and the limbs on that side, are symbolical of *strength*. It is the *right* hand of the

Lord " that doeth valiantly and is exalted, that is become glorious in power," in the Psalms ; and it was fit that the Candidate, having to kneel in adoration to the Deity, and in humility at the altar to receive his obligation, should have the *right* knee prepared to be pressed naked on the earth. When Joseph blessed Ephraim and Manasseh, he laid his *right* hand, as the superior in blessing, on the head of Ephraim, the younger, though Jacob remonstrated, because the younger was to become greater than the elder, and his seed a multitude of nations. "*From this right hand went a flame of Law for them,*" said Moses, blessing the children of Israel before his death.

Every Masonic Lodge is styled a TEMPLE; and you have been made a Mason " in a room and place representing the Outer Court* of King Solomon's Temple." Among all the Oriental nations the Priests and others were required to be barefooted on entering holy places. "*Put off thy shoes from off thy feet!*" said the Angel of the Lord, in a flame of fire out of the midst of a bush, to MOSES, "*for the place whereon thou standest is holy ground!*" "*Loose thy shoes from off thy feet!*" said the Prince of the Lord's Host to JOSHUA, "*for the place whereon thou standest is holy!*" When DAVID fled from Jerusalem, upon the

---

* אולם, Aulam or Avalam, the Porch, where the columns Y∴ and B∴ stood, —ὁ πρόναος, *Vestibulum, porticus;* 1 K. vii. 6; Ez. xl. 7.

rebellion of Absalom, "he went up by the ascent of Olivet, and wept as he went up, and had his head covered, *and he went barefoot.*" "*Go!*" said the Lord to ISAIAH, "*and loose the sackcloth from off thy loins, and put off thy shoe from thy foot!*" and he did so, walking naked and *barefoot*, THREE YEARS, for a sign and wonder upon Egypt and Ethiopia, and a premonition of the captivity to Assyria. "Forbear to cry! make no mourning for the dead! bind the tire of thy head upon thee, *and put on the shoes upon thy feet!*" said the Lord, by the mouth of EZEKIEL, to the Jews.

In Ancient Egypt, the Hierophant, sacrificing to the sun, first laid aside every ornament of a metallic nature.

The Initiate into the Hindū mysteries was invested with a CORD of THREE threads, so twisted as to make three times three, and called *Zennâr.* It was an emblem of the Deity, three in one, BRAHMA, VISHNU, and SEEVA, Creator, Preserver, and Destroyer. Hence the CABLE-TOW, placed three times around your neck. But this cable-tow has to Masons a peculiar and significant symbolical meaning concealed in its name, which seems to be merely an antiquated English word.

The Hebrew word חבל, *Khabel*, means a *rope*, and especially a *measuring-line* or cord; and hence a *field* measured, an *inheritance* or *possession.*

" *She let them down by a khabel through the window*"
(Josh. ii. 15). . . . " *Or ever the silver khabel be
loosed*" (Eccles. xii. 6). . . . " *Thy land shall be
divided by a khabel*" (Amos vii. 17). . . . " *And
he smote Moab, and measured them with a khabel*"
(2 Saml. viii. 2). . . . " *As he that lieth upon the.
end of a khabel*" (Prov. xxiii. 34). . . . Here
Gesenius thinks the word means a large *rope* on a
vessel, perhaps the *cable* attached to the anchor.

The same word, as a verb, means to *tie a rope*, to
bind some one by a *pledge;* and hence, as a noun, a
PLEDGE ; also, *received as a pledge*, or *in pledge.* "*For
thou hast taken a khabel from thy brother*" (Job xxii. 6).
. . . " *Take a khabel of him for a strange woman*"
(Prov. xx. 16 ; xxvii. 13). . . . " *For he taketh
a man's life as khabel*" (Deut. xxiv. 6). . . .
" *Nor take a widow's clothing to khabel*" (Deut. xxiv.
17). . . . " *If thou take thy neighbour's clothing to
khabel*" (Exod. xxii. 25). . . . " *They take the
widow's ox for a khabel*" (Job xxiv. 3) ; " *and take a
khabel of the poor*" (Job xxiv. 9). . . .

Elsewhere it means a *sailor, i.e.,* one who handles
the *ropes;* as " *Rab ha-khabel,* the chief *sailor;*
Jonah i. 6 ; whence *khabali,* mariners ; Ezek. xxvii.
8, 27, 29. The plural of the noun is חבלים, *khabalim,*
bonds or *bands.* " I took unto me two staves, one I
called *Beauty,* and the other *Khabalim, Bands* (or
bonds). I cut asunder mine other staff, *Khabalim,*

that I might break the *brotherhood* between Judah and Israel." Zech. xi. 7–14.

And the third person singular possessive pronoun "his," is indicated by חט, *to*, affixed to the word, and accordingly we find, Ezec. xviii. 7, חבלתו חוב ישיב, *Khabel-to khavab yashayab: Hath restored to the debtor* His Pledge.

Hence, when you had been obligated, and so were bound to us by a stronger *tie* or *pledge*, you were freed from the cable-tow; and so, when a Candidate is required to do certain acts, " if within the length of his cable-tow," the meaning is, *if within the* SPIRIT *of his* PLEDGE *or* OBLIGATION. "The *letter* killeth, but the SPIRIT maketh alive."

The CABLE-TOW, therefore, is the Hieroglyphic of a Pledge or Obligation, and it not only means the Candidate's pledge and obligation, which, to become a Neophyte, he must take to the Order and to every individual Brother; but that, wearing it, he represents men and nations, all whose rights of property, liberty, conscience and life, and they themselves, chattels in the form of human creatures and peoples, are pledged to their masters, as an article of clothing or of furniture is to the pawnbroker.

On your first attempt to enter the Lodge you were repelled by . . . . You were told what that was to teach you; but it was also to teach you that those among whom you desired to enroll yourself were men, knowing their rights, and possessed of arms to defend them; and that they were prepared to meet with the sword, the symbol of loyalty and Honor, the emissaries of Tyranny, the spies or mercenary soldiery of Power, the delators of the most hideous of tyrannies, that of the populace. This portion of the ceremony comes to us from the mysteries of Mithras, in Persia, where the Candidate, entering the Cavern of Initiation after his novitiate, was received in the same manner, and slightly wounded. A people, rising in its majesty to assert its rights, must be baptized in blood.

You made three several journeys, in each of which you made three times the circuit of the Lodge, so completing the sacred and mysterious number, NINE, the square of THREE. These circuits you made travelling from the East, by way of the South, to the West, and thence by the North to the East. The East of every Lodge is that end at which the Master sits. The Senior Warden is in the West, and the Junior Warden in the South. In the York Rite the guide of the Candidate is asked:

" Whence come you, and whither do you go?"

" From the West to the East," he answers.

" Why do you leave the West and journey to the East?"

"In search of Light."

And, in the Hindū or Indian Mysteries, as the Candidate made his three circuits, he paused each time he reached the South, and said, "*I copy the example of the Sun, and follow his beneficent course.*" Daily the Sun rises in the East, journeys by the South, and sets in the West; and yearly leaving the Equator at the Autumnal Equinox, he falls more and more to the South or the ecliptic, until, at the Winter Solstice, the feast of Saint John the Evangelist, he reaches the Tropic of Capricorn. Then seeming to pause for three days, he again gradually ascends, crosses the Equator at the Vernal Equinox, continues northward, and pauses at the Tropic of Cancer at the Summer Solstice, the Feast of Saint John the Baptist.

In the Druidical Mysteries, the Candidate was conducted nine times around the Sanctuary from East to West. Your attention will be continually directed to the number three and its combinations. With perhaps a few hints, it will be left to yourself to fathom the meaning of that part of our symbolism.

We have already spoken at large of the symbolism of your purification. Engrave upon the tablets of your heart these solemn words of the Prophet ISAIAH:

" *Wash you! make you clean! Put away the evil*

of your doings from before mine eyes! Cease to do evil! Learn to do well! Follow justice! Relieve the oppressed! Defend the fatherless, and see them righted! Plead for the widow!"

Your three purifications also allude to Ezekiel's description of that out of which came the likeness of the four mystic creatures of his vision and of the Apocalypse, each having four faces—the face of a MAN and the face of a LION on the right side; the face of an Ox and the face of an EAGLE on the left side; each with four wings, and the hands of a man under their wings on their four sides. These creatures of flame, over which was the throne of God, and which flashed to and fro like lightning, came out of the midst of a whirlwind from the North, a great cloud, and a fire infolding itself; and thus the three elements, the air of the whirlwind, the water of the cloud, and the fire, are mysteriously connected with the four symbolic animals. Study for yourself the hidden meaning, and, in the meantime, remember that nations, like men, to be free must first be virtuous. For them, too, the purification of fire and blood. "When the Lord shall have washed away all the uncleanness of the daughter of Zion, and shall, by the spirit of justice and the efficacy of fire, have purged Jerusalem of the blood shed therein," only then can she possess the holiness of Freedom. On the lips of the NATIONS also must the Seraphim lay the live coals from the altar of God, that their iniquity may be taken away and their sin purged.

You have taken upon yourself an obligation of secresy, in the antique form, as solemn as those taken by the ancient Initiates. The crime of violating it would deserve, though it should not receive, the fearful punishment which the old law imposed.

In the Island of Crete, Jupiter Ammon, or the Sun in the Zodiacal Constellation of the Ram (in which constellation the Sun then was at the Vernal Equinox), had a tomb and a religious Initiation; one of the principal ceremonies of which consisted in clothing the Initiate with the skin of a white *lamb*. This is the origin of our apron of white lamb-skin. The Apron itself is modern; adopted when the Order concealed itself under the mask of a handicraft, and took as symbols the working-tools of Stone-Masonry. It is not only a symbol to us of LABOR and WORK, but of Purity and Innocence, and to all *Christian* Masons, of their faith in " the Lamb of God that taketh away the sins of the world;" a figure and symbol taken from the old Hebrew ceremonial, according to which either seven or twice seven lambs were sacrificed on each of the ten days of the seventh month, on which solemn convocations were held; while, on each, only a *single* goat or kid was sacrificed as a *sin*-offering; the latter being peculiarly sacred to the Principle of Evil, and sent, loaded with the sins of the People, to Azazel, in the desert. The whole symbolic character of the Apron is lost when a piece of cotton or linen is substituted for the lamb-skin.

As a symbol of expiation, it must continually teach you that it is your duty and privilege, as a Mason, to sacrifice yourself, if need be, for the welfare of the Order or of your country. So to become, in some sort, the Redeemer of a People, is the highest glory and loftiest honor of Humanity, and connects the Human Nature with the Divine. To build up in men's minds the idea of Progress, to forge those liberating dogmas which are swords by the pillows of the Generations; to work and to suffer with the People, even, if need be, to the extreme of sacrifice, is the destiny and duty which a true Mason accepts.

*   *   *   *   *   *

This is what is asked and answered in the Cate-chism in regard to the Lodge:

Q∴ What form has your Lodge?

A∴ An oblong square.

Q∴ What is its breadth?

A∴ From the East to the West.

Q∴ What is its length?

A∴ From the South to the North.

Q∴ What is its height?

A∴ From the earth to the heavens.

Q∴ What is its depth ?

A∴ From the surface of the earth to the centre.

Q∴ Why?

A∴ Because Masonry is universal.

☉∴ Our Lodges are situated, or should be situated, due East and West: because, our Catechism says, all Temples are so situated ; and these are so, because the Gospel was first preached in the East, and afterward extended into the West. The reason given in the York Rite is, that the Tabernacle of Moses was built East and West, and that Solomon, in imitation of it, so built the Temple. The Tabernacle was a movable tent ; but whenever set up it was probably placed with its mouth to the rising Sun, since the North, South, West, and East sides are spoken of in its description and the description of its Court. The Temple, like the Pyramids, was built by the cardinal points ; and Ezekiel saw in his vision the Glory of the God of Israel coming from the way of the East, and entering into the House by the way of the Gate toward the East. It was an oblong square, sixty cubits long by twenty wide ; the Oracle or Holy of Holies at the West end, twenty cubits square ; the Inner Court, forty cubits by twenty ; with a porch the whole width of the building, and ten cubits deep, in which was a wide gateway.

The three Sublime Lights of the Lodge are the

SUN, or OSIRIS ; the MOON, or ISIS ; and Mercury, HORUS, HERMES, or KHIR-ŌM, the Master of Light, Life, and the Universe. This leads you to the threshold of all the mysterious doctrines of the old philosophies, to the gates of the Kabalah and the Vedas. It is not yet time for you to enter in, or to know the meaning of the equilateral and right-angled triangles ; of the tesselated pavement in alternate lozenges of black and white ; of the number THREE so constantly presented to you, in the threefold cord around your neck, the three raps at the door, the three circuits, the three columns of the Lodge, the three greater and three lesser lights, the three officers of the Lodge, and its three jewels, movable and immovable, the three purifications, the three articles of furniture, the three ornaments, and, above all, the three triangles interlaced, white, red, and black. You must study, my Brother, be patient, and wait.

Yet we shall not entirely refuse to enlighten you ; by hints, which, if you are an apt Disciple of the Sages, you may understand. Meanwhile, we again refer you to the Volume of Morals and Dogma.

   *   *   *   *   *   *

You will find in the Volume of Morals and Dogma all that is to be made known to an Apprentice in regard to the Symbolism of the PLUMB, the LEVEL, and the SQUARE. Of the Ashlars we have already spoken there ; and we only add, as a hint to induce reflection and persuade to study, that the Oraculum, or Holy of Holies, the Kadosh Kadoshim, or inner apartment of the Temple at Jerusalem, was a perfect cube, twenty cubits square, and the same from floor to ceiling.

The Tracing or Trestle-Board is an oblong square on which designs are drawn by the Master Workman for the government of those under him, in the erection of edifices. It is therefore a symbol of Instruction, Education, and Law ; and thus has both a moral and a political meaning. The Master of the Lodge represents Wisdom or Reason, and the Trestle-Board teaches us, morally, that our conduct should always be regulated in accordance with the dictates of sound Reason, and not by Passion or Impulse. Every man, being a rational being, should have a *plan* of life and conduct, and should steadily pursue it, following always the Compass of Reason, and not permitting the winds of circumstance to blow him from his course.

And, although in a free State the Law must be the expression of the will of the People, yet it should be, not the utterance of its follies, ignorance, or passion, but of its wisdom. The power of making the laws should be committed to the wisest, to the men of knowledge, and the men of intellect. Then there will be harmony, consistency, stability, and permanency in the laws. And the Trestle-Board is an apt symbol of those Free Constitutions, solemnly adopted by the general will, irrevocable and unalterable, except in accordance with their own provisions, which are intended to survive the shocks of time, to guarantee private rights and an equitable exercise of the Powers of Government, to make usurpation of tyrannical authority impossible, whether in peace or war; and to be the resplendent Ægides of Liberty, the Great Charters of Human Rights.

*   *   *   *   *   *

My Brother, for the present your instruction as an Apprentice is about to end. In addition to that which you will find in the Volume of Morals and Dogma, you may obtain the monitorial instruction in the Liturgy published for the use of the Craft in the Southern jurisdiction of the United States.

Brother Master of Ceremonies, place this new Brother at the head of the Column of the North. . . . That is the place, my Brother, which you will occupy in this degree. There, laboring assiduously, and studying zealously, you may earn the right, in due time, to be admitted to the more secret and higher mysteries, and to receive those favors which the Lodge never denies to those who prove themselves worthy.

⊙ now raps o, and each Warden repeats it. Then

⊙∴ Rise! and to order! my Brethren! Brethren Senior and Junior Wardens, inform the Brethren who grace your Columns that I am about to proclaim the Neophyte an Apprentice Mason and Member of this Respectable Lodge!

⊕∴ Brother Junior Warden, Brethren who grace the Column of the North, the Venerable Master informs you that he is about, etc.

⊙∴ Brethren who grace the Column of the South, etc.

⊙∴ I do proclaim the Brother A...... B...... an Entered Apprentice Mason and a Member of this Respectable Lodge, P......, No. .....   And I do accordingly require all the Brethren to recognize him for the future as such, and to give him aid and assistance whenever he may need the same; and on all proper occasions, counsel, warning, and advice.

[⊕ and then ○ repeat this.]

⊙∴ ♪ Brethren Senior and Junior Wardens, request the Brethren of your Columns to unite with me in congratulating ourselves upon the acquisition, by this Lodge, of a new Brother and Friend!

⊕∴ ♪ Brother Junior Warden, and Brethren, etc., the Venerable Master requests you to unite with him, etc.

⊙∴ ♪ Brethren who grace, etc.   . . .   †It is announced, Brother Senior Warden.

⊕∴ ♪ It is announced, Venerable Master.

⊙∴ My Brother, you are now a Mason. Masons, in the highest sense of the word, are Architects, who erect not only houses for ordinary dwelling-places, but palaces, churches, Cathedrals and Temples. There has always been a symbolic meaning attached to the words "House," "Building," and "Builder." The Ancient and Accepted Scottish Rite has been always called The Masonry of Herodom, of the Holy House ; that is, of the House of the Temple of Solomon. "According to the grace of God," says the Apostle Paul, "which is given unto me, as a Wise Master-Builder, I have laid the foundation, and another buildeth thereon. But let every man take heed how he buildeth thereupon. . . . Every man's work shall be made manifest. . . . If any man's work abide, which he hath built thereupon, he shall receive a reward." . . . "If our earthly house of this Tabernacle were dissolved, we have a building of God, a house not made with hands, eternal in the Heavens. . . . We are the Temple of the Living God. . . . Ye are built upon the foundation of the Apostles and Prophets, Jesus Christ himself being the Chief Corner-Stone, in whom all the building, fitly framed together, groweth unto a holy temple in the Lord ; in whom ye also are builded together, for a habitation of God, through the Spirit. . . . Be ye, as living stones," says the

Apostle Peter, "built up a Spiritual House, a holy Priesthood, to offer up spiritual sacrifices!"

There were ample reasons, therefore, why the founders of this Order, to conceal its true purposes, used the name of "MASONRY," in preference to that of any other trade or employment. The Symbolism was ready to their hand. The House and the Temple were accepted Symbols of a moral and virtuous character, of a free State, of a true system of Philosophy, of a spiritual worship. The Brethren are the living stones of the edifice, cemented together by the cement of Brotherhood. As an Apprentice, you are to build up this moral Temple in your own heart, and to aid in erecting the Universal Temple of Liberty upon the Earth. It is the Mason who erects fortifications; and in a free country Freemasons are to build them against the enemies of Freedom, against Error, Intolerance and Usurpation, Luxury and Corruption, Fraud and Ambition.

The Ancient Poets, in their allegories, said that NEPTUNE and APOLLO offered themselves as Masons to Laomedon, to help him build the walls of Troy. They meant that these Gods dictated to him the Laws and eternal principles of Truth, and of Civilization sustained by Material Force.

In the confident belief that you will prove yourself a good and faithful Craftsman, the Lodge which receives you into its bosom is now about, according to the ancient form, to applaud your initiation, and to salute and congratulate you by the consecrated signs, battery, and acclamation. With me, my Brethren!

*   *   *   *   *   *

The new Brother returns his thanks, if he sees fit, with such remarks as may occur to him, and then gives the sign, battery, and plaudit; or the Master of Ceremonies does it for him.

Then his thanks are *covered*, the battery and plaudit being again given by all, at the order of the Venerable Master.

⊙∴ ♪ Be seated, my Brethren!

⊙∴ Venerable Master, I should like to be satisfied that the new Brother has not forgotten the Sacred Word; and I ask, therefore, that he may write it down in the presence of the Brother Secretary, that its orthography and meaning may be kept in his memory.

△ will present a pen and paper to the Brother.

O. 31.   *   *   *   *   *   *

⊙∴ See how feeble and liable to error is human nature, when we follow our impulses and instincts, without sufficiently reflecting on what we are about to do! Be seated! and always remembering how you were about, in the very presence of the Altar, to err and fall, be merciful to error in others.

O. 32.   *   *   *   *   *   *

XIX.

ORATION—ADDRESS TO VISITORS, ETC.

☉∴ BROTHER Orator, if you have any piece of Architecture prepared, the Lodge will be greatly gratified to hear it.

It is the business of ☿ to be prepared with an address, either upon the ceremonies of initiation, or Masonry generally. If there are distinguished Visitors, he will, at the conclusion, address them, to elicit responses. If he is not prepared, ☉ will pass on to other business. If he is ready, ☉ will say:

☉∴ ♪ Brethren Senior and Junior Wardens, be pleased to request the Brethren on your Columns to give their attention to the piece of Architecture with which the Brother Orator is about to favor us!

This is done by each Warden in the usual form. Then ○ informs ⊕, and he informs ☉, that it is announced.

☉∴ Brother Orator, you have the floor.

*   *   *   *   *   *

When the Orator concludes:

☉∴ ♪ Brethren Senior and Junior Wardens, request the Brethren on your Columns to join you and myself in thanking our Brother Orator for his piece of Architecture.

It is announced by each, and each declares it announced.

☉∴ ♫ Rise, and to order, my Brethren!

Then ☉ returns thanks and compliments to the Orator; and, at the end, says:

☉∴ With me, my Brethren!

The sign, battery, and plaudit are given.

☉∴ ♪ Be seated, my Brethren!

If any Visitor replies, he is responded to by the sign, battery, and plaudit.

☉∴ ♪ Brethren Senior and Junior Wardens, be pleased to make known to the Brethren on your Columns that if any one has anything to propose or offer for the good of the Order in general, or of this Lodge in particular, the floor is offered to him.

It is announced by each Warden. Any Brother wishing to speak, obtains permission in the manner stated under the head of proposing and electing Candidates. If none speak, or when all are done:

○∴ ♪ Brother Senior Warden, silence reigns on my Column.

⊕∴ ♪ Venerable Master, silence reigns on both Columns.

☉∴ ♪ Brother Master of Ceremonies, be pleased

to take around the pouch of Propositions! Brethren
Senior and Junior Wardens, you will please inform
the Brethren on your Columns that the pouch of
Propositions is about to be presented to them.

Each Warden does so, and replies that it is announced. The
Pouch is taken round, and each Brother will put in his hand,
as if putting in a paper. Motions and Resolutions may be
signed or anonymous. When it has passed around, the pouch
is taken to the Secretary. Whatever business it contains is
disposed of as the Lodge may order. When all business is disposed of, ☉ says:

☉∴ ♪ Brethren Senior and Junior Wardens, be
pleased to request the Brethren on your Columns to
assist me in returning our thanks to the worthy
Brethren who have now visited us, and assisted in
our labors.

This is done; and each Warden delares it announced.

☉∴ ♫ Rise! and to order, my Brethren!

☉ addresses the Visiting Brethren in such terms as he deems
appropriate. Either of the following may be used, if the
Master pleases:

ADDRESS TO VISITORS.

My Brethren, the bond which unites us, and makes
of all the Masons in the world one living soul, has
brought you here to assist us in our labors. We accept this as an assurance that you will also toil with

us beyond the doors of the Lodge, in the great labors
which belong to Masonry. Whether Catholics, Pro-
testants, Israelites, Mahometans, Sabæists, believers
or doubters, we meet here to build up, by united
effort, the Altar of Toleration in the Temple of Freedom, because we all follow the Law of Love, which
is the efficient principle of morality. For us, the
odious distinctions of the Profane world, dividing it
into parties and nationalities, have no existence. We
are Brethren: worshippers at the same shrine. The
spirit of Provincialism disappears before the unity
of Idea; and personal interest sacrifices itself to the
general interest of universal civilization and happiness. Receive the sincere expression of our thanks
for the favor you have done us; and permit us to
salute you by the mysterious numbers of the degree!

ANOTHER.

My Brethren, in the name of all the toilers in the
great and sublime work of the regeneration of man,
and especially in behalf of the Brethren of this
Lodge, I thank you for coming to our assistance, and
encouraging us by your presence, to-night. A little
knowledge of human nature teaches us that such
visits, especially of the learned and eminent, are
great incitements to emulation and the attainment of
excellence, and almost indispensable to prevent assemblies of Masons from sinking by degrees, and

almost without a struggle, into the quicksands of discouragement and apathy, into the dull, cold, heavy repetition of formulas, to that condition of the Church in Laodicea, when their works are neither cold nor hot, but lukewarm; when they think themselves rich and increased with goods, and in need of nothing, and do not know that they are spiritually wretched and miserable, and poor, and blind, and naked, occupied only with the dead formulas of the ceremonial.

Continue, my dear Brethren, to assist and encourage us, and incite us to assist and encourage each other. Men easily become faint-hearted, and are as easily encouraged and elated; so that with little cost to himself, of trouble or exertion, one may, by his mere presence, work much good, inciting his brethren to works, and service, and charity, and faith, and patient hopefulness which is strength. Let us not forget, my Brethren, either within the Lodge or without, that the word "Charity" does not mean the giving of Alms, but Affection and Loving-Kindness; nor how often a word of sympathy, kindness, and encouragement saves the wounded, distressed, discouraged, doubting soul from total disbelief in the goodness of God, from sinking in the leaden waves of despair and crime; the man from becoming a drunkard and a criminal; the woman from plunging into the sewers of vice; and both from self-abandonment, ruin, and pollution.

Grateful for your presence, the Lodge will be still more thankful for any words of counsel and good cheer. Meanwhile, permit it to salute you by the mysterious numbers of the degree, after the ancient custom. . . . With me, my Brethren!

The Lodge gives the sign, battery, and plaudit, the Visitors giving the sign only.
If any Visitor or Visitors respond, the highest in rank says, when the address or addresses are ended:

V∴ My Brethren, who have to-night been gratified and benefited by the excellent labors of this Respectable Lodge, let us thank the Venerable Master and Brethren for their hospitality, and wish the Lodge Health, Prosperity, and Continuance, by the mysterious numbers, and according to the ancient custom.

All rise, including the Brethren of the Lodge. The Visitors give the sign, battery, and plaudit. Then ☉ says:

☉∴ My Brethren of the Lodge, let us cover the salute of our distinguished Brethren! With me, my Brethren.

The Master and Brethren give the sign, battery, and plaudit, the Visitors giving the sign only. Then all will be seated, by order of ☉.
When the applauses are finished, ☉ will say:

☉∴ ♪ Brother Senior Warden, does any other duty remain to be done?

⊕∴ The poor ye have always with you.

⊙∴ It is true, my Brother. ♪ Brother Master of Ceremonies, take around the box of fraternal assistance! Brethren Senior and Junior Wardens, make known to the Brethren on your Columns that the box of fraternal assistance is about to be presented to them, with the usual charge!

⊕∴ ♪ Brother Junior Warden, Brethren who grace the Column of the North, the Venerable Master informs you that the box of fraternal assistance is about to be presented to you. Let us do good unto all men, especially unto them that are of the Household of Faith! According as every one hath received the gift, so minister the same one to another, as good stewards of the manifold favors of God! Charge them that are rich in worldly wealth that they do good, that they be rich in good works, ready to distribute, willing to share their wealth with others, laying up in store for themselves a good foundation against the time to come, that they may lay hold on eternal life!

⊙∴ ♪ Brethren who grace the Column of the South, etc. . . . ♪ Brother Senior Warden, it is announced, with the charge.

⊕∴ ♪ Venerable Master, it is announced with the charge.

The box is then taken round; first to any Inspectors-General, then to the Master, Wardens, and other officers, including the

Tiler, then to the Visitors, and then to the Brethren. ♃ then puts in his own contribution, and hands the box to the Secretary. If any Brother desires that the amount received should be bestowed in a particular manner, he may rise and ask for the floor, and so propose, giving the name afterward, in a whisper, to the Master. If the Lodge approves this, the amount will be handed to the Proposant. If no such motion is made, it is counted, the amount noted by the Secretary, and the sum handed to the Almoner. Then ⊙∴ says:

⊙∴ ♪ Brother Secretary, you will read the fugitive leaves of the work of to-night! Brethren Senior and Junior Wardens, make known to the Brethren on your Columns that the Brother Secretary is about to read the fugitive leaves of the work of to-night, that they may aid us to correct anything amiss therein!

This is announced, and so declared.
When the Minutes have been read:

⊙∴ ♪ Brethren Senior and Junior Wardens, be pleased to inform the Brethren on your Columns that if any one has any observations to make in regard to the fugitive leaves, the floor is offered to him.

This is announced, and so declared. Any Visitor whose name is omitted, or who is wrongly described in the Minutes, will make it known. When all corrections have been made,

O∴ ♪ Brother Senior Warden, silence reigns on my Column.

⊕∴ ♪ Venerable Master, silence reigns on both Columns.

☉∴ ♫ Rise, and to order, my Brethren! Let us return thanks to the Great Architect of the Universe for the works of this day, and implore His aid and favor!

PRAYER.

Grand Architect of the Universe! Immortal and Inexhaustible Source of Light and Life! The workmen of the Temple give Thee a thousand thanks, ascribing to Thee whatever that is good, useful, or glorious there may be in the works of this day, and thanking Thee for a new addition to their numbers and strength. Continue, we pray Thee, to protect them! Guide them onward in the way that leads toward Perfection! and let Harmony, Peace, and Concord ever cement their work! Let Friendship and Good Works ever adorn this Temple, and here dwell and inhabit! Let Generosity, Loving-Kindness, and Courtesy always characterize the Brethren of the Lodge! and in the outer world help them to shew, by their words and conduct, that they are true Children of the Light! AMEN.

ALL. SO MOTE IT BE.

The Venerable will give one rap, and all will be seated. Then the Lodge will be closed.

XX.

TO CLOSE.

O. 33.   ✻   ✻   ✻   ✻   ✻   ✻

When the work ends early, the Catechism of the degree is gone through with between ⊙ and ⊕ before closing, and immediately after the Minutes are read and approved.

MEMORANDA AS TO THE WORK.

When anything is to be announced, through the Wardens, the Master, giving one rap, will say:

⊙∴ ♪ Brethren Senior and Junior Wardens, be pleased to make known to (or inform) the Brethren on your Columns that, etc., etc., etc.

The Senior Warden, rapping once, will say:

⊕∴ ♪ Brother Junior Warden, Brethren who grace the Column of the North, the Venerable Master makes known to you (or informs you) that, etc., etc.

The Junior Warden, giving one rap, will say:

O∴ ♪ Brethren who grace the Column of the South, the Venerable Master makes known to you (or informs you) that, etc. etc.

Then, rapping once, the Junior Warden will say:

O∴ ♪ Brother Senior Warden, it is announced.

And the Senior Warden, rapping once, will say:

⊕∴ ♪ Venerable Master, it is announced.

Throughout the three degrees this formula is followed. The character (♪) indicates a rap.

Three raps call up all the Brethren.
Two, in opening and closing, call up the Wardens.
One, in opening and closing, calls up all the officers except the Wardens.

During a prayer, the Brethren will kneel on the right knee.

XXII.

TABLE LODGE, OR BANQUET LODGE.

ARRANGEMENT OF THE LODGE.

THE Hall in which the banquet is held should be so situated that no one without can see or overhear anything.

The Table is to be, as nearly as possible, in the shape of a horse-shoe. The Master sits on the outside, at the summit; the Wardens at the extremes.

The Orator is at the head of the Column of the South, and the Secretary at that of the Column of the North. The East is occupied by Visitors, or by the officers of the Lodge, if there are no Visitors.

No other officers than those named have any fixed place. If there are Visitors of the higher Degrees, who fill the East, then the other Visitors will be at the heads of the Columns.

The articles and implements used are called as follows:

The Table............	Workshop.
The Table-Cloth.......	Veil.
The Napkins.........	Flags.
Plates...............	Tiles.
Dishes..............	Platforms.
Spoons	Trowels.
Knives.............	Swords.
Forks..............	Mattocks.
Bottles.............	Barrels.
Glasses.............	Cannons.
Lights.............	Stars.
The Chairs...........	Stalls.
The Snuffers.........	Pincers.
The Meats...........	Materials.
The Bread...........	Rough Ashlar.
The Wine............	Strong Powder (red or white).

The Water............Weak Powder..
Cider or Beer.........Yellow Powder.
Liqueurs...............Fulminating Powder.
Salt..................Sand.
Pepper...............Dust.
To Drink............To discharge a Cannon.
To Eat..............To Masticate.
Mustard.............Paint.

When all are seated, the Venerable will use his pleasure in regard to the first Health; whether to give it before masticating anything, or after masticating the soup, or at some other period.

When he wishes to give the first Health, he raps once with his mallet. If there are serving Brothers, they withdraw immediately from the interior of the horse-shoe, and retire to the West. So they do at each Health. All cease to eat. Ordinarily, the Brother Master of Ceremonies is alone within the horse-shoe, fronting the Venerable, to be better at hand to receive his orders, and see them executed. Sometimes he sits at a small table, between the two Wardens. When ☉ raps ♃ rises, and ☉ says:

☉∴ Brethren Senior and Junior Wardens, assure yourselves that our works are well tiled.

Each Warden ascertains that all on the two Columns are Masons, by running the eye over them, and recognizing them as such.

◯∴ Brother Senior Warden, I answer for my Column.

⊕∴ Venerable Master, the Junior Warden and myself are satisfied that all are Masons on both Columns.

☉∴ I answer for all in the East. Brother Tiler, perform your duty!

Meanwhile the Brethren put on their scarfs. It does not need they should wear aprons.

The Tiler closes and locks the door, and takes out the key. After this, no one comes in or goes out.

O∴ Brother Senior Warden, our works are well tiled.

⊕∴ Venerable Master, our works are well tiled.

☉∴ ♪ My Brethren, our works, which have some time been suspended, are again in full vigor.

NOTE.—If the Lodge had been closed before repairing to the banquet, it would be necessary to open it anew.

⊕∴ Brethren on my Column, our works, etc.

O∴ Brethren on my Column, our works, etc.

☉∴ To order, my Brethren.

FIRST HEALTH.

☉∴ Brethren Senior and Junior Wardens, invite the Brethren of each Column to prepare to charge and align for the first obligatory health.

⊕∴ Brethren of the Column of the North, prepare to charge and align, etc.

O∴ Brethren of the Column of the South, prepare, etc.

☉∴ Charge and align, my Brethren!

NOTE.—No one must touch a barrel until this order is given, otherwise there will be confusion in the work.

Each pours into his glass so much as he pleases. If any one drinks water only, he is under no obligation to use wine.

As soon as each has filled his cannon, he sets it as far from the edge of the table as half the diameter of his tile: thus the cannons are aligned in an instant.

The barrels and stars are aligned on a second line.

When all is in line:

O∴ Brother Senior Warden, all is aligned upon the Column of the South.

⊕∴ Venerable Master, all is aligned upon both Columns.

⊙∴ The East is so likewise.   Stand, and at order!

All rise.   The flag is over the right fore-arm.   The Brethren having the high degrees, throw it over the right shoulder. Thus all are at order.   If the table is a horse-shoe, the Brethren within it remain seated.

⊙∴ ♪ Brethren Senior and Junior Wardens, be pleased to announce upon your Columns that the first obligatory health is that of THE PRESIDENT AND THE CONGRESS OF THE UNITED STATES!   We will add to this health our wishes for the success of the arms of the nation in War, and its honor and prosperity in Peace.   It is a health so dear to us, that I invite you to deliver your fire as handsomely as possible. I claim for myself the words of command.

⊕∴ ♪ Brethren on the Column of the North, the first obligatory health is that of the President and the Congress of the United States!   We will add to this health, etc.

⊙∴ ♪ Brethren on the Column of the South, etc.

⊙∴ Attention, my Brethren!

1. Right hand to the Sword!
2. Carry Sword!
3. Salute with the Sword!
4. Sword to the left hand!
5. Carry Arms!   [The Cannon is raised and held out. See below.]
6. To the cheek!
7. Fire!
8. Good fire!
9. The sharpest of fires!
10. Advance Arms!
11. One! Two! Three!!
12. One! Two! Three!!
13. One! Two! Three!!
14. Advance Arms!
15. One! Two! Three!!
16. Right hand to the Sword!
17. Carry Swords!
18. Salute with the Sword!
19. Rest Sword! .   .   .   [The knife is laid down.]

At 5 the Cannon is raised, and held out in front, at arm's length. . . . At 6, it is brought near to the cheek. 7. Drink, and again carry the Cannon to the front at arm's length. . . . 8. Drink again, and do the same. . . . 9. Drink again, to the bottom, and hold the Cannon nearly at the height of the chin, in front of the right shoulder, arm at full length. . . . 10 and 11. Present Arms! One, bring the Cannon to the left breast; Two, bring it to the right breast; Three, Carry it to the front. . . . 12. The same. . . . 13. The same. . . . 14, 15. Bring back the Cannon to the left breast, then to the right, and then set it on the table, all doing this at the same instant.

Then all applaud, with a triple battery and triple huzza.

Then ⊙ says:

⊙∴ Let us resume our seats, my Brethren!

Each Warden repeats.

So long as the work continues in vigor, the Brethren may continue to eat; but it must be in silence.

SECOND HEALTH.

Sometimes, and it is most convenient for all, as less interrupting the service, ⊙ orders the Second Health immediately after the first.

If he should not see fit to do so, he should suspend the work.

If he does this, work must be resumed before the second health. If the work has not been suspended, he proceeds at once, saying:

⊙∴ Brethren Senior and Junior Wardens, invite the Brethren on each Column to prepare to charge and align, for the second obligatory health!

The Wardens, in succession, report.

⊙∴ Charge and align, my Brethren!

The Wardens announce that all is charged and aligned, as before.

⊙∴ Brethren Senior and Junior Wardens, the second obligatory health, which I have the honor to propose, is that of The Governor and Legislature of the State of A........   We will add to this health our wishes for its continued Sovereignty, Independence, and Freedom; and that it may ever vindicate its honor, assert its authority, and protect its Citizens against usurpation. The health is so dear to us that I invite you to deliver your fire as handsomely as possible.

The Wardens repeat the announcement.

The salvo is fired: the plaudit is given as before.

If there be any officer of the State Government present, he may now respond to the Toast. While he does so, all will remain standing. He, and any other officers of the Government, will not have drunk at first: he will do so after the response, and then applaud. The Lodge will cover the plaudit.

☉∴ ♪ My Brethren, let us resume our seats!

Then he may, as before, suspend the works, or leave them in full vigor.

THIRD HEALTH.

This is given according to the same formula. It is, "The Judicial Departments and Officers of the United States, and of the State of A........" We will add to this health our wishes that the Independence of the Judicial Power may be always maintained: that it may never be oppressed by the Military Power, and that its capacity to protect the property, liberty, and life of the Citizen, may never be diminished.

This may be responded to, with plaudit covered as before.

The works may be suspended or continued in vigor.

FOURTH HEALTH.

Is prepared for as before. It is:

"The most Puissant Supreme Council of Sovereign Grand Inspectors-General of the 33d Degree, for ...., whose See is at ...." We will add to this health our wishes for the prosperity of the Masonic Order in general. Be pleased to invite the Brethren of each Column to join me in delivering the most Masonic and fraternal fire.

The Wardens report, and the fire is given as before.

If any member of the Supreme Council is present, he will remain seated. Then he will respond, drink the toast, and give the plaudit, which will be duly covered.

☉∴ My Brethren, let us resume our places!

The work may be suspended or remain in vigor.

FIFTH HEALTH,

Given as above, is that of "The Grand Consistory of Sublime Princes of the Royal Secret, of the 32d Degree of the Ancient and Accepted Scottish Rite, for the State of A............," if there be a Consistory in the State in which the Lodge is holden.

SIXTH HEALTH.

Given as above:

"The Most Worshipful Grand Lodge and Grand Master of Ancient, Free, and Accepted Masons of the State of A........" We will add to this Health our fraternal wishes for its Prosperity and continuance, and that of the Brethren who constitute its Masonic People.

SEVENTH HEALTH.

At such moment as the Wardens deem proper, and, above all, when nothing is to be served, the Senior Warden raps once. ☉ repeats it, and then,

☉∴ What is your pleasure, Brother Senior Warden?

If the works are suspended, ⊕ will request the Venerable Master to restore them to vigor, which he will do in these words:

☉∴ My Brethren, at the request of the Brother Senior Warden, our works, which have been some time suspended, are resumed and in full vigor.

The Wardens repeat the announcement.

Then ⊕ raps once. O repeats, and then ☉.

⊕.·. Venerable Master, be pleased to order the Brethren to charge and align, for a health which the Brother Junior Warden, the Brother Orator, and myself will have the honor to propose.

This will be done as before. When it is announced that all are aligned, ☉ will say:

☉.·. Brother Senior Warden, announce the health which you desire to propose!

⊕.·. It is yours, Venerable Master. Rise and to order, Brethren, Sword in hand! The health which the Brother Junior Warden, the Brother Orator, and myself have the honor to propose to you, is that of the Venerable Master who directs the labors of this Lodge, and of all who are near and dear to him. Be pleased to join us in delivering the best possible fire!

O reports, saying: "The health which the Brother Senior Warden, the Brother Orator, and myself have the honor to propose, is," etc.

ʊ repeats the same announcement.

⊕ says, " With me, my Brethren!" and gives the words of command, or requests the Junior Warden to give them, as he prefers. After the health, the plaudit is given. Meanwhile ☉ remains seated. All the others continue standing, and at order.

☉ returns his thanks. Then ⊕ says:

⊕.·. Out of respect to our Venerable Master, his plaudit will not be covered. Let us resume our seats.

EIGHTH HEALTH.

After a time the Venerable Master causes the works to be resumed, if they are not in vigor, and causes all to charge and align for a health.

It is that of "The Brethren Senior and Junior Wardens," with such additional remarks as the occasion may suggest. The Orator and Secretary repeat the announcement.

The Venerable gives the commands. All the Brethren remain seated. The Wardens alone rise. ⊕ returns thanks. ⊙ causes their plaudit to be covered.

NINTH HEALTH.

At what seems a proper time, ⊙ directs that all charge and align. The health is "The Visiting Brethren who honor us with their presence." "To this we add the health of all Lodges affiliated or corresponding with ours. Union!—Contentment!—Wisdom!"

During this health the Visitors remain standing. The plaudit is given. One or more of the Visitors reply, and the plaudit, given by them, is covered.

After this health, any of the Brethren may sing Masonic songs, or read brief essays, demanding the floor for the purpose.

TENTH HEALTH

Is of "The Officers and Members of the Lodge." "To this we will add the health of the Brethren recently initiated," if there are any such.

Only ⊙, ⊕, O, and the Visitors drink this toast, the officers and members standing. The Orator returns thanks for the officers; the oldest Brother for the members; and one of the Initiates, if there are any, for all.

Their plaudit is covered.

ELEVENTH AND LAST HEALTH.

If there are serving Brothers, ⊙ directs ♃ so to introduce them.

They come with their flags and cannons, and are placed on the West, between the two Wardens.

Then ☉, ♪, directs all to charge and align for the last obligatory health.

Each Warden announces the same.

☉∴ Charge and align, my Brethren!

When informed that all are charged and aligned,

☉∴ Stand! and at order!

All rise. Each gives an end of his flag to the Brother on his right and on his left, and with his left hand takes an end of each of theirs. This permits him to hold his sword with his right hand. The serving Brethren make the same chain with the Wardens, ♃ being in the middle of them.

☉∴ ♪ Brethren, Senior and Junior Wardens, the last obligatory health is, that of all Masons spread over the whole surface of the earth, whether in prosperity or adversity. Let us, with reverence, invoke for all the favor of the Grand Architect of the Universe! that it may please Him to succor the unfortunate, and bring them into good harbors! Be pleased to invite the Brethren on your Columns to unite with us in delivering for this health the most efficient of fires.

The Wardens repeat.

Then the Venerable begins the closing song, in which all join.

PARTING SONG OF MASONS.

1. A - dieu! a heart-foud, warm a - dieu! Dear brethren of the Mys-tic Tie!

Ye fa-vored, ye en-lightened few, Whose se-crets Gold nor Power can buy:

Though far a - part our paths may lie, Still to our ob - li - ga-tion true;

With melt-ing heart and brim-ful eye, You'll think of me, and I of you.

2. Oft have we met, a social band,
  And spent the cheerful festive night;
Obedient to our chief's command,
  The sons of Honor and of Light.
And by that Hieroglyphic bright,
  Which none but Craftsmen ever knew,
Strong memory on our hearts shall write,
  "You'll think of me, and I of you!"

3. May Freedom, Harmony, and Love
  Unite us in the Grand Design,

Beneath the Omniscient eye above,
  The Glorious Architect Divine!—
May we still keep the unerring Line,
  Act by the Plumb in all we do,
Answer the Summons and the Sign!—
  "You think of me, and I of you!"

4. Honor to all whose right and claim
  To wear our sacred badge is clear;
And triple honors to each name
  To Scottish Masons justly dear
We part, perhaps no more to hear
  In the same Lodge words wise and true;
But o'er whatever seas we steer,
  "You'll think of me, and I of you!"

Then ☉ says:

☉∴ Attention, my Brethren!
  Right hand to the Sword!
  Carry Sword!
  Salute with the Sword!
  Sword to the left hand!
  Carry Arms!
  To the cheek!
  Fire!
  Good Fire!
  Triple Fire!
  Advance Arms!

The last two verses are sung again.

One! Two! Three!

One! Two! Three!

One! Two! Three!

Advance Arms!

One! Two! Three!

Right hand to the Sword!

Carry Sword!

Rest Sword!   [The swords are laid down without noise.]

PLAUDIT.

Then the following song is sung:

CLOSING SONG.

1. Now our so-cial la-bors clos-ing, Homage of our hearts we pay;
2. Let us each in Time's com-mo-tion Heavenly Light and Truth im-plore!

Each in con-fi-dence re-pos-ing, Kindest thoughts that ne'er de-cay.
Thus we'll pace life's storm-y o-cean, Land-ing on a hap-pier shore.

3. Soon we part, the word once spoken,
    Friend from friend in kindness goes,
Thus, till Time's last ties are broken,
    Be the claim each Brother knows.

4. On the Level now and ever
    May we stand, upright and true ;
Part upon the Square, and sever
    With a better world in view!

After this, ☉, rapping once, which the Wardens repeat, directs inquiry if any Brother has anything to propose, for the benefit of the Order in general, or of the Lodge in particular.

If any, they are heard; disposed of, if it can be done briefly; and if not, postponed until the next meeting. Then:

The box of fraternal assistance is passed around. After which:

☉∴ ♪ Brother Senior Warden, what is your age?

⊕∴ Three years, Venerable.

☉∴ At what hour is it our custom to close our labors?

⊕∴ At midnight.

☉∴ What is the hour?

⊕∴ Midnight, Venerable.

NOTE.—It is a French custom to give the fraternal kiss before parting. The Venerable gives it to the Brother on his right, and it goes round, and returns to him on the left. Then he raps thrice, and each Warden repeats this, and directs the Plaudit.

Finally,

☉∴ ♪ My Brethren, our labors are closed, let us retire in peace.

Each Warden, rapping once, says the same.
All lay aside their insignia, and retire.

NOTE.—In announcing the healths, the Venerable and Wardens need not adhere to the protocols given. They will, if persons of talents, vary them continually, thus adding to the pleasures of the entertainment.

9

FELLOW-CRAFT.

—

COMPAGNON.

INDEX.
FELLOW-CRAFT'S DEGREE.

———

FELLOW CRAFT.

—

I.

OPENING.

The Lodge being opened in the Degree of Entered Apprentice, the Venerable Master, rapping o, says:

☉∴ ♪ Brethren Senior and Junior Wardens, be pleased to announce on your Columns, that it is my intention now to suspend the labors of the Lodge in the Degree of Entered Apprentice, for the purpose of passing to those of Fellow-Craft.

⊕∴ ♪ Brother Junior Warden, Brethren who grace the Column of the North, the Venerable Master informs you, etc.

☉∴ ♪ Brethren who grace the Column of the South, etc. . . . ♪ It is announced, Brother Senior Warden.

⊕∴ ♪ It is announced, Venerable Master.

☉, ⊕, and ○, each in succession, rap ⌶.

☉∴ Rise! and to order, my Brethren!

All rise, and come to order as Apprentices.

☉∴ With me, my Brethren!

All give the sign, the battery, and the Plaudit.

☉∴ The labors of this Lodge, in the Degree of

Entered Apprentice, are suspended. Let the Lodge be tiled!

The Apprentices withdraw.

The Tracing Board of the Second Degree is substituted for that of the first, and one point of the Compass, on the Altar, is raised above the Square.

⊙∴ ♪ Brother Senior Warden, what is the first duty of a Warden in a Lodge of Fellow-Craft Masons.

⊕∴ To assure himself that the Lodge is duly tiled, Venerable Master.

⊙∴ Be pleased to assure yourself of that, my Brother, and cause the Tiler to be informed that we are about to pass to the labors of the Fellow-Craft, that he may tile accordingly.

⊕∴ ♪ Brother Junior Warden, be pleased to ascertain if the Temple is duly tiled, and cause the Tiler to be informed, etc.

○∴ ♪ Brother Junior Deacon, ascertain if, etc.

♂ does so, as in the first degree, using the Fellow-Craft's battery. Then, returning to his place, and sheathing his sword:

♂∴ Brother Junior Warden, the Temple is duly tiled.

⊙∴ ♪ Brother Senior Warden, the Temple is duly tiled.

⊕∴ ♪ Venerable Master, the Temple is duly tiled.

⊙∴ ♪ How tiled, very dear Brother?

⊕∴ With secrecy and brotherly love. By a

worthy Brother Master-Mason without the door, with a drawn sword.

⊙∴ His duty there?

⊕∴ To guard against the approach of all cowans and eavesdroppers, on the hills or in the vales, and to see that none enter here except such as are duly entitled, and have the permission of the Venerable Master.

⊙∴ It is well, very dear Brother. What is the second duty of the Senior Warden in a Lodge?.

⊕∴ To know with certainty that all present are Fellow-Craft Masons.

⊙∴ ♪ Brethren Senior and Junior Wardens, you will please assure yourselves, in due form, that all present are Fellow-Craft Masons.

* * * * * *

⊙∴ In the name of God, and of Saint John of Scotland, under the auspices, etc., and by virtue of the authority with which I am invested as Master of this Respectable Lodge, I declare it to be duly opened in the Degree of Fellow-Craft. No Brother may speak aloud, or pass from one Column to the other, without first obtaining permission; or may engage in political questions or controversy, under the penalties prescribed by the General Statutes of the Order. . . . With me, my Brethren!

† 2. * * * * * *.

Then, putting on his hat, and giving one rap:

☉∴ ♪ Brother Secretary, be pleased to read to us the engraved plate of our last labors as Fellow-Crafts.

When the Record is read and approved:

☉∴ ♪ Brother Master of Ceremonies, be pleased to repair to the ante-room, and ascertain if there are any Visitors.

♃ obeys, and returning, makes his report.

II.

PRELIMINARIES OF RECEPTION.

When it is proposed to pass an Apprentice to the degree of Fellow-Craft, the following provisions are to govern.

An Apprentice cannot be passed until he has served his time; that is, has been present at five meetings of his Lodge, for instruction. He *ought* to be twenty-three years of age.

When it thus becomes permissible, the Apprentice will apply for the second degree, making his application specially to ◯, in whose Column, and under whose inspection, he will have worked.

At a proper time during the work, ◯ will say:

◯∴ Venerable Master, the Brother A........ B........, an Apprentice of this Respectable Lodge, has requested me to ask for him the favor of being passed to the degree of Fellow-Craft.

⊙ will cause the Apprentice to be seated between the two Wardens, where he will undergo a strict examination upon the instruction of the first degree; after which ho will be directed to retire. Then,

⊙∴ ♪ Brethren Senior and Junior Wardens, be pleased to invite the Brethren on your Columns to offer such remarks as they may see fit, in respect to this application of the Brother A........ B........

This is done. When any discussion is over (in which the Apprentices may take a part), ⊙ directs the Apprentices to re- tire. Then it is that the Lodge passes to the labors of the Fellow-Craft.

The works of the Fellow-Craft being opened, ⊙ says:

⊙∴ ♪ Brethren Senior and Junior Wardens, an- nounce on your Columns that the Brother A....... B....... is proposed to be passed to the degree of Fellow-Craft; and invite the Brethren to offer any remarks they may think proper.

Each Warden does so, and reports it announced.

Then the Lodge will take into consideration the present and previous remarks, and may postpone the proposition to another day, if there be not time to discuss the matter fully, or if further information is desired.

If it is not proposed to postpone, ☿ will conclude for passing or delay. Then the ballot will be taken, as to his conclusions, in the manner directed in the Apprentice's degree.

It requires a unanimous vote of the Brethren present to per- mit the candidate to pass. If the result is favorable, the Master directs the Plaudit.

Then the Fellow-Craft's labors are closed, and those of Ap- prentice resumed.

Then, the Apprentices being admitted, ⊙ will announce that it has been determined to permit the Brother, A..........

B.........., to pass to the degree of Fellow-Craft, or that the matter is postponed, as the case may be. He will then fix a day for conferring the degree.

All the Brethren of the Lodge must be summoned to attend the meeting when the Candidate is to be passed, and the summons should inform them that there will be a reception in the second degree; so that any who could not attend the previous meeting may be present at this, and object, if they have any good cause. The summons to an Apprentice will not mention any work at which he cannot assist.

On the day of Reception all the Brethren will be admitted to the Lodge. The Lodge of Apprentices will be opened, and, after reading and approval of the Record of the previous meeting, the Master will direct the Apprentices to retire.

But if there be no work to be done in the Apprentices' Lodge, nor any banquet, the Apprentices need not be summoned. In that case the Record of the Apprentices' Lodge will remain unread until a meeting of that Lodge, when all are present.

After any family affairs of the Fellow-Crafts are disposed of, and Visitors received, and if no one objects and shows good cause, the Reception will proceed as follows.

III.

RECEPTION.

When all is ready, ☉ says:

☉∴ ♪ Brother Master of Ceremonies, be pleased to go and prepare the Candidate in due form, and in that condition bring him to the Lodge.

♃ goes to the Preparation-room, where the Neophyte will be in waiting, in charge of a Brother, and will prepare him.

† 3.   *   *   *   *   *   *

♂∴ Brother Junior Warden, the Apprentice has worked the due time. He believes his Master is satisfied with him, and it is of his own free-will and accord he makes this request.

☉∴ ♪ Brother Senior Warden, the Apprentice, etc.

⊕∴ ♪ Venerable Master, the Apprentice, etc.

☉∴ How does he dare hope to obtain this favor?

⊕∴ Brother Junior Warden, how does he dare hope, etc.?

☉∴ Brother Junior Deacon, how does he, etc.?

♂∴ Brother Master of Ceremonies, how does this Apprentice dare hope, etc.?

♃∴ By his proofs of devotion to the great cause in which we are engaged, and by his proficiency in the instruction of the first degree.

♂∴ Brother Junior Warden, the Apprentice hopes to obtain the favor he asks by his proofs, etc.

☉∴ Brother Senior Warden, the Apprentice hopes, etc.

⊕∴ Venerable Master, the Apprentice hopes, etc.

☉∴ Let him enter! and place him between the Columns.

⊕∴ Brother Junior Warden, it is the order of the Venerable Master, that the Apprentice be permitted to enter, and that he be placed between the Columns.

☉∴ Brother Junior Deacon, it is the order, etc.

♂∴ Brother Master of Ceremonies, it is the order, etc.

As ♃ and ✠ enter the Brethren rise, and stand with drawn swords. The

MUSIC

plays a slow march. They take the March of Apprentice, and salute the East, West, and South as Apprentices. When the

MUSIC CEASES,

the Master, rapping once, says:

☉∴ ♪ Brother Junior Warden, you command the Columns of Apprentices. Has this Apprentice served his time, and are you and the Brethren of his Column content with him?

○∴ Venerable Master, he has served his time, and we are content with him.

☉∴ Do all the Brethren consent that he shall advance?

All extend the right hand.

☉∴ ♪ Brother Master of Ceremonies, our very dear Brother, the Junior Warden, asks for this Apprentice an increase of wages. Remove the veil, and let him be seated.

He then addresses him as follows:

☉∴ A short time only has elapsed, my Brother, since you were initiated an Entered Apprentice

Mason. If found qualified you may now advance, having attended five meetings of a Lodge, for instruction. It is said that, anciently, five *years* were required to elapse; which was the time during which those who attached themselves to some sects of Philosophy were required to study.

The degree of FELLOW-CRAFT is *Fellowship*, Education, Science. Like the Apprentice's degree, it deals exclusively with the moral and political meanings of our Symbols, except so far as the Philosophical and Spiritual necessarily mingle with and interpenetrate Morality and Political Science.

Before you can proceed, we must know that you have made due proficiency in the preceding degree. To understand the instruction of this degree, that of the former must have been understood, and must be constantly kept in mind. If you have not taken the trouble of engraving that on your memory and on the tablets of your heart, or if you are not capable of doing it, self-respect would forbid our casting any further instruction before you. We shall, therefore, proceed to examine you in regard to the symbolic meaning of the points of your entrance, and of the Lodge and its details.

IV.

EXAMINATION.

☉∴ My Brother, what is Freemasonry?

    etc. . . . etc. . . . etc. . . .

The second and third Sections of the Lecture or Catechism of the first degree will be gone through with. The aspirant must have them well in his memory, or his reception must be postponed. The business of hurried half-examination, and of permitting Brethren to pass who are "*substantially*" acquainted with what they ought *perfectly* to *know*, is not to be continued.

When the examination is concluded, ☉ continues:

☉∴ You are now about to make Progress in Masonry. The Fellow-Craft's degree *is* PROGRESS. It teaches Brotherhood, Education, Science. In them and in Moral Improvement, true Progress, for the Individual or the Nation, consists. If you would realize what Progress is, call it *To-morrow*. To-morrow performs its work irresistibly, and it performs it *to-day*. It always reaches its aim through unexpected means. It ever goes on, not always steadily, but, more often, fitfully. It is a workman to whom no tool comes amiss. It adjusts its divine work to the man who strode over the Alps, and the feeblest, tottering invalid. It makes use of the Cripple as well as the Conqueror, of the Knave as well as the Saint.

The delay required to elapse after you were initiated, before you could be permitted to receive the second degree, was intended to give you the needful time in which to prepare yourself, by imprinting on your memory, so that its characters should remain indelible, the instruction of the first degree, to fit you to make progress in the second. In the Ancient Mysteries that interval was of several years. Thus the Egyptian Priests tried Pythagoras before admitting him to know the Secrets of the Sacred Science. He succeeded, by the patience and courage with which he surmounted all obstacles, in obtaining admission to their Society, and receiving their lessons. In Palestine, the Essenes admitted none among them until they had passed the tests of several degrees.

*   *   *   *   *   *

In this degree, the five years of study required by Pythagoras are symbolically represented by five Circuits, in each of which, following the Sun, you will imitate his annual course, going by the North and East to the South and West, which represent the Solstices and Equinoxes. At the end of each you will receive the appropriate instruction.

You have entered here, bearing the RULE, or Twenty-Four-Inch GUAGE, one of the working-tools of an Apprentice. Its meaning was explained to you in that degree. Keep it in mind in this! Disorder is the law of weakness. Let the RULE still be to you the symbol of LAW, Order, Intellect, controlling and regulating Force. Rule, in the Latin *Regula*, is government, restraint, the limitation and management of Force. But remember, also, that it is *Motion* that gives *Method* on the earth, as in the skies—that reveals Power, as among the electrical elements. Movement is the result of an alternating preponderance. The scales of the balance must alternately rise and fall. Immobility would be stagnation and death.

♪ Brother Master of Ceremonies, let this Apprentice lay aside the RULE, and take the MALLET and the CHISEL. Then take him upon the first of his five journeys.

V.

THE FIRST CIRCUIT.

MUSIC.

♃ takes the Rule, and puts a Mallet and a Chisel in the Candidate's left hand. Then, taking him by the right hand, he leads him once, slowly, around the Lodge, and halts with him near the Junior Warden. Here he gives one rap.

MUSIC CEASES.

† 4.   *   *   *   *   *   *

⊙∴ In this journey, symbolical of the first year

of study of the disciples of Pythagoras, you have borne the MALLET and the CHISEL. The latter, used by means of the force of the former, serves the workman for smoothing and polishing, with constant and intelligent labor, the materials for his creations. It is, above all, the chief tool of the sculptor, with which he cuts away the envelope that, in the rough block of marble, conceals and hides the statue, and by which he develops the Gladiator, symbol of Strength, the Jupiter of the Capitol, symbol of Majesty, or the Venus, symbol of Beauty.

The Apprentice, working with the GAVEL, employs FORCE alone, cutting down the stone to certain straight lines, marked by the unbending, inflexible RULE, under the directions of the Master. The Sculptor, using the CHISEL, uses it with *judgment*, and with judgment applies the FORCE of the MALLET, whether he carves the beautiful and delicate vase, in accordance with the lines of beauty, creating the graceful wreath and exquisite foliage, or invests the statue with the poetry of his art. Even the stone-cutter, shaping the cube, the oblong stone, or the column, and more especially the Corinthian or composite capital, must exercise his skill and judgment in the use of the CHISEL.

The morality of the LINE and RULE is not sufficient for the Fellow-Craft. These will give Honesty, Uprightness, Truthfulness, Punctuality, Puritanism.

The work of the CHISEL is wanting, or the character
is hard, dry, and ungenial. It is perfected by those
genial virtues and fine graces which are not dictated
by the stern rules of law or the Ten Commandments,
but by Generosity, Liberality, Courtesy, Amiability,
Gentleness, the soft relentings of forgiveness; by all
the graces and beauties, which are as the flutings
and capital of the column, the curves, the flowers, and
foliage of the vases.

It is GENIUS that directs the Chisel of PHIDIAS
and CANOVA; the genius that produced the Laocoön,
the Dying Gladiator, the works of Benvenuto Cellini,
and all the immortalities of Sculpture. In the STATE,
also, besides the mathematical formulas of the LAW,
and the harsh lines of the RULE of Intellect, there
must be Genius in those who govern, and the graces
and beauties of science and the arts; or we have
Lacedæmon and not Athens; Holland, with its inter-
minable right-lines of ditches, and not the seven-
hilled Rome, with its magnificence of beauty; or
classic Greece, with its Temples amid olive-groves;
or England, with its picturesque scenery, and hedge-
rows blossoming with beauty in the Spring.

*   *   *   *   *   *

In the Apprentice's degree, as in a lower school,
are symbolized exact discipline, and the training of
the faculties for future use. In *this*, as in an *upper*

school, you must *train* thought, that it may at once be wedded with healthy act. In this life all should be workers. There should be no idle spectators. Everywhere, man is man's brother. None belong to the Planet Neptune. The nation is but the family. Rather, it is the individual, with concentrated strength, and the like enlarged accountability. Men are assembled, not only to think nobly, but to act accordingly. The heart of the world should be all heroic. All men are copartners in the great world-business. The worthiest should be the Directors, but all are shareholders. The franchise is the light that should illumine all—the white that comes from many colors.

Love the Truth! Abhor the Untruth! That is the first requisite. Without that you can neither improve yourself nor serve the People. Let the MALLET and CHISEL first rid you of all duplicity, dissimulation, equivocation, and dishonesty. Until then, you are no man, but a sham, only waiting for circumstances to make you a wretch or villain.

Then rid yourself of the love of lucre. It will require heroic resolution; for it is the deepest-seated of all passions in the human heart, and prostrates the noblest minds, as if they had been born to run like the lizard. Yet there is no hope till that citadel is breached.

To secure moral and intellectual freedom to an

individual, or political freedom to a nation, is a work
of Thought, Patience, and Perseverance. When a
nation has *secured* liberty, it has been because it was
enabled, by long experience, to undertake the management of its own affairs. It is a work that goes on
by slow steps, and the harder the toil with which a
people hew the steps out of the solid rock, the surer
is the first ascent. Yet, at the instant when Freedom touches a nation on the shoulder, it is enlisted
in her cause for life. So it must be with *you.* You
enlisted in her service as an Apprentice, and received the bounty. There is no discharge or fur-
lough in that war. If there is any earnest work on
earth, it is where the road to Freedom is being
paved. The tree of liberty must come up on the
spot, from the seed, and not be transported bodily in
the bulky growth. Empire is a high enterprise. It
begins, like charity, at home ; and it is after much
tribulation that this kingdom is entered, and with
much and constant exertion it is maintained. There
are not only the fierce fight of brethren, but the march
in the wilderness. It is not the vivid *moral* sentiment only that can bring the pilgrims to the promised land. The Thought must explain the trials
of the Time ; but the march in the desert gives the
discipline, and Temperance will give the triumph.

*   *   *   *   *   *

Thought, the noblest characteristic of the isolated

man, is also that of a People. Our purpose now is
to lead you to think. Men may become wise without
many books. It is true that he is fortunate who has
the leisure to study and add to his knowledge. The
Fellow-Craft ought, if possible, to obtain a knowledge
of the natural sciences. The more he knows of the
universe the better he knows its Author. And these
sciences, especially geology, necessarily lead the
student to think and reflect. But the intelligent
man may obtain great results by thought alone.
Freemen are serious. They have objects at heart,
worthy to engross attention. It is reserved for
slaves to indulge in groans at one moment, and to
laugh at another.

Your first journey, our ancient instruction says, is
a symbol of the term of one year, which a Fellow-
Craft was required to pass in perfecting himself in
the work of cutting and smoothing the stones which,
as an Apprentice, you learned how to rough-hew. This
work, with the chisel and mallet, is to teach you that
the degree of perfection which an Apprentice can
attain, is far from finishing his work; that the
materials consecrated to the building of the Temple
which he rears to the GRAND ARCHITECT, and of
which he is at once the material and the workman,
are not yet ready for the building, and that he must
still undergo the hard and toilsome labor of the
mallet, and learn accurately, and with precision, to

use the chisel, never varying from the lines traced for him by the Masters. You must interpret and apply this for yourself. Give me the sign of an Entered Apprentice Mason.

He gives it.

⊙∴ What does the sign mean and remind you of?

✠∴ It reminds me of my obligation ; and it means that I will rather †5 . . . . . . than reveal the secrets of Masonry unlawfully.

⊙∴ Let it also remind you, henceforward, that, as a good and true Mason, you must rather incur the risk of being beheaded, like Saint John the Baptist, than betray the cause of the People, or become the instrument or apologist of their oppressors.

♪ Brother Master of Ceremonies, take from this Apprentice the Mallet and Chisel, arm him with the COMPASS and RULE, and let him, under your guidance, make his second journey.

VI.

THE SECOND CIRCUIT.

♃ takes the Mallet and Chisel, and puts in his left hand the Compass and Rule, takes him by the right hand, and leads him again around the Lodge, in the same direction as before, while there is solemn

MUSIC.

When the circuit is made, he places him between the Columns, and

MUSIC CEASES.

⊙∴ My Brother, this second journey represents the second year of the studies of the disciples of Pythagoras. It is said that during that year they studied Geometry, to which Arithmetic is the introduction. In the theory and practice of Geometry the COMPASS and RULE, or SCALE, are indispensable, and that is one reason why you have borne them in your journey.

The Compass, also, is the symbol of the circle which it describes, and of the celestial spheres. In conjunction with the Rule, it represents that Divine element, intermingling with the laws of morality and the rules of political science, by which alone perfection, symbolized by the cubical stone, can be attained, or even approached unto.

A man may strictly comply with every positive obligation imposed on him by the law, and even with all contained in the moral code, and yet be detestable. A community of men, in which each should punctiliously observe the law, and that code, would be one in which no generous soul could live. If the Divine, in morals, did not intermingle with the Human, the world would be intolerable. How little the strictly moral man is often the benefactor of men we all well know. Strictness of morals may belong to the

driest, and hardest, and most ungenial character; and
often the vicious and dissipated more benefit society
and their race than the strictest moralists. One
must go far beyond *those* rules to imitate the Beneficent and Glorious Deity. Loving-kindness, Generosity, Devotedness, Sympathy—these, and the like,
are of the Divine. The Rule is not a symbol of
Fraternity, nor even of the kindnesses one owes his
neighbor.

The Compass also, by which, round a fixed point,
we describe the circle, emblem of Deity or the
Supreme Wisdom, is itself an emblem of that Wisdom. With its aid, too, upon the base laid down by
the Rule, we erect the Equilateral Triangle, symbol
of many things, and, to a Fellow-Craft, especially of
Liberty, Fraternity, and Equality.

*   *   *   *   *   *

This second journey, like the first, signifies Preparation—the Study of Principles, which fits a
Fellow-Craft to do the Work; whether by the Fellow-Craft is meant an individual or a People. The
practical elements must be acquired before they can
be applied. The elements of Mathematics must be
thoroughly understood, and its problems demonstrated, by the aid of the figures traced by the Compass and Scale, before they can be applied in Survey-
ing, or the measurement of land; in Navigation, or

that of courses and distances on the pathless ocean; in Coast-Surveying, which marks the shoals and reefs that cause shipwreck, and, with the aid of the Compass, of his reckonings and observations, and the logarithmic tables, enables the mariner, in the darkness of night, and amid the terrors of the frightful storm, to find safe harbor; or in Astronomy, which measures the distances, orbits, specific gravity, and mass of the planets, and enabled Leverrier and Adams to ascertain, before their telescopes discovered it, that another planet existed, by the measured perturbations of its neighbors.

To all this Science attained, by the use of those simple instruments, the Compass and Scale. The Circle and the Line are their symbols. From moral rectitude, and the wisdom that teaches Love and Faith, result the perfection of the individual man, the interpenetration of the Human by the Divine; and from justice and wisdom results good government in the State. Rule, Law, Order, Justice, Rectitude in dealing with other Nations, inflexible adherence to sound policy, stability in measures, consistency and absence of vacillation in Legislation—these, in a State, are symbolized by the SCALE—the law of merit and demerit; reward for the worthy and punishment for the unworthy, office and honor to the best; a scale of Honors according to merit; and Wisdom, Prudence, Foresight, and Forethought,

Toleration, generous, and liberal, and enlarged policy as to matters at home and abroad, lenient indulgence tempering strict justice, are symbolized by the Compass—again the Divine interpenetrating the Human ;—by the *Rule*, LAW ; by the *Compass*, EQUITY.

For the RULE is the symbol, naturally, of *direction* and *control* by rule, regularity, inflexible, unbending Principles. *Regulæ juris*, the Rules of Law, do not shift and vary with the fluctuating tides of circumstance, nor disappear in the presence of necessity or expediency. These are only for to-day. Principles are for all time, the same yesterday, to-day, and to-morrow ; as the Deity is all that was, is, or is to be. To-morrow, necessity and expediency will have disappeared like the mists of morning : the principles will remain and shine with undimmed lustre, like the stars. Every man and every people, without fixed principles, is like a vessel without a rudder or compass, beaten by the baffling winds, and by the invisible currents of the ocean carried hither and thither. But there must also be wisdom in the administration of affairs according to these principles. In the individual it consists greatly in temper. Even in the game of Honors which is played at Courts, we obtain success less by our talents than our tempers ; and nations, more frequently even than individuals, lose by loss of temper, which is lack of Wisdom, and a chief weakness of Republics ; which, therefore, in the end, always lose.

The Fellow-Craft is, in pursuing his studies, to lay up Principles for future use. Remember that, in all cases, the use of a *doctrine*, and the only reason for its being promulgated and accepted, are its translation into *action*. Even the sublime doctrine of Christ is of no great use to the every-day violators of it, how bitterly soever they may hate all dissenters from the truth. Men who act sincerely up to what doctrines they may have accepted, either as hereditary or as creations of their own, be they of Christ, Buddha, Zarathustra, or Mohammed, are virtuous in proportion to their sincerity, if the doctrine itself teach virtue ; that virtue by no means consisting in the *thinking* or *believing*, which is an accidental, inevitable matter, where the man is sincere ; but in the *doing*, which depends solely on himself.

♪ Brother Master of Ceremonies, take from this Apprentice the Compass, give him the CROW or LEVER, and let him, under your guidance, make his third journey!

VII.

THE THIRD CIRCUIT.

♃, leaving the RULE in his left hand, places on his left shoulder a CROW, or LEVER, which, also, he holds with his left hand. Then he takes him by the right hand, and leads him in the same direction as before, once around the Lodge, while there is martial

MUSIC.

When the circuit is made, he places him near the Senior Warden, and the

MUSIC CEASES.

† 7.   *   *   *   *   *   *

☉∴ My Brother, this third journey represents the third year of the studies of the disciples of Pythagoras. It is said, in our old Ritual, that during this year an Apprentice is taught how to move and place in position the stones for the foundation of the building, which is done with the RULE and CROW, or LEVER. The LEVER, it is also said, is the symbol of the power of KNOWLEDGE, which, adding to our individual strength, enables us to do and effect that which, without its aid, it would be impossible for us to accomplish.

"Behold," it is said in Isaiah, "I lay in Zion for a foundation a STONE, a tried stone, a precious cornerstone, a sure foundation : he that believeth shall not make haste. Judgment also will I lay to the line, and righteousness to the plumb."

"The God of Jacob," it is said, in Genesis, "is the stone of Israel."

"The stone which the builders refused," it is said, in the Psalms and elsewhere, "is become the head of the corner."

"Ye are no more strangers and foreigners," Paul says to the Ephesians, "but fellow-citizens with the Saints, and of the Household of God ; and are built upon the foundation of the Apostles and Prophets, Jesus Christ being the chief corner-stone, in whom all the building, fitly framed together, groweth a holy Temple in the Lord."

You are now to commence the erection of that Temple of virtue, morality, and freedom of the mind and soul, which is symbolized by the TEMPLE of SOLOMON. That edifice was erected by SOLOMON on Mount Moriah, purchased by David.

"The King commanded, and they brought great stones, costly stones, and hewed stones, to lay the foundation of the House. And Solomon's builders and Huron's builders did hew them, and the Stone-Squarers," or men of Byblos—the Giblemites.

The length of the House was sixty cubits, or one hundred and two and a half feet, and its breadth twenty cubits, or thirty-four feet. There was also a porch, or portico, ten cubits, or seventeen feet, wide, along the whole eastern front, making the foundation an oblong square, measuring nearly one hundred and twenty feet by thirty-four. Solomon's own house was much larger, being, with the porch, two hundred and twenty-one feet long, by eighty-five wide.

It is the uses for which the Temple was intended that make it symbolical. It was for the public worship of the Deity ; and in the Oracle, Holy of Holies, or KADOSH-KADOSHIM, the western room, the SHEKINAH, or Divine Presence, was supposed to dwell between the Cherubim.

To the Fellow-Craft, as you already know, the Temple symbolizes an Individual and a State. The foundation of the moral or political Temple is to be laid by the help of the symbolic LEVER, to the lines laid down by the RULE; and it is laid of great, costly, hewn, symbolic stones, like the Cyclopean work of the Etruscan Architects, yet to be seen in the ancient foundations of Rome. The foundation-stones of the Temple still remain, some of them twenty-four feet in length by four in width, bevelled on the edges, of a very white limestone, resembling marble, and forming, when cemented together, a perfectly solid wall or foundation, which only a convulsion of the earth could demolish.

Thus firm, solid, stable, and durable should be the foundation of the character which makes the MAN, of the knowledge which makes the Scholar or the Statesman, of the STATE that is to endure. Courage, resolution, decision, firmness, persistence, endurance, hopefulness, self-respect, self-reliance, the chief ingredients of manliness; forethought, temperance, fortitude, hardihood, energy, justice, rectitude, fairness, lovingkindness, faith and faithfulness, devotedness and disinterestedness, these are the chief of the great, costly, hewn stones of the foundation of an admirable character. Classical learning, the natural and physical sciences, the law of nations, the laws of trade, knowledge of great commercial currents and financial phenomena, and familiarity with great Constitutional principles, are those of the foundation of the learning of the Statesman. The great principles embodied in Bills of Right and Magna Charta, and Constitutions written and unwritten, are the foundations of a Free State.

Force of Will is the great individual Lever. Force of public opinion is the great Lever of a free State.

*　　*　　*　　*　　*　　*

Let the Fellow-Craft, therefore, and even the humblest Apprentice, be encouraged to work, not apprehensive, in whatever direction he may work, that his labor will be lost. No Force, nor any action of any Force, is lost in this universe. There are no blows struck in the void. Paul, after his conversion, was not a person of much consideration, and the sphere of his labors was the preaching of a new and unpopular faith—anti-idolatry in an idolatrous world. He wrote a few letters, no one of them as long as a single modern speech of some windy Boanerges—letters to handfuls of obscure individuals in the great Empire City, Rome, and the great Provincial Cities of Corinth and Ephesus, and in some Roman Provinces, and to the obscure persons, Timotheus, Titus, and Philemon: and what a wonderful work in the world those letters have wrought! What, by the side of them, or of Luther's sermons even, are Moscow expeditions and Waterloo? The great works of the world are done unexpectedly, like the invention of printing, by obscure men. Let us all take courage, therefore, and work!

♪ Brother Master of Ceremonies, take from this Apprentice the Crow, and give him the SQUARE; and let him, under your guidance, make his fourth journey.

VIII.

THE FOURTH CIRCUIT.

℣ takes the CROW, and places the SQUARE in his left hand, with the RULE. Then, taking him by the right hand, he leads him once around the Lodge, in the same direction as before, while there is joyful

MUSIC.

When the circuit is made, he places him in the North, and the

MUSIC CEASES.

† 8.   * * * * * *

⊙∴ This voyage, my Brother, it is said in our Ancient Rituals, represents the fourth year of the service of an Apprentice, during which he is employed in the erection of the body of the edifice, and in accurately placing in position the stones of which it is built: and it teaches you that only application, zeal, and intelligence can raise a Fellow-Craft above the general level of his fellows.

The Square is not only used as the only certain means by which the workman is enabled to cut into rectangular shape the stones for the building; but also in laying them, and making true, just, and square, the corners of the edifice.

The Fellow-Craft is said to have passed from the PERPENDICULAR or PLUMB to the SQUARE; the Square being the Plumb and Level united, and at right angles with each other. The Perpendicular is a single straight line, vertical. The Square is two lines, forming a right angle. When you become a Master, the third line will complete the right-angled triangle, and exhibit the 47th Problem of Euclid, the favorite and little understood symbol of Pythagoras, expression of the great Secret of the Universe.

In the Orient, the Aspirant, after undergoing the severest, or rather the most cruel trials, was proclaimed the Soldier of Mithras, and could, like the modern Apprentice, call all Initiates his companions in arms, that is, his Brethren.   Next, he became a LION, a name embodying the idea of STRENGTH, the peculiar expression of the modern Fellow-Craft.

Your fourth journey symbolizes the building up of the enduring and harmoniously-proportioned fabric of virtue and morality in the individual Soul, and in Society and the State.

There is nothing peculiar or eccentric in the morality of Masonry.   It is the same that was taught by Confucius to the Chinese, by Zarathustra to the Bactrians, by Socrates and Seneca, and by Him whom Power, Priestcraft, and the Mob sacrificed on the Cross.   All its precepts may be read in its Liturgies and Rituals, and to these we chiefly refer you.

It is especially political truths that are symbolized in this degree.   The letter G is not displayed as the initial letter of the word GEOMETRY, but of the more significant Greek word GNOSIS, *Knowledge.*   "*Know thyself!*" was an old maxim of the Sages.   To learn that we know nothing is the first step in the acquisition of knowledge.

By the Holy House of the Temple, to a Fellow-Craft Mason, is especially symbolized the fabric of a State.

*   *   *   *   *   *

A throne, whether of king or free people, should stand on the golden backs of strong lions, bound by the wisdom of the circling serpents, and canopied by the silver doves of mercy. But wisdom cannot be entailed. The lust of idleness is a disease that preys alike on People, Peers, and Princes. History proves that the sense of right and public duty cannot secure exertion. Families perpetually wear out, by the unwillingness of nature to propagate the useless plants.

The Masonry of the Ancient and Accepted Scottish Rite, my Brother, based on the foundations of morality and manliness, is, first of all, hostility to Tyranny. It is the Apostle of LIBERTY, FRATERNITY, and EQUALITY. Under a despotism, therefore, it is revolutionary.

In free countries Masonry must labor to maintain, perpetuate, and improve free Institutions. It has it peculiarly in charge to resist usurpation, especially by the military power, out of which Despotisms and Dynasties have generally grown; to protect the Constitution against violation by force or fraud, and zealously to defend the natural and guaranteed rights of the people; and especially to guard, as the sacred Palladium of Liberty, the right to the writ of Habeas Corpus, secured ages ago to Englishmen, and confronted by which *lettres de cachet* are harmless, and the law breaks down the gates of the Bastille and the doors of the dungeons of the Inquisition and of military prisons alike.

A free people may speak its mind with fullness; but, after decision, it must obey, as well as the serf.

Respect for the law should be greater in free States than in those that have Masters, and where public opinion has not cut and deepened the great channels. For it is the law made by themselves for themselves. Reverence for the law is self-reverence. For Officers, Civil and Military, who violate it, and usurp power, and crush Constitutional guarantees, the mandates of the Law should be concise and stern, like those of the Twelve Tables. LET THEM DIE THE DEATH! Remember that a hatred to ill-government is an antipathy wonderfully strong in wise men, and wonderfully weak in fools; and when usurpation is once in the saddle, it is not easily unseated. The title ripens by prescription; and if the people become a little used to it, only the most intolerable outrages will rouse them to annihilate the new-born despotism. Always remember that you entered here by the right of being free-born, and therefore oppose the very beginnings of tyranny.

Law distinguishes the criteria of right and wrong; teaches to establish the one, and punish, prevent, or redress the other; employs in its theory the noblest faculties of the soul, and exerts in its practice the cardinal virtues of the heart. It is a science universal in its use and extent, accommodated to each individual, yet comprehending the whole community. It is, or ought to be, the perfection of human reason; the expression of experience and wisdom, gathered from the whole human family, and applied to the wants of communities. It is founded first on the study of the universal human nature, and that study is a science in itself. It is a moral as well as a practical science. Law is morality in office. It is progressive as man himself, following him with equal steps. It is a heroic work to amend the law.

A country that puts itself into the hands of its demagogues is lost, the question of its ruin being only a question of time. Encounter these, and oppose them with all your might everywhere! Never consent to, much less aid in, the elevation of the shallow, the showy, the frivolous, the half-informed, the sprightly without depth, the trickster, or the liar! Before you vote for the creature who electioneers for himself, writes praises of himself, and bribes the public journals to puff him, lay aside your Masonic clothing, and withdraw forever from the Lodge. To be the pimp of the Great is one of the saddest sights in this world : to be the pimp of the Small is an unspeakable abasement. A Statesman should not only be the true representative of his constituents, but of his nation ; nay, a grand Representative of human nature. If a free people produces men who can master the material world, who can ride dauntless and keep a steady seat in the spiritual realm, and yet is represented in the noble art of ruling by men who can neither run, nor ride, nor walk, but only creep and grope in their blindness, this is as much misrule as if it were still in the den of despotism. The trained men of a free people ought to be superior to the most gray-headed servants of the most sagacious monarch. And yet Free States are often ruled by pigmies, that loom through the mists like real giants.

Choose the men, if you can find them, worthy to lead the people in the hour of deep despondency and wintry gloom; to strike with living electric force the most torpid human feeling; to utter the burning words that move the great public heart to heroic strength and endurance; that give faith and the light of hope in the darkest hour of trial, and stir the meanest of mankind to unselfish sacrifice; not merely those who can speak punctually to the purpose as a clock; and still less the tinselled popinjays that craft and cunning always pull by wires, whose orations are deserts of common-place, so many yards of frieze or fustian, with here and there a tawdry bit of tinsel stuck on with paste.

Remember that State-*Craft* is not State-WISDOM; and mistake not cunning and craft for greatness! The national affairs of a free people are transacted in open day. It hides no counsels in palace-chambers, and sends out no edicts from an invisible throne. Ambidexterity is out of place in a republic, and no qualification for a republican Statesman.

Simplicity, and not show, honest administration, and not corruption, the silent rule of the law, and not the glittering and noisy empire of arms, are characteristics of free government. Kings parade their power before the people in the midst of armed men, and their reviews are as much meant for their subjects as for the enemy. A free country is not meant for spectacle. They that rule themselves are conscious of their strength, and simplicity becomes splendor. The People grants or revokes the Commissions of its Generals, the patents of power of its rulers. The allegiance of the willing hearts is beyond that of the bayonets. Conscious strength is silent. The national acts would hardly be known but for the press. Mankind may not be better than of old; there may be the same old love of lucre, the same lust for power, the same hunger for patronage. But the people act and speak through the Press, sit in perpetual oversight of men and the things they do, and drag to light the deeds that delight in darkness. Through it they tell those in power that they are not immortal, and that their power is but a *brief* trust. If there be trafficking in forbidden wares, the veil is drawn aside at last in open market. In the end, all things are tested by the SQUARE and RULE.

The old Romans gave official nobility. They allowed a man to bear the surname of Africanus, Capitolinus, or Coriolanus, and thus linked a noble name to a noble deed—a possession and an example forever. This privilege inspired the family more than a peerage held in heirship. True, the love of excellence is different from the love of distinction, and better. It consists in the desire to do good deeds, and it longs for the words on earth, that many will hear only in Heaven—"*Well done! thou good and faithful servant!*" But the love of distinction is natural and laudable; and distinction is valuable when conferred on excellence alone. The badge of Honor, or the office, which mediocrity and trickery can attain, loses its value in the estimation of honorable minds. A free people should take care not to cheapen its rewards. It is more fatal and more foolish than to depreciate its currency by shamelessly breaking its faith. Wages to the workman; honor to the worthy! A man were better hang himself with the garter of nobility, than wear it when he has not earned it. He only who has borne the cross is worthy to wear it. Let men be bribed and bought with money, if you will, but not with place or honor. Appoint the fittest, and promote the best. Honors distributed by any other rule are *dishonors*. If you have a vote, you have a voice, indirectly, in the conferring of all honors; and how much or how little soever your vote may weigh, if you do not give it for the best, you, to that extent, undermine the foundations of the State.

Youth will naturally vote for youth; and its knowledge is ordinarily superficial, its counsels rash and impetuous. It is apt to prefer the shallow and the sprightly to the profound and solid. A single House of Legislators, composed chiefly of young men, would prefer the swift speed of impulse to the slow progress of Prudence. Hence, in free governments, the Legislature is generally divided into two bodies, a lower and more numerous, and an upper, of fewer men, and these of greater age. A free people are ever young, and have the impatient temper of youth. Hence an appeal lies naturally to age; from the man to the sage; from the hour to the year. Age sits in the seat of Posterity, and considers its judgment. In this House ought to be gathered up the golden harvest of wise experience. It should be a real "assembly of the notables," of the wise men and elders, deputed by common consent. In a free land the wise men ought to be seen as plainly as the mountains or the monuments.

So, in part, with the SQUARE and the RULE, should the House of the Temple of a State be builded. Fortunate the workman who can use well the tools!

♪ Brother Master of Ceremonies, take from this Apprentice the Square and Rule, and let him, under your guidance, make his fifth journey.

IX.

THE FIFTH CIRCUIT.

*   *   *   *   *   *

⊙∴ My Brother, this fifth journey represents the fifth year of the studies of the disciples of Pythagoras. It was devoted chiefly to Astronomy and Numbers. It is said in our old rituals, that during this year the Apprentice studied the theory of Architecture. And he was advised that it was not sufficient for him to be well grounded in the principles of morality and virtue, but that it would require continual effort and constant self-denial to approach toward perfection.

You have made this fifth journey without working-tools.

† 10.   *   *   *   *   *   *

The Sword is, as you are aware, the symbol of Loyalty and Honor. Now, and to you, it is symbolical of armed resistance to tyranny. It is the significant emblem of the Military Power, as the Defender of Liberty.

Loyalty was for ages a chivalric blind devotion to the Monarch or the Leader. It has exacted life, not only in hecatombs, as in the days of Cæsar and Timour, but in fragments also, as when one serf of an Eastern Despot hastened to stab himself, and another to throw himself from the rock, that his master's absolute power, and the devotion of his subjects, might be manifested to the envoy of another monarch. Surely there *is* something noble in human nature; and the presence of the Divine in it explains its contradictions, notwithstanding the shrieking of the sophists and the groaning of misanthropes, and all that is sordid and base in Humanity. For man has, in all ages, offered his life freely on all kinds of pretexts—for religions of all sorts, for money, for enterprise, for whims and oddities, and even for the worthless tyrants. It is more difficult to live than to die. Shame on the Mason who could *not* die for his Order and the Cause, if the Order and the Cause required it.

There is a spiritual loyalty, from Thermopylæ, and Curtius leaping into the gulf, to the latest noble self-sacrifice of heroism. The loyalty of man to man is such, that he will not only kill himself, but his idol, as when Virginius slew his child, and the Roman freedman killed his master, to save from worse. Loyalty to kings has been common. A thousand breasts have often been bared to save the hero from the swords of thickening foes. Napoleon's dying veterans, at Waterloo as at Austerlitz, in direful defeat as well as in glorious victory, uttered with feeble voices their old cry of devotion. The man personified the principle. Men die for Glory, Honor, and Duty. The loyalty of the Knight to the leader and lady; of the Jesuit to his Order and the successor of Loyola; of the Templar, the Knight of St. John of Jerusalem, and the Teutonic Knight, to his Order and Grand Commander; that of the Crusaders to the Cross, were all developments of the Divine. When men ceased to reverence kings, Loyalty became obedience to the Law, the love of constitutional liberty, the fidelity of the soldier to his colors and captain, the love of the sailor for his ship and flag. Thus personal loyalty was sublimated into Patriotism and the cardinal virtues.

No one yet knows, or can calculate, the immense force of Loyalty to a Flag, to a free Government, a Union, an idea. It will be written, some day, in letters of blood and fire. In the days of true allegiance, personal loyalty is one of the virtues: when the true type is lost, it is a superstition. It is so in Priestcraft, and in all the crafts. *Cræft* meant strength. It afterwards degenerated into cunning. There is always the shouting loyalty; the homage to Cromwell, followed by that to Charles. But the world still continues to be loyal to its great men, worshipping them during life, and deifying them after death. If Men sometimes make mistakes, and deify the sham hero and spurious great man, it only proves that they are so anxious for some one to whom to be loyal, as to do homage to a Pretender, because he *seems* to be a King and Priest of Heroism or Thought.

Loyalty to the State is indispensable to the State. Without it, the mass of people have not become a State, but only an organized mob. It is the cohesion that binds the free State together. Remove it, and you have only a heap of grains of sand. Cemented with it, the State endures. From this Loyalty come the resolution to maintain her ancient glories, and the laying down of life for an idea or a political theory. What a potent loyalty is that in Poland and Hungary! loyalty to the idea of State Sovereignty and Nationality.

Every man can help enlarge and strengthen this Loyalty to the State. The self-sacrifice of the humblest, as an example, has a wonderful power. Who can estimate the effect, now and in the future, not only upon individuals, but on a whole people, of the heroism of the sailor who nails the colors to the mast, and cheers manfully as the ship goes down: of the widow, who furnishes the inflammable arrows to burn her own house, made a fortress of by the enemy? The circles produced by such actions not only widen continually, but the ripples become immense waves of enthusiasm and patriotism as they enlarge, and recede from the centre.

It is a truth in morals, that the soul may brutalize

the body, as much as the body may degrade the soul. There is reciprocal sympathy between them. The body is not flung beneath the brazen wheels of the car of Juggernaut, until the miserable spirit of the man has already all but perished in the dust before the foul idol. A religion of craven fear and abortive hopes, without love, as without light and liberty, ends, like the enchantments of Circe, in transforming men into brutes. A sound and healthy and vigorous morality depends upon a healthy religious faith. To get that is one chief object of your last year of study. We shall, in time, come to resemble whatever God we believe in. Theory always crystallizes into practice. A cruel God will have cruel worshippers. Man becomes the image of the God of his creed.

*   *   *   *   *   *

Every true word is the word of God. He is the great Fountain of Truth. All true Thoughts are inspirations. The true Orator is a Prophet: the babblers are the prophets of Baal. Thoughts, spoken and printed, are the great levers by which nations are moved; the storm-words that lash the great heaving popular ocean into convulsions; the word of Christ that stills the restless waves. But, unfortunately, all speech is not the utterance of true Thoughts, or even of any Thoughts whatever; and babble is often more available with the people than genuine speech.

See to it that you do not mistake the loquacious babbler for the truly great man. No mistake is more fatal to republics. For speech, even if it consist chiefly of sound, is Power, as often for evil as for good. The Press is the Fourth Estate. Its license is a mighty evil. To preserve its freedom and curb its license, to keep it the minister of Good, and not permit it to become wholly the Demon of Evil, is a great problem that must in some manner be solved. No cause will hereafter be so fruitful of national disasters as the licentiousness of the Press, not even the pitiful littleness of public men, and the knavery of the basely ambitious, the venal, and the corrupt.

The Mason must be ever ready to defend, with arms, the old flag of the Order, on which are emblazoned the magical words, great always, though sometimes misunderstood, "LIBERTY! EQUALITY! FRATERNITY!" Among the soldiery of this Army of Freedom may well be that boundless ambition which is the spur of Renown. In it there is no barrier which merit cannot pass. There is an instinct in all freemen that courts the danger leading to an eminence, and makes life weigh little in the scales against Glory and Honor. Let the career be open to the talents, and Liberty may always have its army of

Ironsides, like those of Cromwell, whose deeds survive the shrieks of Faction ; men intelligent as brave, loyal as Paladins, fearing God as much as they feared not the face of man. Such an army might be trusted to elect its own leaders, lifting them, like the old Germans, on their shields.

It will not do for even despotisms to commit the tremendous error of mistaking the obedience of the soldier for the acquiescence of the nation. That fond delusion ruins thrones. Great armies always incline to confer dictatorship, and therefore, in building up a free State, it must be solemnly secured, that always, in peace as well as war, the military power shall be in strict subordination to the civil authority. It will not do for either the People or the Tyrants to fall asleep, whether in the shade of a Upas tree, or in the shadow of an army.

Every free State ought to beware, not only of wars which exhaust, but of governments which impoverish. A waste of the public wealth is the most lasting of public afflictions ; and the Treasury which is drained by extravagance must be refilled by crime.

The Apprentice is a youth who has not attained his majority. The Fellow-Craft is the Citizen entitled to vote ; and also entitled, if he can attain it, to office and power. If you should embark in the game of chances called Public Life, make the SQUARE and the RULE, uprightness and fair and equal dealing, your rules of action. Cease not to be the gentleman, if you become the Candidate. Offer yourself for office, and no more. Become not base in the whining beggary for votes ; or baser, by trickery and the sowing of slanderous lies against an opponent. Neither expect to escape slander, nor cease to be patriotic when misunderstood and reviled. When your motives have been pure, men will see a fault in the conduct, and calumniate the motives : when your conduct has been blameless, they will remember its former errors, and assert that its present goodness arises only from some sinister intention. You will be termed crafty, when you have, in reality, been rash ; and that will be called the consistency of interest, which, in reality, is the inconsistency of passion. The chief business of Party is to traduce the great and elevate the small.

Finally, if you discover that you are wanting in foresight, be honest, cease to mislead the people, and retire to private life. Apply the same rule mercilessly to others. The man who blunders to-day will blunder to-morrow. Near-sightedness of the Intellect does not improve by age, like that of the eyes. Foresight is the most indispensable of all requisites for the Statesman. Blunders, in Statesmanship, are worse than crimes ; and, indeed, it is nothing less than crime for the incompetent pilot to oust the competent, and undertake to steer the ship in the dark night, through the tempest and among the shoals. Shrewd knavery is preferable, in Statesmanship, to honest stupidity, shallow uprightness, and well-meaning superficiality. A dishonest politician *may* serve the State well. It will often be most profitable for him to do what is right and wise. But even interest cannot secure wisdom in the action of the stupid, the narrow-minded, and the silly.

The wise Statesman sees in advance the coming distractions and calamities of the State. It is madness longer to trust the Politicians who do not. Incompetency is always incompetency. Want of foresight is chronic. The real Statesman is aware of the first breath of Revolution : he listens for it as the old Prophets listened for the words of Jehovah. When the true Tempest is arising, even nature and the animals comprehend the mystery of the few first whispers. The stagnant atmosphere, the mountains veiled darkly with prophecy, veined with blood-streaks, coming closer to the old homes, darkly but clearly visible ; the rivulets running with the voice of ocean, the moaning woods, the perplexed flocks and herds, the hush of birds, the dumb consternation of nature— all these have their parallels in the signs and portents that precede the organic disturbances of States. What is the sham leader to do who has not read them, when the white watery winds sweep the heavens' concave, amid the bending perilous trees, the harried harvest, the mute or clamorous horror of the people, the terrible hurricane, the crash of ruin in the day of doom? Will you still trust these incapables when the storm roars? will you intrust to them the work of renovation? Let the harriers sleep in their kennels rather, and the near-sighted read the Book of Revelations, and the true seers, who *foresaw*, take the helm.

♪ Brother Master of Ceremonies, let this Candidate now do his last work as an Apprentice!

X.

THE MYSTIC STAIRWAY.

† 11. * * * * * *

☉∴ My Brother, the degree of Fellow-Craft realizes the hopes of him who desires to learn, and of him also who is wise. For in it the secret of our mysteries begins to be opened, and the veil which covers them to be drawn aside. And while he who as yet knows not that secret sees that every one may comprehend it, the Sage is glad to find himself among his Peers.

Upon the tracing-board of this degree you see the representation of the front of King Solomon's Temple, with a winding stairway of *three, five,* and *seven* steps.

It is the great symbol of our Order, and has more than one meaning. Whether you will learn them all will depend upon yourself. The value of the secret is in proportion to the intelligence and excellency of him to whom it is entrusted. The man to whom Virtue is but a name, and Liberty a chimæra, will little value the light you have already received; and he to whom Philosophy is foolishness will less value that which is perhaps to be given you hereafter. The bats and the owls prefer the obscure twilight to the light of noon-day. As little can the selfish and heartless value as an emblem the chain which encircles the Temple, with its eighty-one mystic knots. They can neither appreciate the Brotherhood of an Order like ours, nor that electric chain of sympathy, which, causing the fate of every man, and his conduct, to be influenced and controlled by the actions and fortunes of others, makes of a people, and even of the whole human race, a single individual.

The Temple is, among other things, a symbol of science. The man who is familiar with the mechanism of the universe and its phænomena; with the laws that govern the movements of the spheres, singularly connected as they are with numbers; with the laws of generation, growth, and crystallization; with the world of vegetation, the organic revolutions of the earth in past ages, and the marvellous wonders of minute life disclosed by the microscope, will have developed his Reason and parted with the absurd notions of childhood and ignorance. The natural and philosophical sciences are the great, costly, hewn stones of the Temple of Science. Your journeys by the North, South, East, and West symbolize the great circle of these Sciences, and the Fellow-Crafts' Lodge *should be* a school of instruction for them.

Pythagoras inscribed on the door of his Temple these words: " *He to whom Geometry is unknown, is not worthy to enter into this Sanctuary.*" By Geometry, we have already said, is meant the mathematics, or the science of numbers. Mathematical demonstration attains its results with unerring certainty. Numbers, to Pythagoras, were the first principles of things ; and the natural laws of the distances and orbits of the spheres, and the forces of gravity and attraction are singularly connected with them. It has not been deemed irreverent to characterize the Deity as the Great Geometrician, as well as the Grand Architect of the Universe.

It is not difficult for one to obtain a sufficient general knowledge of Zoology or the animal creation, of the mechanism of the frame-work of animals, their habits and wonderful adaptations ; of Geography and Geology, Mineralogy and Botany, to attain to enlarged ideas of the Power, Wisdom, and Beneficence of the Deity. His studies in these are symbolized by his first journey ; Geometry and the science of numbers by his second; Astronomy by his third; in the fourth journey he prepares himself to persuade and convince other men by the graces of Rhetoric and the demonstrations of Logic; and in the last, he learns the principles of the highest Political Science.

The true Fellow-Craft is, therefore, the man of science and virtue, learned, and an artist. The Compass, the Square and Rule, the Lever and the Sword, are all symbols of his characteristics and qualifications. If he applies them to their proper symbolical use, he cannot but become a good man, and a useful and patriotic citizen.

Entering between the two great Columns, symbolical, as their names show, of the *Active*, Divine, Generative ENERGY or STRENGTH, and the *Passive*, Productive STABILITY and PERMANENCE of Nature; symbolical, also, of the Divine WISDOM and UNDERSTANDING, of the Divine JUSTICE and MERCY, you ascended *three* steps, and then *five*, and saw above you *seven*.

Three, *five*, *seven*, and *nine*, are the peculiarly mysterious numbers in Masonry.

Much of the mysterious knowledge of the Ancients was concealed in the symbolism of numbers. We are not permitted, in this degree, to explain these at any length. They are all philosophical and religious. Philosophy is a domain into which you do not as yet enter, and we shall say only so much as may serve to arouse your curiosity and incite you to study.

* * * * * *

The Masonry of the York Rite applies the number *five* particularly to the Orders of Architecture—the *Tuscan, Doric, Ionic, Corinthian*, and *Composite;* and the number *seven* to what were once styled the Liberal Arts and Sciences—*Grammar, Rhetoric, Logic, Arithmetic, Geometry, Music*, and *Astronomy. Five* is also remarked upon as connected with the Senses. It has selected the least striking illustrations or applications of these numbers; and the rudimental information it gives on these subjects may be read in any of the Monitors.

The first three steps of the Temple of Individual Perfection are FAITH, HOPE, and LOVING-KINDNESS; the five next, number of the aggregate of the Senses and of that of the Orders of Architecture, symbolize the aggregate of the manly virtues and moral excellencies. The seven, number of what were once called the Liberal Arts and Sciences, symbolize the aggregate of learning and intellectual acquisitions which adorns and completes the character.

In the STATE, the three steps are LIBERTY, EQUALITY, and FRATERNITY; the five, the great institutions of the State, which are, the *Executive* Power, the *Legislative* Authority, the *Judicial* interpretation, the

Church, and the *Army :* the seven symbolize the Arts and Sciences, fostered by, and adorning the State.

The five Orders of Architecture may also be symbolic of the five principal divisions of the religious—*Polytheism ;* the *Philosophic Paganism* of Athens and Alexandria, of Socrates, Plato, and Hypatia ; *Hebraism, Mahommedanism,* and *Christianity ;* and also of the five different forms of Government—the *Patriarchal,* the *Despotic,* the *Oligarchic,* the *Republican,* and the *Limited Monarchical :* thus opening to the Fellow-Craft a vast field of Study.

The BLAZING STAR is the symbol of Civilization and Enlightenment ; the letter G, of the Deity, of Geometry and all the Arts and Sciences, of Government, and of Gnosis or Spiritual Knowledge.

Our old Rituals say that the Blazing Star is the emblem of that Genius which soars to the loftiest heights ; and the symbol of that sacred fire with which the Grand Architect of the Universe has endowed us, by the light of whose rays we must discern, love, and practice Truth, Justice, and Equity.

"The Delta," they said, " which you behold all blazing with light, offers you two great Truths and two sublime ideas. You behold the name of God, as the source of all Knowledge and all Science. It is symbolically explained by Geometry. This sublime science has for its essential base the profound study and infinite applications of triangles, under their

ОBLIGATION AND SECRETS.

veritable emblem. All these mysterious truths will develop themselves to your eyes in succession, and in proportion as you advance in our sublime art."

Your toils as a Fellow-Craft are now to begin. You have completed your work as an Apprentice. Your obligation as a Fellow-Craft will not only bind you to secrecy, but also to the performance of the chief duties of Brotherhood. It will contain nothing at variance with your duties to your God, your country or your family. Are you ready to assume it?

✠∴ I am.

XI.

THE OBLIGATION.

☉∴ ♪ Brother Master of Ceremonies, bring the Candidate to the Altar, in due form, to take upon himself his obligation as a Fellow-Craft Mason!

† 12.   *   *   *   *   *   *

☉∴ Go now, my Brother, accompanied by the Master of Ceremonies, and give the Brother Senior Deacon the Signs, Words, and Tokens, to the end that he may make you to be recognized as a Fellow-Craft.

This order is obeyed. When ♄ has received the signs, words, and tokens, he says:

♄∴ Venerable Master, the signs, words, and tokens are right.

⊙∴ ♪ Brother Master of Ceremonies, re-conduct this Brother to the place from which he came, and there let him be re-invested with that whereof he was divested, and return to the Lodge for further instruction.

MUSIC.

When the Candidate is re-clothed, he works his way into the Lodge, salutes the officers, and is then conducted to the East.

MUSIC CEASES.

⊙∴ Hereafter, my Brother, you are to labor upon the pointed cubical stone, or the cube, with a pyramid erected on one face; and you will receive your wages at the Column Boaz. And this new work, say our old Rituals, should remind you that a Fellow-Craft, whose business it is to keep the building in repair, ought to use every exertion, not only to conceal the faults of his Brethren, but, by his example and counsel, to persuade them to reform. Always we encounter the same trivial and commonplace explanations.

The Cube, with the Pyramid superposited, is the symbol of a Free State. The Cube represents the People. The four faces of the Pyramid are the Departments to which the People commits its Powers— the Executive, Legislative, and Judicial, and the Church. These unite in the single point of unity of Will and Action.

On this you are to work. It is therefore necessary you should have working-tools. Those of a Fellow-Craft are the SQUARE, the LEVEL, and the PLUMB. The SQUARE, you already know, is the Jewel of the Master; the PLUMB, of the Senior Warden; and the LEVEL, of the Junior Warden. They symbolize the building squarely up, with great stones laid truly and horizontally, the perpendicular walls of the fabric of individual character, and that of the State. They are also symbols of the three great Powers of the State, on the healthy and independent action of each of which, and the performance by each of its appropriate functions, depends the continuance of the State.

The SQUARE is a symbol of *Control*, and therefore of the Executive Power, vested in a hereditary or elective Chief Magistrate.

The PLUMB is a symbol of *Rectitude* or *Uprightness*, of inflexible Law and Regulation, and therefore of the Legislative Power.

And the LEVEL is a symbol of *Equality* in the sight of the law, and of *Impartiality*; and therefore of the Judicial Power.

They are POWER, WISDOM, JUSTICE.

The law is the same for the State as for the individual: calamity shall follow as the consequence of wrong. "He that walketh righteously and speaketh uprightly; he that despiseth the gain of oppressions;

that shaketh his hands from holding of bribes; that stoppeth his ears against bloody advice, and shutteth his eyes from seeing evil; he shall dwell on high; his stronghold the impreguable rocks; bread shall be supplied him, and water not fail."

In this degree you see one point of the Compass on the Altar raised above the Square. You are now half way between the things of Earth and those of Heaven; between the moral and political, and the philosophical and spiritual.

In the ancient English work of this degree, the staircase consisted of *eleven* steps, in five Divisions, the mystic numbers, 3, 5, 7, and 11, following each other. The number Five, it was said, reminded the Candidate of "the five remarkable points in the ever-blessed career of our Lord and Saviour Jesus Christ," and Eleven, "of the miraculous preservation of Joseph, who preceded his eleven Brethren into Egypt." These are mere puerilities.

The numbers and stairway are Kabalistic. In that system of Philosophy there are, including DAATH, eleven Emanations from the Deity, or SEPHIROTH, through which one ascends in thought to the ABSO-LUTE, Nameless, Unmanifested Deity. 3, 5, 7, and 11, added together, make 26.

The Hebrews attached a numerical value to every letter. The great name of the Deity, which we render "JEHOVAH," was composed of *four* letters, or *three*, with one repeated—Yod, He, Vav, He; and the numerical value of these letters, in the same order, was 10, 5, 6, 5, which, added together, make 26, and 5, 10, 6, are expressed by the token of the Apprentice.

† 13.　　　＊　　　＊　　　＊　　　＊　　　＊　　　＊

XII.

SANCTIFICATION BY THE CROSS.

The Cross is a symbol of devotedness and self-sacrifice. From the time of the Crusades it has belonged to Fellow-Craft Masons. Pointing to the four quarters of the Compass, consisting of two lines intersected at right angles by each other, so that, though infinitely prolonged, no two of the extremities could ever meet, it was honored as a striking symbol of the Universe by many nations of antiquity, and imitated by the Hindus and Celtic Druids in the shape of their Temples. The *Crux Ansata* was a Cross, with a serpent in a circle above it. The *Tau* Cross is a most ancient symbol. "And the Lord said unto him," says Ezekiel, "Go through the midst of the City, through the midst of Jerusalem, and mark the letter Tau upon the foreheads of those that sigh and mourn for all the abominations that be done in the midst thereof." The TAU was the emblem of LIFE and SALVATION. It was set on those who were acquitted by the Judges, as a symbol of innocence; and the Military Commanders placed it on soldiers who escaped unhurt from the field of battle, as a sign of their being saved by the Divine Protection.

STAT CRUX, DUM VOLVITUR ORBIS—*the Cross stands, while the world revolves*—was the device given his Order by MARTIN, the Eleventh General of the Carthusians. So let Freemasonry always stand, true to her ancient principles, the Champion and Tribune of the People, the advocate of the rights of man, whatsoever revolutions there may be in the profane world!

In your studies you will have constant occasion to remark how extensive has been the corruption of words, how general the loss of the true meaning of the symbols. A Rite which transmuted *Pythagoras*—in French, *Pitagore*—a native of *Crotona*, into *Peter Gower*, an Englishman resident at *Groton*, in England, owes it to accident if it has preserved *anything* accurately. Take, for example, the word SHIBBOLETH. A Roman name of Jupiter was *Lapis*, a stone; or *Lapideus*, stony. In making bargains, the swearer held in his hand a flint stone, and said: " *If, knowingly, I deceive, so let Diespiter, saving the City and the Capitol, cast me away from all that is good, as I cast away this stone.*" Whereupon he threw the stone away. Hence the origin of the term, "SEBOLITHŌN, *I keep the stone,*" applied among our Ancient Brethren as a testimony of retaining their original vow uninfringed, and their first faith with the Brotherhood uncorrupted.

♪ Brother Master of Ceremonies, let this new Brother begin his work as a Fellow-Craft, going to it by the march of this degree!

† 14.   *   *   *   *   *   *

The Orator, or the Brother occupying his place, pronounces the discourse.

Then ♃ conducts the new Brother to a place between the Columns.

☉∴ ♪ Brethren Senior and Junior Wardens, announce on your Columns that we are about to applaud, in token of the satisfaction of this Respectable Lodge, at numbering our Brother, A...... B......, among its Fellow-Crafts.

The Wardens announce this.

☉∴ ♫ Rise, and to order, my Brethren!

All rise. ☉ gives the sign, battery, and acclamation of Fellow-Craft, conjointly with all the Brethren.

The new Brother returns his thanks, or requests ♃ to do it for him.

The thanks are covered.

The Pouch of Propositions is presented to all the Brethren, by ♃ or a Deacon, as ☉ may direct.

The Almoner takes or sends round the box of fraternal assistance. The amount contributed is disposed of as in the Apprentice's Lodge.

XIII.

CLOSING.

☉∴ ♪ Brethren Senior and Junior Wardens, inquire of the Brethren, who compose your Columns, whether they have anything to propose for the good of the Order in general, or for that of this Respectable Lodge in particular.

The Wardens do so.

☉∴ ♪ Brother Secretary, be pleased to read the sketch of the labors of to-day. Be silent, and listen, my Brethren!

△ reads his minutes.

☉∴ ♪ Brethren Senior and Junior Wardens, inquire of the Brethren if they have any observations to make in respect to the minutes of the labors of the day.

The Wardens do so, and the matter is disposed of as in the Apprentice's Lodge.

XIV.

INSTRUCTION.

Note—The Catechism is repeated before closing, when it is thought proper and there is time, or it may be done at another meeting.

† 15.　　*　　*　　*　　*　　*　　*

XV.

TO RESUME LABOR IN THE APPREN-TICE'S DEGREE.

If it is desired, for any purpose, instead of closing, to resume labor in the Apprentice's Degree, it will be done as follows, in lieu of the whole closing ceremony:

⊙∴ ♪ Brethren Senior and Junior Wardens, be pleased to inform the Brethren on your Columns, that I am about to suspend the labors of this Lodge in the Fellow-Craft's degree, for the purpose of resuming labor in the degree of Entered Apprentice.

Each Warden, rapping once, makes the announcement, and then each responds that it is announced.

† 16.   *   *   *   *   *   *

Then the business of the Lodge is transacted, and, at the proper moment, it is closed.

ΟΥΡΑΝΟΣ.

CŒLESTE: SPIRITUALE.

ΠΝΕΥΜΑ.

ΣΩΜΑ.

TERRESTRE: MATERIALE.

ΓΑΙΑ.

न

———·•·———

ꜰꝯꝼꝯꝼ.

MASTER.

———

MAÎTRE.

INDEX.

———

MASTER MASON.

MAÎTRE.

I.

ESSENTIAL INTRODUCTION.

THE Preparation Room is styled "*The Chamber of Reflection.*" It should have a sombre and gloomy appearance, being hung with dark gray cloth, and lighted by a single large candle of yellow wax.

In the middle of this room is an altar, eighteen inches square, and three and a half feet high, covered with a black cloth. By it stands

* 1.   *   *   *   *   *   *

In the goblet red wine.

There is one small table, covered with black cloth, and one chair. On the table are the working-tools of the first two degrees, all broken.

On the altar is

* 2.   *   *   *   *   *   *

In different places on the walls are the following inscriptions, painted or printed in large letters:

"*Through the frowning gates of death lies the way of eternal life.*"

"*Time ever digs the grave where we must lay our sins or our sorrows.*"

"*He that would die well and happily must lead an upright life.*"

"*Let us ever keep our house in order, that we may be fit to die.*"

"*By a wise and virtuous life, make the best preparation for a peaceable death.*"

"*The Dead are with us always.*"

"*Blessed are the dead who die in the cause of Truth.*"

"*All death is new Life.*"

"*Birth, Life, Death! God the Creator, Preserver, Destroyer!*"

"*It is the Dead that govern. The Living only obey.*"

"*The world is filled with the voices of the Dead.*"

"*The Just that is dead condemneth the wicked that are living.*"

"*He that overcometh shall not be hurt of the second death.*"

"*To him that overcometh will I give to eat of the Tree of Life.*"

"*The dust returns to the earth as it was; and the spirit to God, who gave it.*"

The Senior Deacon is to prepare the Candidate. He should thoroughly understand his duty; and by appropriate remarks in regard to the solemnity and importance of the degree, should arouse expectation and excite the imagination. The grave dignity of his manner will much tend to make the ceremonies imposing.

THE MIDDLE CHAMBER.

The Lodge-room is so called. It must be wholly hung with black, both walls and ceiling, and no light be admitted from without.

Here and there on the walls are death's-heads and cross-bones, in white; and silver tears, in groups of 3, 5, and 7.

The Lodge is lighted by nine lights, three in front of each Dignitary, forming an equilateral Triangle.

On the Altar are the Hebrew Bible, the Compass and the Square, both points of the Compass being above the Square. On these are

* 3.   *   *   *   *   *   *

In the middle of the chamber is

* 4. * * * * * *

Round this is a movable railing, seven feet in height; and black Curtains, hanging from this to the floor, surround and enclose the .... forming a close apartment, ten or twelve feet in length, and six or eight in width.

* 5. * * * * * *

TITLES.

In the Master's Lodge the MASTER is styled " *Worshipful.*"
The WARDENS are styled "*Most Venerable.*"
The MASTER MASONS, " *Venerable.*"
These titles are *indispensable.*

CLOTHING.

At a reception all the Masters should be dressed in black, with a slouched black hat and weeper of crape, white gloves, apron, and blue sash. In strictness, they ought to wear long black dominoes, and a white plume. All wear swords, and sit covered. The Worshipful Master should wear a long blue velvet mantle.

II.

OPENING.

☉∴ ♪ My Brethren, I am about to open here a Lodge of Master Masons for the dispatch of business. I will thank you to give me your attention and assistance. The Officers and Brethren will clothe themselves, and the Dignitaries and Officers repair to their respective stations and places.

* 6. * * * * * *

PRAYER.

O Lord! Thou art excellent in truth, and there is nothing great in comparison to Thee! Enlighten us, we beseech Thee, in the true knowledge of Free-masonry! Let us not be numbered among those that know not Thy Statutes nor the divine mysteries! Grant us knowledge and understanding, that we may obtain wisdom! Enable us to decipher and read the Great Book of Thy Revelation, whose pages are always open before us, and therein to find Thy Statutes and Commandments, and the Keys to Thy Holy Mysteries! Bless our undertakings! enable us to serve Thee aright! and let all our actions tend to Thy glory and to our own advancement in excellence and virtue! Help the distressed and struggling nations to become free; and though neither our eyes nor those of our children shall behold it, make of the whole Earth Thy Holy Temple! Amen!

After the Prayer an opening Ode or Hymn may be sung. Then ⊙ says:

⊙∴ In the name of God and of Saint John of Scotland, and under the auspices, etc. . . . . and by virtue of the authority in me vested, as Worshipful Master of this Lodge of Master Masons, I declare it to be duly opened, and its labors in full force. No Brother may speak aloud, etc.

* 7.   *   *   *   *   *   *

The same formalities as in the Apprentice's degree are used in respect to the reading and sanctioning of the record, and the introduction of visitors.

III.

PRELIMINARIES OF RECEPTION.

A Fellow-Craft cannot be raised to the third degree until he has worked his time—that is, until he has been a Fellow-Craft at least three months and a half.

This means that he has been present at seven meetings, *which is indispensable* (these being supposed to be held once a fortnight).

Moreover, he must be twenty-five years of age, in the absence of a dispensation as to age from an Inspector-General.

When thus duly qualified, he prefers his request to ⊕, who, at an opportune moment, will say:

⊕∴ Worshipful Master, the Brother A.......... B........., a Fellow-Craft of this Lodge, asks the favor of being raised to the degree of Master Mason.

⊙∴ Brethren Senior and Junior Wardens, announce on your Columns that the Brother A........ B........ is proposed to be raised to the degree of Master Mason. Invite the Brethren to offer their remarks.

This is done. If the applicant is present, he asks permission to withdraw. After the debate, if any, is concluded, or if there be none, the Apprentices and Fellow-Crafts withdraw.

Then the Master's Lodge is opened. The Worshipful Master again invites remarks. If any are offered, ☿ concludes, and, finally, a ballot is taken. If it is unanimous in favor of the applicant, the plaudit is given, the day for reception will be fixed, and the Secretary will enter all on his minutes.

If there be a black ball, the matter is postponed, and cannot be again brought forward until the expiration of the time fixed by the statutes. This must be at least three months.

When the matter is settled, and if the Reception is not to take place at once, the Master's Lodge will be closed, and the works resumed in the Fellow-Craft's degree, if these had been suspended. In that case, the Fellow-Crafts are called in. If the Lodge had not been working in the Fellow-Craft's degree, those of Apprentice may be resumed, as they may, after resuming and then closing those of Fellow-Craft, and all the Brethren will re-enter.

All the Masters will be summoned to attend the meeting when a reception is to take place. The writs of summons will mention that a Fellow-Craft is to be raised, and direct the Masters to appear in black.

At the proper hour the Lodge may be opened, in the first instance, in the Master's degree; or it may be opened in the first, second, and third, in succession. The others are included in the Master's Lodge, and opening it opens them.

IV.

RECEPTION.

*8.   *   *   *   *   *   *

The Candidate being in the Chamber of Reflection, ♄ takes his sword and hat, and sends them by ♃ to ☉.

On the table of each Warden is a thick roll of pasteboard, eighteen inches long, and nine in circumference.

The lights are now extinguished. Only a single one will remain burning; a candle of yellow wax, in a large lantern, on the Master's table; or an antique lamp, suspended in the middle of the Lodge. Each Dignitary may, in preference, have a dark lantern, or a candle shaded by a box.

The Brethren will sit in two lines, lengthwise the hall, leaving room between their benches and the wall for the Candidate to pass around behind them. All will have their swords drawn.

V.

PREPARATION OF THE CANDIDATE.

♄ will conduct the Candidate into the Chamber of Reflection, and say to him:

♄∴ My Brother, you are about to pass through a solemn and impressive ceremonial. It is fit that you should prepare for it by serious and solemn reflection. One's own thoughts are either the best or the worst of companions. I shall leave you alone for a time with yours. Until I return, read and reflect upon the sentences inscribed upon these sombre walls. Do not deceive yourself! Masonry is real and earnest. Its laws are stern and imperative; and the Master Mason must not shrink from duty, even if it lead him to the grave.

He then goes out, and leaves the Candidate alone. Every sound should be excluded, except the audible ticking of an unseen clock. When ten minutes have elapsed, ♄ returns, and says:

♄∴ It is well for man to remember that he is mortal, and to consider what is meant by his mortality. The constituents of his body are the same as those of the bodies of the other animals. Their bones, and flesh, and muscles, their organs and nerves, are composed of the self-same materials as his. His blood and theirs are alike. Their hearts beat by the same mechanism, and perform the same functions, as his. The anatomist discovers no radical difference between the brain of the ape and that of the man. Our food becomes part of our body, whether it be of the fruits of the earth or the flesh of beast, bird, or fish; and continually what we receive from the animals returns to them, and that which is part of our body to-day is part of that of the bird or beast to-morrow.

Continually we eat and drink of the bodies of the dead; and the particle of matter that once was part of the body of Socrates or Plato, of Moses or of Mahomet, may to-day be part of yours or mine. The head and the body are not THE MAN; for these belong to the universe of matter, continually come and go, and, after death, enter into new combinations.

You seek to penetrate the inner or greater mysteries of Freemasonry. Are you not already surrounded by mysteries enough; by mysteries sufficiently incomprehensible? BIRTH, LIFE, DEATH!— are not these mysteries appalling and tremendous enough? Perhaps you think that Masonry may *explain* what Faith only enables you to believe, without comprehending the enigma. Why should you imagine this, since Science and Philosophy only add to the number of those mysteries and insoluble enigmas that oppress us with a blind terror, and too often sink the soul in the profound abyss of despairing skepticism?

I promise you nothing. Does any degree of progress really bring us nearer that Light, which is infinitely distant? The secret of Masonry is perhaps only a more inexplicable mystery. Death is certain. Beyond that all is clouds and darkness. The Stars that set in the Ocean rise again; but none of us have seen the dead return to life. Yet the Thoughts and Influences of men survive their mortal bodies: and that is an Immortality. So the Sun's light continues when he is beneath the earth. Life is the electric spark, the manifestation of a spirit itself unknown.

Our Lodge is now in mourning for the dead, oppressed with the weight of a great calamity. It may refuse, during its period of mourning, to permit you to be exalted, and to know the Greater Mysteries. If you are bold enough to make the attempt, and incur the danger that may attend the intrusion, the time is at hand; and when you shall have been duly and truly prepared, I will endeavor to procure you admission.

* 9.   *   *   *   *   *   *

When ✠ is thus prepared, ♃ will enter at a given signal, and take him in charge, and ♄ will return into the Lodge.

VI.

ENTRANCE ASKED FOR.

Then ♃ knocks at the door, with the battery of the Fellow-Craft. ♂ partly opens the door, and asks:

♂∴ Who comes here to disturb the Masters of Freemasonry in council?

♃∴ It is a Fellow-Craft, who, having diligently done his work upon the Temple, now asks to be allowed to pass from the Square to the Compass, and to be raised to the sublime degree of Master Mason.

☉∴ says, in a loud voice, and sternly:

☉∴ How dare a Fellow-Craft venture to disturb the Masters in council? Does he not know that a terrible crime has been committed, and that while the guilty remain undiscovered, suspicion attaches to all the Fellow-Crafts? Is this a time for selfishness to seek advancement, and personal ambition to prefer its imaginary claims, when the Craft mourns, and lamentation is heard in all its Lodges? What insolence and effrontery! So one might act who was an accomplice of the murderers. Arm yourselves, my Brethren! Perhaps, by that fatal fascination which often follows crime, one of the wretches has returned to the place where the victim was sacrificed. Or, perhaps, it is some spy or emissary of Tyranny, a wolf in sheep's clothing, a Jesuit, or an Inquisitor.

Arm, my Brethren! Danger is ever nearest when we feel most secure. Is the intruder alone?

⊕∴ Venerable Brother Junior Deacon, is the intruder alone?

♂∴ He is not. The Venerable Brother Master of Ceremonies accompanies him.

⊕∴ The intruder is not alone, Worshipful Master. The Venerable Brother Master of Ceremonies accompanies him.

☉∴ Does he vouch for him, that he is a true and loyal Fellow-Craft?

⊕∴ Venerable Brother Junior Deacon, inquire of the Venerable Brother Master of Ceremonies, if he vouches for this person, that he is a true and loyal Fellow-Craft.

♂∴ Venerable Brother Master of Ceremonies, do you vouch for this person, that he is a true and loyal Fellow-Craft?

♃∴ I do not. I received him from the Venerable Brother Senior Deacon.

♂∴ Most Venerable Brother Senior Warden, he does not. He received him from the Venerable Brother Senior Deacon.

⊕∴ Worshipful Master, the Venerable Brother Master of Ceremonies does not vouch for him. He received him from the Venerable Brother Senior Deacon.

☉∴ Venerable Brother Senior Deacon, do you

vouch for this person, that he is a true and loyal Fellow-Craft?

♄∴ Worshipful Master, I do not. Finding him in waiting in the Chamber of Reflection, I supposed him to be the Fellow-Craft whom the Lodge consented to raise to the degree of Master Mason.

☉∴ Do the doors of the Temple open, then, to receive all who wish to enter? Venerable Brethren Senior and Junior Wardens, take with you four armed Brethren, seize, and carefully examine from head to foot this justly suspected person! Especially look for the marks of blood on his hands and garments! Take from him his apron, and bring it hither. It may testify against him. See to it that you do not overlook any mark or trace that may bear witness against him, that he is either an accomplice of the assassins, or a spy!

♄, ♂, and four Brethren wearing masks, and all with drawn swords, go to the Chamber of Reflection, take the Candidate's apron roughly off, and examine him carefully. Then ♄, leaving him in charge of ♂ and ♃, and surrounded by the four armed Brethren, returns into the Lodge (the door remaining half open), and hands the apron to ☉, saying:

♄∴ Worshipful Master, we have obeyed your orders, and diligently examined the suspected person, but find upon him no mark or trace of guilt, or that he is a spy or emissary of Tyranny, or Jesuit, or Inquisitor. His garments are bloodless, his hands clean, and his apron, as you see, without spot or stain.

⊙∴ Brother Junior Warden, be pleased to repair to the Chamber of Reflection, and see if you recognize this person as a true and loyal Fellow-Craft, and no spy or impostor!

O goes to the Chamber of Reflection, and examines ✠ in the first section of the Fellow-Craft's instruction. Then he returns into the Lodge, and, at his station, says:

O∴ Worshipful Master, I have carefully examined the Brother now in the Chamber of Reflection, and find him to be a Fellow-Craft Mason, duly passed and received.

⊙∴ Most Venerable Brother Senior Warden, be pleased to repair to the Chamber of Reflection, and see if this Fellow-Craft is worthy and well qualified, understanding the perfect points of his entrance.

⊕ goes to the Chamber of Reflection, and examines ✠ in the second section of the Fellow-Craft's instruction. Then he returns to the Lodge, and at his station, says:

⊕∴ Worshipful Master, I have carefully examined the Brother now in the Chamber of Reflection, and find him worthy and well qualified, understanding the perfect points of his entrance.

⊙∴ Most Venerable Brother Senior Warden, is this person known to you as a Fellow-Craft, or to the Most Venerable Brother Junior Warden?

⊕∴ Worshipful Master, we have often seen him toiling faithfully and zealously among the Fellow-Crafts.

☉∴ Is he the same whom we were willing, before this sorrow came upon us, to raise to the sublime degree of Master Mason ?

⊕∴ Most Venerable Brother Junior Warden, is this Brother the same whom we were willing, etc. ?

◯∴ He is.

⊕∴ Worshipful Master, he is.

☉∴ Then our suspicions were ill-founded, for which the Great Architect of the Universe be thanked ! But we know not the authors of the crime which has clothed the Lodge in mourning, nor but that it may have been perpetrated by emissaries of the enemies of the human race among the Fellow-Crafts. Tyranny never wants for tools and instruments. Therefore it behooves us to take all possible precautions that no such servants of Azazel obtain admission among the Masters. If this Fellow-Craft is innocent and loyal, he knows the sad occasion of our sorrow. Brother Senior Deacon, examine this Fellow-Craft further !

♄ goes to the door, and stands on the inside.

☉∴ What is it he now desires of the Lodge ?

♄∴ What is it you now desire of the Lodge ?

✠∴ To be permitted to pass from the Square to the Compass.

☉∴ Does he deem himself worthy and well qualified ?

♄∴ Do you deem yourself worthy and well qualified?

✠∴ I do not.

☉∴ How, then, does he expect to obtain what he asks?

♄∴ How, then, do you expect to obtain what you ask?

✠∴ As we obtain mercies from our Father in Heaven, notwithstanding our unworthiness.

☉∴ Why does he seek advancement when all the Craft is in distress?

♄∴ Why do you seek advancement when all the Craft is in distress?

✠∴ To be the better able to serve the Order, avenge innocence, and punish crime.

☉∴ By what further claim does he expect to obtain the great favor he asks?

♄∴ By what further claim do you expect to obtain the great favor you ask?

✠∴ By the benefit of the Password of a Master Mason.

☉∴ Most Venerable Brother Senior Warden, my suspicions are renewed. How can this person, being but a Fellow-Craft, be in possession of the Password of a Master Mason?

⊕∴ Most Venerable Brother Junior Warden, our suspicions are renewed. How can, etc.

○∴ Venerable Brother Senior Deacon, our suspicions, etc.

♄∴ How will you give the Password of a Master Mason? Who made it known to you?

♃∴ Venerable Brother Junior Deacon, he has it not. I have promised to give it for him, being his guide.

♄∴ Most Venerable Brother Junior Warden, the Fellow-Craft has not the Password. The Venerable Brother Master of Ceremonies, being his guide, has promised to give it for him.

☉∴ Most Venerable Brother Senior Warden, etc.

⊕∴ Worshipful Master, the Fellow-Craft, etc.

☉∴ Receive the Password, Most Venerable Brother Senior Warden!

⊕ goes and receives it, returns to his place, and says:

⊕∴ Worshipful Master, the Password is right.

☉∴ Most Venerable Brethren Senior and Junior Wardens, is it your opinion that we may safely admit this Fellow-Craft?

○ goes to the West, and he and ⊕ seem to consult. Then ○ returns to his station, and ⊖ says:

⊕∴ Worshipful Master, since the consequences of over-confidence may be so fatal, we demand that this Candidate shall be submitted to the extraordinary tests.

☉∴ Proceed, then, very dear Brethren, to do your duty!

⊖ and ○, drawing their swords, repair to the Chamber of Reflection; and ⊕ says to the Candidate:

⊕∴ Fellow-Craft, you are most rash and indiscreet to present yourself here at a time when you and all your fellows justly labor under suspicion. We are not satisfied with your professions; for guilt or criminal intentions may wear the mask of innocence, and the Traitor's heart is too often coupled with the Patriot's tongue.

* 10.   *   *   *   *   *   *

⊕∴ The signs of sorrow and consternation which you witness, and the broken working-tools before you, all testify to the grief and confusion among the laborers upon the Temple. When Death, in the natural course of events, takes from us those who are dear to us, our tears flow freely, and we refuse to be comforted; but when it is inflicted by violence, the blow, more sudden and unexpected, is terrible, and wrings the soul with agony and horror. We no longer suspect you of being an accomplice; but we must be equally assured of the innocence of your intentions and the purity of your motives. For that we require your solemn oath. Most Venerable Junior Warden, place this Fellow-Craft in due position to take that oath!

* 11.   *   *   *   *   *   *

The Candidate is now told to rise, and the Wardens return to their stations in the Lodge. Then ⊕ says:

⊕∴ Worshipful Master, the Candidate has been

submitted to the extraordinary tests, and we consent that he may enter.

⊙∴ ♪ Venerable Brethren, if you also consent, give me the sign!

All raise the right hand.

⊙∴ Let the Candidate enter, and be seated in front of the East!

He enters, and is seated facing ⊙, who says:

VII.

ENTRANCE.

⊙∴ You have come here, my Brother, seeking to be initiated into the Greater Mysteries. Still you are in search of Light.

You have already heard somewhat as to the nature and purpose of those ancient ceremonies of which Freemasonry is the successor. Heretofore, like the Ancient Neophytes, you have been occupied with the study of moral and political truth alone. Now you are to ascend also into the region of Philosophy, the region of that higher and more sublime light which each one values in proportion to his intellect and capacity.

The true object of Initiation was to be sanctified, and to SEE; that is, to have just and faithful conceptions of the Deity, the knowledge of whom was the LIGHT of the mysteries. It was promised the Initiate at Samothrace, that he should become pure and just. Clemens says that by Baptism souls are *illuminated*, and led to the pure LIGHT, with which mingles no darkness nor anything material. The Initiate, become an *Epoptēs*, was called a SEER. "HAIL, NEW-BORN LIGHT!" the Initiates cried, in the mysteries of DIONUSOS.

Once more we remind you, that the first learning in the world consisted chiefly of symbols; and that even Modern Philosophy uses them far more than it does definitions. The wisdom of the Hindus, Chaldæans, Persians, Egyptians, Hebrews, of Moses, Zarathustra, Pythagoras, Pherecydes, Socrates, Plato, of *all* the ancients, that has come down to us, is symbolic. It was the mode, says Samanus, on Plato's Symposium, of the ancient Philosophers to represent Truth by symbols and occult images.

"All that can be said concerning the Gods," says STRABO, "must be by the exposition of old opinions and fables; it being the custom of the ancients to wrap up in enigma and allegory their thoughts and discourses concerning nature; which are therefore not easily explained."

Masonry still follows the ancient method of teaching. Her symbols are her instruction. The Lectures are but hints and helps toward the interpretation of her symbols. Each Initiate must study, interpret, and develop the symbols for himself.

For in all ages the profoundest truths have been wisely covered from the common People as with a veil. By these, everywhere, what was originally revered as the symbol of a higher Principle, became gradually confounded or identified with the object itself, and was worshipped ; until this proneness to error led to the most degraded forms of idolatry. And where, at the present day, they no longer worship idols and images made with the hands, they form and fashion ideas, images, and idols in their minds, which are not the Deity, nor like the Deity, and worship *them*. The common notions of our own day are as absurd as those of Paganism ; and in the vulgar mind the same efficacy is attributed to rites and ceremonies as at any time in the ancient world. Still it continues literally true that most men worship Baal, and not God.

The mysteries were carried into every country, in order that, without disturbing the absurd popular belief, Truth, the Arts, and the Sciences, might be known to those who were capable of understanding them, and to maintain the true or Sacred Doctrine incorrupt ; which the people, prone to superstition and idolatry, have in no age been able to do ; nor, as many strange aberrations and superstitions of the present day prove, any more now than heretofore. The doctrines that assign to the Creator the passions, and so lower Him to the level of Humanity, prove that now, as always, the old Truths must be committed to a few, or they will be overlaid with fiction and error, and irretrievably lost. The people must have a God near to them; a Personal Deity, after their own image, sitting above the clouds, and with whom they can be familiar; one who will save them, and damn their enemies and the heterodox; one with the emotions, passions, and sympathies of Human Nature: and to teach them to believe in the absolute, supreme, unembodied Wisdom, is to present them, virtually, with Atheism. Now, as ever, they worship the symbol and the image.

♪ Brother Master of Ceremonies, take this Candidate, and let him, duly guarded, make his first three symbolic journeys.

VIII.

THE CIRCUITS.

* 12.　　*　　*　　*　　*　　*　　*

"Remember now thy Creator in the days of thy youth, while the evil days come not, nor the years draw nigh when thou shalt say, I have no pleasure in them; while the Sun, or the Light, or the Moon, or the Stars, be not darkened, nor the clouds return after the rain; in the day when the keepers of the House shall tremble, and the strong men shall bow themselves, and the grinders cease because they are few, and those that look out of the windows be darkened; and the doors shall be shut in the streets when the sound of the grinding is low; and he shall rise up at the voice of the bird, and all the daughters of music shall be brought low. Also, when they shall be afraid of that which is high, and fears shall be in the way; and the almond-tree shall flourish, and the grasshopper shall be a burden, and desire shall fail; because man goeth to his long home, and the mourners go about the streets: or ever the silver cord be loosed, or the golden bowl be broken at the fountain, or the wheel broken at the cistern. Then shall the dust return to the earth as it was; and the spirit shall return unto God who gave it."

When the three circuits are completed, the Candidate is halted in front of the East, and the

MUSIC

plays a slow and solemn air. When the

MUSIC CEASES,

the Deacons and armed Brethren retire to their seats, and 2. says:

2∴ Worshipful Master, the Candidate has made his first three symbolic journeys.

⊙∴ Let him be seated.

A seat is given him, and ♃ retires to his own seat.

⊙∴ You have now made the first three of the seven symbolic Circuits or journeys. To call them symbolic is to announce that they have a mystic meaning. You must discover this for yourself.

Three Planets were deemed by the ancients to be above, and three below the Sun; and the natural order of all, proceeding upward from the earth, was deemed to be, The Moon, Mercury, Venus, The Sun, Mars, Jupiter, Saturn. To these, in the same order, were assigned the Seven Archangels, ISAPHIEL, RAPHAEL, HAMALIEL, ZARAKIEL, AURIEL, GABRIEL, and MICHAEL. All these are combinations of one Hebrew word, AL, the name of the Deity originally worshipped by the Hebrews.

* * LITURGY C. * *

In your first three Circuits, your soul has passed symbolically, in its ascent toward its home, through the spheres of *Saturn, Venus,* and *Jupiter,* called by the Hebrews *Sabatai, Nogah,* and *Tsadōc;* symbolized by the metals, *Lead, Copper,* and *Tin;* and their colors, *Black, Blue,* and *Scarlet.*

At the sphere of SATURN, the Ancients said, the Soul, ascending, parted with its *Falsehood* and *Deceit.* Are you now free from those most common vices of

Humanity, which infect alike the conduct of the Individual and the policy of the State?

Look around you, and see how few men are habitually and perfectly frank, sincere, true, and loyal! Interrogate yourself, and admit that you have too often, under temptation, and to attain a coveted object, been false and deceitful!

What is more common among men than the pretence of friendship, coupled with the reality of enmity or ill will? What more common than professions belied by practice? How constantly are the Masonic pretences and professions of Brotherhood mere empty, idle words!

*　　　*　　　*　　　*　　　*　　　*

You laid your hand, not long since, on the bosom of what seemed to be a corpse, the victim of violence or revenge. Even if you supposed it to be actually what it seemed, you could safely swear, and we knew it, that you were not the accomplice or accessory to the supposed crime. Perhaps you thought the scene absurd. But, like everything in Masonry, it was symbolic, and your protestation was a pledge. That body represented a State once free, and whose freedom was its life; now no longer living, but dead, and ready for its burial. Interrogate your own conscience, if you are a citizen of a free State, and ask yourself if you have done nothing to destroy the State; if you have done anything to avert the doom that seems to have been pronounced by Omnipotence against all Republics, as the enactment of a general law of decay and dissolution ? If you have ever aided Falsehood to prevail over Truth, Incapacity to impose on the People's ignorance, Pretence and Plausibility to win office, Inexperience to hold the reins of State, Dishonesty to distribute Patronage, a corrupt Press to deceive the People, the Insolence of Civil or Military Power to accustom them to usurpation, the Constitution to be smitten with asphyxia, the Civil Courts to be set at nought, if you have permitted the despotism of party or of private interest to control your vote and cause you to aid in excluding capacity, intellect, and honesty from office, you will not be held guiltless when calamity and ruin overtake the State.

Remember that the Mason is, above all things, a true man and a loyal citizen. Falsehood and deceit, in man or nation, are ignoble and dishonorable. Let them become common as they will, until a profitable lie has its market-price, and falsehoods swarm in the putrid carcass of the body politic; until fraudulent bankruptcies no longer diminish respectability, and no trust is too sacred to be violated, no oath too solemn to be broken, no pledge of public or private honor strong enough to bind the soul; until the State or Nation contemptuously disregards her pledges, violates the obligation of her contracts, does more than that for which she incarcerates her citizens for swindlers; still, if you believe you have a living soul, and if you hope for its reascension to its home beyond the Stars, you must purify it of falsehood, fraud, and deceit.

At the sphere of VENUS, said the ancients, the Soul, ascending towards its home, shakes off its sensual appetites and passions. If it be not impossible to part with these in this life, it is at least impossible to do so, except by accepting that unnatural and artificial stagnation, that apathy and immobility, that emasculation of the Soul, which are the Death of all that is manly and heroic.

The appetites and passions are the gifts of God, for good and wise purposes. Allowed to predominate and control, they become our Tyrants, and are frightful vices and leprous diseases of the Soul. Lust, and gluttony, and drunkenness, brutalize the Soul equally with the body, and make greatness and goodness impossible. They turn Wisdom into Folly, and Intellect into Idiocy. They debauch, corrupt, and infect the whole man. But when the just equilibrium is preserved between the appetites and passions, the moral sense and the Reason, the first are spurs and incentives to exertion, the springs of vigorous manliness, the sources of Love, Effort, and Heroism.

Vice and Luxury have, in all ages, sapped the

foundations of States. Manliness and Virtue, the Family Affections, Temperance, Frugality, and Economy, are the only sure preservatives of Republics. Debauchery and vice are a syphilitic poison in the arteries of a Commonwealth. Extravagance and luxury lead to dishonesty and peculation, and to the prostitution of place and office; to lavish expenditures, oppressive debts, ruinous taxation, and the ultimate subjugation of Labor by Capital. Public corruption is the mother of private dishonesty. Repudiation, resorted to for relief, sanctions and encourages private rascality, and the State becomes a great lazar-house of pestilence, rotten, like that poor debauchee, Louis XV., before its final dissolution. Nothing can be so disgusting and offensive as a diseased and leprous soul, of man or State, dying by inches in a diseased and rotten body.

If you would truly become a Master Mason, purify your own soul, and resolve to do your utmost to purify the State of profligacy and debauchery. Keep your appetites and passions ever under due control. Be not their slave, but their master. Discourage vice, luxury, and extravagance among the people and in the State; and remember that a nation also has a soul that may be brutalized; and if the baser animals have their types among men, so also they have among States. Remember that public debt and the luxury of the rich breed pauperism among the people, and diseases that at last culminate in Revolution; and that, invariably, the anarchy of the Revolution of the poor against the rich leads to the tyranny of the Despot and the atrocities of absolute Power.

At the sphere of JUPITER, the ascending Soul parted, it was said, with its *avarice*. It is a vice which Civilization, Commerce, and Freedom largely develop. Wealth always tends, in prosperous States, to become the Supreme good, the highest merit, the aggregate of all the virtues; and Poverty to be less a misfortune than a misdemeanor. Inordinately valued, and giving power and consequence, Money becomes a God.

*   *   *   *   *   *

Avarice has, in all ages, been deemed an ignoble vice. Like the process of petrifaction, it turns the heart to stone. When it has become the tyrant, all the kindly sympathies that bind man to man die out. When the disease infects a whole people, they seem insane. Health, comfort, home affections, the improvement of the intellect, rest and recreation, patriotism and charity, all alike cease to be cared for. Charity is a plant that withers in the shade of Avarice, as it does in that of Luxury.

There may be an avarice even of knowledge. All wisdom which extends no further than ourself is unworthy of us. A life sacrificed to subtle speculations, like one sacrificed to the accumulation of wealth, is a life wasted. The more gifts one has received, the better use Providence commands him to make of them. He who has only knowledge to dispense, should dispense that liberally. He may so excite to doing good in other ways, even those who may have no other motive for deeds of benevolence than that of serving their own interests. Time may teach them the knowledge of higher things.

Free of avarice himself, the Mason should endeavor to shame into deeds of benevolence those who are not so. It matters little to the poor who are succored, whether it is mere ostentation or genuine Charity that relieves them. He should spread the example of his benevolence beyond the circle of those only who are wise and good, and every day widen the sphere of his usefulness among his fellow-creatures, convinced that the life he will then lead will be the most acceptable of all lives to the Supreme Being.

*   *   *   *   *   *

The Hebrew name of *Jupiter* is TSADOC, the JUST. Let the Mason whose soul has passed symbolically through that planetary sphere, strive, by honest exertion and honorable means, to secure a competency for himself and for his children, since that is laudable, and just, and wise ; but let him not become diseased with the leprosy of avarice, nor seek to amass wealth by those speculations which enrich one by the robbery of many, or by the loss and calamity of the State. Let him aid his Country to attain greatness and secure prosperity by the ways of justice, and honor, and noble and heroic enterprise, and not by the acquisition of territory wrested or stolen from the weak, or by a commercial supremacy obtained by a selfish policy, and retained by disregarding all the Divine obligations of sympathy, justice, and generosity.

♪ Brother Master of Ceremonies, let this Candidate now under your charge and that of our Venerable Deacons, make his last four symbolic journeys.

Conducted and accompanied in all respects as before, the Candidate passes four times around the Lodge, in the same direction as before. At the end of the fourth circuit he is again halted in front of the East, and those who conducted him return to their places when his arrival has been announced.

While he makes these circuits, there is soft and solemn

MUSIC.

When he halts, the

MUSIC CEASES.

♃∴ Worshipful Master, the Candidate has made his last four journeys.

☉∴ Let him be seated.

My Brother, according to PLATO, the Soul cannot re-enter into Heaven until the revolutions of the universe shall have restored it to its primitive condition, and purified it from the effects of its connection with the four elements.

If you would understand the ancient mind, and be enabled to interpret the allegories and explore the symbols in which the old Sages endeavored to delineate the ideas that struggled within them for utterance, and could be only inadequately expressed by language, you must study the connection between the secret science and mysterious emblems of Initiation, and the Heavens, the spheres, and the constellations.

Conducted and accompanied by seven Brethren, each bearing a *sword*, the symbol of Spiritual Truth, and a *Light*, and these seven representing the seven Archangelic Intelligences of the Planets, you have now symbolically passed through the spheres of *Mercury, Mars,* the *Moon,* and the *Sun,* symbolized by the metals *Quicksilver, Iron, Silver,* and *Gold;* and to which are assigned the colors, *Green, Flame-colored* or *Orange, White,* and *Purple* or *Violet.*

At the sphere of MERCURY, the Soul was said to part with all inclination to *Injustice* and *Hypocrisy.*

Nothing is so difficult as for a man to be entirely just. If he be so in his conduct, no man is always so in his opinions, and his judgment of the conduct of others. To nothing are we so prone as to uncharitable judgment; and yet there is nothing of which we so much complain, and with so much reason, against men and public opinion, in our own case. We know that even when there is the most apparent reason for such judgments, there are extenuating circumstances unknown to the world, good motives at bottom, stress of temptation, weakness and error, more than intentional wrong, which, if the world knew, it ought, in justice, to modify, if not to reverse, its stern and pitiless judgment. How rarely do we presume that others, whom we condemn, have like excuses or justification! The only just judgment is that which is charitable and merciful. Even the Infinite and Perfect Justice is in equilibrium with the Infinite and Perfect Mercy; the Infinite WISDOM, above both, holding the beam of the balance.

We need no other definition of Justice than that of the Great Teacher, who gave his name to a religion that now too commonly repudiates his precepts: "*All things whatsoever ye would that men should do to you, do ye even so to them: for this is the Law and the Prophets.*"

*   *   *   *   *   *

Avoid, therefore, for the future, as one purified and sanctified, all injustice, extortion, and hypocrisy; and, as a Citizen of the State, help to cast out of office and power all who advocate and countenance injustice, all who flatter the people, and mislead them to betray them; all who clothe schemes of unjust national aggrandizement in the livery of the Apos-

tolate of Freedom, and to the shame of national robbery add the utter baseness of a sanctified hypocrisy.

At the sphere of MARS, the Soul, ascending, was
said to part with the vices of Revenge, Anger, Ingratitude, Impatience, and Querulousness, resuming
in their stead its original virtues of Mercy, Forgiveness, Forbearance, Gratitude, Patience, and Equanimity.

"Love your enemies!" said the Great Teacher ;
"bless them that curse you! Do good to them that
hate you! Pray for them which despitefully use you
and persecute you!" Do this, he said, " that ye
may be the Children of your Father which is in
Heaven: for He maketh His sun to rise on the Evil
and on the Good ; and sendeth rain on the Just and
on the Unjust."

* * * * * *

Ingratitude is hateful, and yet a too common vice.
Even the dog and the horse are grateful for kindness. Man, and the wolf and wild-cat, are ungrate-
ful alike. We need not enlarge upon a fault which
is detestable even in an animal.

A querulous impatience argues an entire absence
of heroism. To complain of and repine at the dis-
pensations of Providence is worse than a folly.
Patience and Equanimity are the inseparable attri-
butes of a truly great soul. " The Commandment is a

lamp," says the Wise King, "and the Law is Light; and reproofs of instruction the way of life." All must bear the Cross; the wisest bear it most patiently. After all, the sadnesses of Life help to sweeten the bitter cup of Death. "*Happy is the man*," said ELI-PHAZ, the friend of Job, "*whom God correcteth; therefore despise not thou the chastening of the Almighty.*" Omnipotent Wisdom created the Human Race. To exist at all, a being of spirit and body united, man could not but be made subject to pain and sickness, to evils, and deprivations, and calamities. After all, is it not always better to have suffered than not to have lived at all? Suffer as we may, lose as we may, we still cling to life, finding in it something to outweigh our sufferings and sorrows.

At the sphere of the Moon, called in the Hebrew, LABANAH, *whiteness*, the Soul, ascending, was said to lay aside its prejudices and preconceptions. These are inseparable from us in this life. No man is without them: there are too few who are not slaves to them. In all ages they have led to bigotry and persecution; and men are generally most bigoted in proportion to the want of real foundations for their faith. One is not satisfied to believe that he is in possession of the truth, unless he can persuade or compel others to follow and adopt his faith. Disputes about creeds are generally disputes about what neither party understands; and the less one comprehends his creed, as where it is in regard to natures infinitely above his comprehension, the more he will be oracular and dogmatical, the more bitter hater of heresy, the more zealous persecutor. To force me to believe what you believe, particularly when you believe it *because* it is impossible, is an impossible undertaking.

*   *   *   *   *   *

We receive our religious and political faiths, as we receive our taste for particular viands, by education and habit. If, therefore, we cannot rid ourselves of our prejudices, we may, at least, agree that others shall hospitably entertain theirs. In them every man has an estate in fee. Why quarrel with the Esquimaux because he prefers train-oil to the most elaborate dishes of our *cuisine?* Why seek, by persecution, to compel the Red Indian to appreciate the music of Bellini and the metaphysics of Cousin? Let us hope to be, by-and-by, freed of our own prejudices and preconceptions; and let us, in the meantime, admit that there is no error so grave as intolerance, and no crime so great as persecution. Let us be neither Jesuits nor Inquisitors, but admit that the greatest of wrongs and follies is to attempt to propagate truth by the sword.

At the sphere of the Sun, called in the Hebrew SHEMESH, the Soul, ascending, was said to part with its aspirations for greatness and Empire. Man naturally covets influence, power, control, and dominion over man, and is not content with controlling the body, unless he can also control the Soul. Hence the love of unlawful and unreasonable power, and Tyranny and Usurpation. Nations covet Empire and Dominion. Propagandists equally of Freedom and Despotism, they are not only bigoted and persecuting, like individuals, but their lust for power and pre-eminence is insatiate.

* * * * * *

Let every Mason be content to be Monarch over himself! Let him seek to control no man against his will, to coerce no man to believe as he believes. Even in a republic, let him tolerate Monarchical opinions. Let him, to convert men from error, use only the weapons of argument and reason! Let him, as a citizen, hold that greatness and empire are not essential to the prosperity of States; that small States, free, are better and happier than large ones enslaved; and that consolidation by conquest is like uniformity of faith procured by persecution. The Man and the Nation that would rise into the highest sphere of excellence, must be free from ambition and the insane desire to rule, since from these flow all manner of injustices, oppressions, and tyrannies, ending at last in calamities unutterable; in Rome, under

Vitellius and Domitian, Spain under the Bourbons, the Ottoman Empire existing by sufferance, a church with the will, but without the power to persecute, the Throne above the volcano, a Republic cemented by blood, and weak in all its apparent grandeur, by the terrible hostility of hate.

At the sphere of the *Sun*, you are in the region of LIGHT.

The God of the Hebrews was not only JEHOVAH, but the Lord of the Celestial Armies, the ELOHIM, ADONAI, AL SHADAI, ALOH, ALIUN, AL, the MALAK, YEHOVAH-ELOHIM, ADONAI-TSABAOTH. "Out of Zion, the Perfection of Beauty, He *Shone*." "He sits in the *Heavens*: He is in His holy Temple: His Throne is in the Heavens: He *lights* the *Lamp* of the Faithful, and *enlightens* their darkness." "He is," says DAVID, "my *Light* and my Salvation." He is a *Sun* and a shield. He is to be an Everlasting *Light* and a *Glory*; a *light* to those sitting in darkness: He sends out His *Light* and His *Truth* to lead His servants. "Thou that dwellest between the Cherubim," they cried to Him, "*shine forth!* Cause Thy face to *shine!* and we shall be saved!" He covers Himself with *light* as with a garment, and makes his Angels *Spirits*, and his Ministers a *flaming fire*. "God is the Lord which hath showed us *light*. His Word is a *lamp* to the feet and a *light* to the path of the Faithful."

You have been in search of that Light. If you still desire to advance toward it, you must now assume a solemn and binding obligation, from which no earthly power can ever free you. It will in no wise conflict with any duties you owe yourself, your family, your friends, your country, the Human Family, or your God; but it will bind you to Secresy and Fidelity, and to the performance of the great duties of Brotherhood. Are you willing to take upon yourself that obligation?

✠∴ I am.

☉∴ ♪ Venerable Brother Master of Ceremonies, conduct this Candidate to the Most Venerable Brother Senior Warden in the West, and let him cause him to advance to the altar of obligation, upon the first degree of the right angle of an oblong square, forming a square on the second degree by two steps, and on the third by a single one: and let him then place him at the altar in proper position to take upon himself, in due form, the solemn obligation of a Master Mason.

The Master of Ceremonies takes the Candidate by the hand, leads him to the West, and says:

♃∴ Most Venerable Brother Senior Warden, it is the will and pleasure of the Worshipful Master, that you cause this Candidate to advance, etc.

*   *   *   *   *   *

IX.

THE OBLIGATION.

* 13.　　*　　*　　*　　*　　*　　*

☉∴ . . . . Your obligation made you an Entered Apprentice Mason, and a Fellow-Craft; but though now again obligated, you are not yet a Master Mason, and may never become so. You are still in search of Light. "*The King of Kings and Lord of Lords,*" PAUL says to TIMOTHEUS, "*who alone has eternal existence, dwelleth in the Light into which no mortal can come.*" "In the WORD," says Saint JOHN, "was LIFE; and that LIFE was the LIGHT of men: the True Light, which lighteth every man that cometh into the world. He that doeth what is Right and True cometh to the Light, that his actions may be manifestly seen to accord with the Divine Will."

He who anciently received the Greater Mysteries was said to become a King and a Priest among men; an Intellectual Ruler, an Interpreter of the Divine. His duty was to dispense Light among the ignorant and uninformed. The Master Mason also is a Ruler among Masons, the Instructer and Guider of the Apprentices and Fellow-Crafts. These are, as it were, his constituents. Remember that the God of Israel said to David, "He that ruleth over men must be just, ruling in the fear of God, and as the light of the morning when the sun rises, of a morning without clouds ; as the light shining clear in the drops upon the tender grass after a rain."

Duty and danger go always, in this world, hand in hand ; and the Master Mason, Apostle of Light and Liberty, must ever say, and on this saying ever act : " The mean consideration of my own safety shall never be put in the balance against my duty. I will own no superior but the laws ; nor bend the knee to any one but Him who made me." Death is not, by far, the greatest evil that can befall a man. To betray a trust, or violate an obligation, is a greater misfortune than to die. In defence of his own rights of free action, speech, and conscience, or of the civil and religious rights of his people, with the God of Armies on his side, the Mason will not fear the hour of trial ; " for though the hosts of his enemies should cover the field like locusts, yet the Sword of the Lord and of Gideon shall prevail."

You are about to pass, symbolically, through a scene of trial, of suffering, and of danger. You know that it is a principle in Masonry that we should engage in no great and important undertaking without asking in prayer, if only by a momentary aspiration, the assistance and support of the Great Architect of the Universe. Prayer strengthens the hands to work, and nerves the soul to meet danger bravely.

Let us, then, invoke the protection and aid of the Supreme Wisdom and Power!

♪♫ Rise, my Brethren! Let us, on bended knees, beseech Him, who dwelleth in the Light, to favor and assist this Candidate, to guide and protect us, and to prosper the work of Masonry!

All kneel, and ☉ offers up this

PRAYER.

Our Father who art in Heaven, hear our reverent supplication! Thou dwellest in the Light: illumine the soul and strengthen the heart of this Candidate! Help him to keep his solemn obligations! Remind him continually of them, that he may not forget them, or become indifferent or lukewarm, and so incur the guilt of perjury! Enable him ever to prefer danger to dishonor, and martyrdom to betrayal of his trust or abandonment of the just cause of the People! Guide and protect us and all good Masons in the discharge of our solemn and sacred duties! Give us courage to prefer a glorious death to a base life! Make prosperous and effectual the work of Masonry, and let it be Thy instrument to aid in the regeneration of Humanity! Make it a force and power! Direct its labors, and shape its course for good! Enlighten us! Illumine us! Instruct us! and let us be able to thank Thee, when we come to die, that by Thy Grace and Favor we have not lived in vain! AMEN!

ALL. SO MOTE IT BE! AMEN!

⊙∴ Rise, my Brethren! Brother A..........
B.........., if you would become a Master Mason
you must now represent one whom Masons believe
to have been their Grand Master at the time of the
building of King Solomon's Temple. To your places,
my Brethren! Venerable Brother Master of Ceremonies, take this Candidate in charge, and make due
answers for him!

A PAUSE OF SOME MINUTES.

⊙∴ The past centuries return: the walls of the
first Temple rise around us in all their grandeur. The
Divine Presence dwells again between the extended
wings of the Karobim in the Holy of Holies, on the
Mercy-Seat: the Past has become the Present, and
the Present the Future.

All the Brethren surround the grave, except the dignitaries
and ♃. ○ is in the South, holding the twenty-four-inch gauge;
⊕ in the West, holding the square; ⊙ in the East, holding his
mallet, and having by him a maul stuffed with wool. ♃ stands
on the right of the Candidate, at the foot of the grave. Lighted
by the single lamp or candle, the Hall is sombre and silent.
Meanwhile there is played a strain of soft, slow, solemn

MUSIC.

When all are in place and ready, the

MUSIC CEASES.

Then, partly recited, partly acted, follows this

X.

LEGEND AND DRAMA.

☉∴ . . . . When David, the King of Israel, had brought the Ark of God from the house of Abi-Nadab, in Gebaah, to the house of Aghbad-Adōm, and thence into the City of David, he proposed to build a house in which it might dwell; but Yehûah, by Nathan, his prophet, forbade it, saying to him, that when his days should be fulfilled, and he should sleep with his fathers, his son should build a House for Yehûah.

Afterwards David purchased the threshing-floor of Arnan or Arunah, the Yebūsai, on Mount Maraiah, to set up there an altar unto Yehûah; the Tabernacle, the Ark and the Altar of Sacrifices being then upon the hill at Gabaon. Then he prepared materials for the building of the Temple, with the help of the workmen sent him by Haïrōm, King of Tsūr, hewn stones, iron and brass, and timbers of cedar in abundance, with a hundred thousand talents of gold and a million talents of silver; saying to Salamah, that Yehûah had forbidden him to build the House, because he had shed much blood and made great wars; and giving it to him in charge that he should build the House of Yehûah his Alohim, and to the Princes of Israel, that they should help Salamah to build the House, the Sanctuary of Yehŭah-Alohim, and bring the Ark of the Covenant of Yehŭah, and the Holy vessels of the Alohim into the House to be so built to the name of Yehŭah.

Accordingly, in the four hundred and eightieth year after the Exodus from Egypt, in the fourth year of the reign of Salamah, in the month Zif, which is the second month, he began to build the House of Yehŭah. Already he had sent to Haïrōm, King of Tsŭr, the firm friend and ally of his father, requesting to be furnished with Tsidunian hewers, to hew cedar trees for the House, upon Mount Lebanon.

Haïrōm cheerfully granted what was asked, and directed that his servants should bring the cedar and pine timbers from Lebanon to the sea, and convey them in rafts along the coast to Yapu, whence they could be taken to Yerŭsalam, Salamah paying for this service with wheat and oil.

Also King Haïrōm or Hŭrōm* sent to King Salamah a skilful workman, a man of judgment, also named Haïrōm or Hŭrōm (the son of a woman of the Tribe of Dan or Naphtali, and whose father was a Tsŭrian), a skilful workman in metals, stone, and wood, and in embroidery and carving, who cast the great columns for the main entrance, and made the furniture and vessels.

To procure the materials, Salamah drafted 30,000

---

* Haïrōm, in Kings; Hŭrōm, in Chronicles; the initial H being Kh.

men of the different Tribes, and divided them into three classes, each of 10,000. Each class labored on Lebanon one month, and was at home two months in every three. There were also 70,000 bearers of burdens, and 30,000 hewers in the mountains; for Salamah built not only the Temple, but also a Palace for himself, and the House of the Forest of Lebanon, larger than the Temple. 3,300 officers superintended the workmen, and so the great costly hewn stones and the timber were prepared.

Thus there were, bearers of burdens, *Sabal*. 70,000

Hewers in the Mountains, *Khatsabim* 30,000

Superintendents or Overseers, *Manatzkhim* . . 3,300

Besides the 10,000 Israelites, and the men of Gebal sent by the King of Tsûr.

The three classes were not only distinguished from each other by the nature of their employment, but the *Sabal* and *Khatsabim* were foreigners. They· were the Apprentices; the men of *Isrāl* and *Gebal*, the Fellow-Crafts; and the *Manatzkhim*, the Masters of the work.

Those of each degree, it is said, had signs and words by which to recognize each other, and to enable them to receive their wages.

To receive these, the Apprentices, it is said, congregated at the column YAKAIN; the Fellow-Crafts at the column BAAZ; the Masters in the middle chamber.

The foundation was laid, as we have said, in the

second month of the fourth year of Salamah's reign.
The Temple was completely finished in the eighth
month, Bûl or Khesvan, of the eleventh year of his
reign ; seven years and six months having thus been
occupied in its erection. On the second day of the
second month, Zif or Aiyar, of the year 1012 before
Christ, the first stone of the foundation was laid. In
the seventh month, Ethanim or Tisri, of the year
1004 before Christ, the House of God was solemnly
dedicated, and the Ark of the Covenant placed in
the Holy of Holies.

But in the meantime, as our Masonic tradition informs us, a tragical scene had been enacted in the
unfinished Temple.

It was promised by King Salamah, that when the
Temple should be finished and dedicated, the most
skilful and faithful Fellow-Crafts should be raised to
the rank of Master Mason, and invested with the
Master's word ; with which, though aliens and not
Hebrews, they might travel into foreign countries,
and earn Master's wages, being by it recognized as
Initiates everywhere.

Fifteen of these Fellow-Crafts, when the Temple
was nearly finished, desiring to return to their own
country, because they were weary of the work, and
had not been industrious enough, nor were skilful
enough, to expect to be selected to receive the Master's degree, plotted together to force Hûrōm, the

Master of the workmen [called Abai and Abaif, Master], to make known to them the Word, intending, when they had forced it from him, to return to their native countries.

Now the Mason's WORD, or the TRUE WORD of a Master Mason, was not yet made known to any of the Master Masons. It was only known by the two Kings and the Master, Hūrōm, and it required *three* to give it, each giving only one letter. The others were not to receive it until the dedication of the Temple.

Twelve of the Conspirators, repenting of their evil design, failed to meet the other three in the Temple at the time agreed upon for putting their wicked plot into execution. The other three, though disappointed, persisted. Their names are *said* to have been YUBELA, YUBELO, and YUBELŌM. In these a mystery is concealed.

It was well known that Hūrōm went to the Temple to pray, at noon, daily, while the workmen rested from their labors. Knowing he was then always alone, and all the workmen absent, the three miscreants selected that hour and opportunity for effecting their purpose. They did not intend the murder of the Master, but thought that fear would induce him to divulge the Word, knowing how often it has constrained men to do the basest things, to which death ought to have been preferable.

Yubela posted himself at the *South* gate; *Yubelo* at the *West* gate; and *Yubelōm* at the *East* gate of the Temple.

In other forms of the legend, Yubela is called *Romvel* or *Gibs;* Yubelo, *Hobhen, Gravelot, Austerfurth,* or *Otterful;* and Yubelōm, *Abiram, Abibal, Akirop,* and *Schterké.*

So these miscreants waited until Hūrōm, having offered up his prayers, was on his way out of the Temple. At first he walked to the South gate. There YUBELA met him, holding in his right hand a twenty-four-inch gauge of Steel, and rudely demanded of him the Master's Word. "You cannot," said Hūrōm, "receive it in this way. You must wait with patience until you have served your time. Moreover, by my oath, I alone cannot give it, but only with the assistance of the Kings of Israël and Tsūr."

* 14.   *   *   *   *   *   *

⊙∴ . . . . The Master, Hūrōm, fled to the West gate, and there found YUBELO, with a heavy square of Steel in his hand, who, seizing him rudely, demanded the Master's Word. Hūrōm refused, as before, and struggling, broke away.

* 15.   *   *   *   *   *   *

⊙∴ . . . . Hūrōm, bleeding from his wounds, fled to the East gate, where he was met by YUBELŌM, the eldest, and strongest, and most determined of the three Edomitish brothers, holding in his hand a heavy Stone hammer. Confronting him, and in an angry and menacing tone, this unbelieving ruffian cried

* 16.   *   *   *   *   *   *

For a little while there is entire silence. Then sounds of labor are heard, and the workmen conversing. Then a bell strikes twelve times, and there is heard slow and solemn

MUSIC.

After which the following

EVENING HYMN OF THE WORKMEN.

Abide with me! Fast falls the Eventide;
The darkness thickens: LORD, with me abide!
When other helpers fail, and comforts flee,
Help of the helpless, O abide with me!

Swift to its close ebbs out life's little day:
Earth's joys grow dim, its glories pass away;
Change and decay in all around I see:
O THOU who changest not, abide with me!

I fear no foe, with THEE at hand to bless;
Ills have no weight, and tears no bitterness.
Where is Death's sting; where, grave, thy victory?
I triumph still, if GOD abides with me.

Reveal THYSELF before my closing eyes!
Shine through the gloom, and point me to the skies.

Heaven's morning breaks, and Earth's vain shadows
    flee ;
In life, in death, O LORD, abide with me!

After the hymn is sung, all is silence again. After a little
while, O, ⊕, and ♄ come to where

* 17.   *   *   *   *   *   *

For a time all is silent. Then a trumpet or bugle blows a call,
and a stir is heard among the workmen. ⊙ assumes his station,
and ☿ takes that of ⊕. Then ⊙, rapping o, asks:

⊙∴ ♪ My Brother Azariah, what is the cause of
the commotion among the workmen of the Temple?

☿∴ My Lord, it is the third hour, and yet the
Most Worshipful Master Hairōm hath not come to
the Temple, and the workmen know not how to proceed with their work.

⊙∴ It must be that he is sick. Is he not in his
own house?

☿∴ My Lord, he is not; nor hath been since the
morning of yesterday ; nor hath he been seen of any
one, since yesterday he remained in the Temple to
prayer.

⊙∴ Some accident must have befallen him. Let
all the workmen make careful search for him around
the Temple, and within the walls of the city.

The Brethren walk around, and go out and return, for a time;
and then ☿, rapping o, says:

☿∴ My Lord, the most careful search has been

made by all the workmen within and around the Temple, and throughout the city, but the Master cannot be found.

⊙∴ Then some violence has been done him, and he is dead or injured ; since, living and well, he was never absent from the post of duty. Yet no man was his enemy, for he had never wronged or injured any one.

h raps are now heard at the door, followed by w.

☿∴ My Lord, some one asks admission as a Fellow-Craft.

⊙∴ Whoever it be, let him enter. Perhaps he may bring us tidings of the Master.

The door is opened.

☿∴ Who seeks admission ?

♂∴ [at the door] Twelve Fellow-Crafts, who ask an audience of our Lord the King.

☿∴ My Lord, twelve Fellow-Crafts ask an audience of our Lord the King.

⊙∴ It is granted. Let them approach !

♂ and several Brethren approach the East, and ⊙ says:

⊙∴ What is it ye seek? Speak, and ye shall be heard.

♂∴ O our Lord the King, let not thy anger consume thy servants, though we have sinned against thee and in the sight of God. We have repented, and our hearts are dead within us. We, who are twelve, with three other of our fellows, wearying of work. and fearing we should not be found worthy to receive the Master's degree at the dedication of the Temple, conspired together to compel the Master Hairōm, by threats of violence, to make known to us the Master's Word, intending then to flee to foreign countries, and there be enabled, as Sons of the·Light, to earn Master's wages. We twelve, reflecting upon the enormity of the attempt, repented and abandoned our wicked purpose. But since the Master is not to be found, we fear that the other three have carried their purpose into effect, and, to conceal their crime, have taken his life.

⊙∴ Who are these others?

♂∴ Three brothers, Edomites and worshippers of Baal, named Yubela, Yubelo, and Yubelum.

⊙∴ My Brother Azariah, let inquiry be made among the workmen; and if these men be found, bring them, bound, before me.

Some of the Brethren go out, and, after a little, return.

☿∴ My Lord, inquiry has been made among the workmen, and the three Edomitish brothers are not to be found, nor have they to-day been seen of any one.

⊙∴ What manner of men are these?

☿∴ Idle, rude, and quarrelsome, my Lord.

☉∴ Then there remains no doubt that the Master is slain. I fear the Master's Word is lost. Bring before me again the twelve Fellow-Crafts who conspired with these three, and who say that they repented.

Some Brethren enter, and approach the East.

☉∴ Ye are those who conspired with the three Edomites to procure the Master's Word by force?

♂∴ Our Lord the King, we are.

☉∴ Have you truly and sincerely repented of your evil design?

♂∴ We have, and prayed to the God of Isräl for forgiveness.

☉∴ Are ye also Edomites?

♂∴ Nay, my Lord; we are men of Gebal.

☉∴ To obtain forgiveness for evil deeds or counsels, it is not enough to have repented. Reparation and good deeds are also needed. Are you willing to search, even as far as the sea-coast and the desert for the Master, or his body, and for those whose accomplices you were to have been, and to make them captives, even at the peril of death?

♂∴ We are.

Several. We are.

☉∴ My Brother Azariah, divide these twelve Fellow-Crafts into four parties of three each. Let three go to the North, as far as Galilee; three to the

South, beyond Hebron and Carmel; three to the East, as far as the river Jordan and along the shores of the Sea of Sadamah; and three to the West, as far as the sea-coast and to Yapu. If they find the Master's body, let them carefully examine it, and bring to us whatsoever they may find upon it, bestowing the body in safety and honor where we may go and give it burial. If they overtake the fugitives, let them take them captive, or die in the attempt. If they do their duty manfully and faithfully, they will have atoned for their fault, and shall be forgiven, and may hope to attain to the Master's degree.

The Brethren go out, and all is silent for a time. Then three raps are heard at the door, and ☿, in the West, says:

☿∴ My Lord, some one desires admission.

☉∴ Learn who it is, my Brother, and if it be proper, admit him or them.

The door is opened and closed again, and ☿ says:

☿∴ My Lord, it is three of the Fellow-Crafts who were sent in search of the Master and of the three fugitives.

☉∴ Let them enter.

Some Brethren enter and approach the East.

♂∴ Our Lord the King, we are the three Fellow-Crafts who were sent to the West in search of the body of our Master, and of the Edomitish fugitives.

When we had journeyed a day, and were near the sea-coast, we heard the first tidings. Meeting a wayfaring man, we learned that he had, some hours before, met three men, foreigners, who swore by Baal, and seemed to be laborers, on the way to Yapu, who, learning from him that no vessels were about to sail. from that port, seemed troubled and alarmed, and with many imprecations, turned back toward the hill-country of Samaria. Believing these to be the fugitives, we hastened after them that night and the next day, and stopping at nightfall to rest in the mountains, we heard voices of men conversing, as we discovered, in a cave near by. We listened, and heard one say, " What folly, to think that such a man as the Master Hûrôm would betray his trust through fear of death!"

Then another said, " We have stained our hands with his blood for nought."

And the third, " Now we shall never obtain the Master's Word, and no doubt the avenger of blood is already on our track."

Then the first voice said, " O wretched Yubela, thou art lost! For murder and sacrilege, the punishment is death by fire in the Valley of Hinnom : to be hunted like a wolf, and then slowly, dying a thousand deaths, to be burned to ashes !

* 18.   ✦   ✦   ✦   ✦   ✦   ✦

Assured that these were the murderers, we determined, though ourselves only three in number, foot-sore, faint, and weary, to enter the cave and seize them, or lose our lives in the attempt, hoping so to atone for our offence, and putting our trust in God and the justice of our cause. We entered; but within it was dark, and the way rough and rocky, and one stumbling and falling, the assassins were alarmed, and fled into the labyrinths of the cave. In the darkness we lost our way, and could not follow them; and when morning came, we discovered that they had escaped by another outlet. Searching in vain for traces of their flight, we at length resolved to return, to make known to our Lord what we had learned, and renew our search for the body of the Master.

☉∴ Alas! O Lord, my God! was there no help for the widow's son! The Master Hûrōm is no more! But he died bravely, refusing to betray his trust, and shall ever be to Masons an emblem of Fidelity and Honor. The murderers cannot escape. The unseen avenger of blood pursues them. I have forbidden the sailing of any vessels from any of my ports, and sent messengers with the tidings to my Brother Hûrōm of Tsûr, and all the tributary Kings and Princes, and even to Damascus and to the King of Egypt. When they are apprehended, each shall receive the punishment he invoked upon himself.

The steps of justice are soft, but sure. Meanwhile, as soon as the other nine Fellow-Crafts return, and if they have not found the body of the Master, let the twelve again go forth, divided into four parties, as before, and search in every direction, for the distance of a day's journey from the city, while all the workmen pray to the God of Isräl to make known to us where we may find the body.

Some of the Brethren go out. Then there is solemn

MUSIC.

When the

MUSIC CEASES,

⊕ and ○ resume their places, and ⊙ rapping o, says:

⊙∴ ♪ My Brethren, I have called you together from the River to the land of the Philistines, and unto the border of Egypt, in consequence of the murder of the Master Hūrōm, and to assist me in finding his body, and giving it Masonic burial. Let the Lodge of sorrow and mourning be duly tiled. . . . Most Venerable Brother Adōn-Hūrōm, why are you, being the Junior Warden, in the South?

○∴ Most Worshipful Master, as the Sun is in the South at high noon, so I stand there to oversee the workmen, and call them from labor to refreshment, and from refreshment to labor again, that the Holy Temple may, in due time, be finished.

⊙∴ Most Venerable Brother Zabūd, why are you, being the Senior Warden, in the West?

⊕∴ Most Worshipful Master, as the Sun stands in the gate of the West to close the day, so I stand there to close the daily labor of the workmen, and, on the sixth day of each week, to pay them their wages, that on the Holy Sabbath they may be content.

⊙∴ And why am I, being the Most Worshipful Master, in the East?

⊕∴ As the Sun stands in the gates of the morning to open the day and dispel the darkness, so stands the Most Worshipful Master in the East, to open and instruct his Lodge, and cause the good to triumph over the evil.

⊙∴ [rising] The Most Worshipful Master stands in the East, and the Wardens stand in their stations. ♫ Let the Most Venerable Brethren Tsadōc and Abiathar, the Priests, offer up their prayers. Kneel, my Brethren!

All kneel, and ♄ and ♂ offer up this prayer:

PRAYER.

♄∴ O Sovereign and Supreme God of Isräl, hear the prayer of Thy servants in their distress!

♂∴ O Thou whom no man hath seen or can see, help us in our affliction! Calamity has fallen upon us, and the waters of sorrow flow over our heads!

♄∴ Thou art our life and our salvation! Have mercy upon us, O Yehūah, and help us in our distress!

♂∴ Let thy Loving-kindness encompass us about, and Thy tender mercies give us strength! We acknowledge our transgressions: our sins are ever before us!

♄∴ Wash us from our iniquities, and cleanse us from our sins!

♂∴ Create in us clean hearts! and renew a right spirit within us!

♄∴ Cast us not away from Thy presence! and take not Thy Holy Spirit from us!

♂∴ Open our lips, and our mouths shall show forth Thy praise!

♄∴ AMEN!

♂∴ So MOTE IT BE!

☉∴ Rise, Venerable Brethren!

☉, ⊕, and ○ rap ʜ, each in succession.

☉∴ This Lodge of Masters is duly opened. Valiant Brother Benaiah, see that the approaches to the Temple are duly guarded! Venerable Brothers Elihoreph and Ahiah, the Scribes, write down the cause of our assembly, and whatever may be transacted. My Brother Azariah, have the Twelve Fellow-Crafts returned?

☿∴ Most Worshipful Master, they have; and, after diligent search, have not found the body.

⊙∴ Then it must be hidden within, or near, the city.   Select nine of the Masters, and let three search within the city, three on the North and East of it, and three on the West and South.   If they find the body, let them carefully examine it, and if there be upon it any seal of gold, let them bring it up to us, and carefully note the place where the body lies, that they may conduct us to it.

Some of the Brethren go out.

MUSIC.

After a time the

MUSIC CEASES.

n raps are heard at the door.

⊕∴ Most Worshipful Master, there is a Master's alarm at the door.

⊙∴ Learn who makes it, and his errand!

The door is opened, and closed again.

⊕∴ Most Worshipful Master, the three Masters who were sent to the West and South of the city have returned, and ask admission.

⊙∴ Let them enter.

Some Brethren enter, and approach the East.

♀∴ Most Worshipful Master, we being ordered to go without the city, and search on the West and South of it, went forth at the gate of Yapū, and thence by the foot of Mount Zion into the valley of Hinnom, and, finding nothing, returned, to enter in at the gate of Zion; but when we had ascended the Mount of Zion, and were near to the Tomb of thy father, David the King, we came to a place upon the brow of the Mount, where the earth seemed to have been newly stirred, and, upon examining, found it to be a grave. Not doubting that the murderers had buried the Master there, and the distance from the Temple not being great, we thought it our duty, before disturbing the grave, to return and make known our discovery, that you might do what should seem good in your sight. And that we might readily find the grave, we took up and placed, upon a mound at the head of it, a small bush of acacia.

⊙∴ It is well done, my Brother. Most Venerable Brother Senior Warden, let all the Masters assemble at the West gate of the Temple, to accompany us to the grave of the Master, that we may disinter the body and bring it into the Temple, at the East gate, for proper burial!

All the Brethren go out, and form in procession in the ante-room. Both doors of the Hall are opened. The procession passes from the ante-room into the preparation-room, thence into and round the Hall, and into the ante-room again. This circuit is made three times. Meanwhile, there is played a slow and solemn

DIRGE.

At the third circuit the Brethren divide, passing on either side of the grave. The curtains are removed, and the

MUSIC CEASES.

⊙∴ Here is the grave, newly made. No doubt it contains the body of the Master. The acacia at its head is a fit emblem of the sublime faith in which he lived and died. Surround the grave, my Brethren!

The Brethren form a circle round the grave, and face to the centre, ⊙ being at the foot of the grave, in the circle, with ⊕ on his right hand, and ○ on his left.

⊙∴ Venerable Brother Azariah, take three of the Masters, and reverently and carefully remove the earth and rubbish that cover the remains of the Master.

* 19. 　　* 　　* 　　* 　　* 　　* 　　*

⊙∴ Venerable Brethren, the Master Hûrôm is dead. So must death shortly overtake us all. If it comes to any of us as suddenly and unexpectedly, may it find us as well prepared, in the strength of virtue and good deeds! He died rather than betray his trust by divulging the Master's Word, because it had been solemnly agreed between him, my Brother the King of Tsûr, and myself, that we should only make it known when all were present. The Word is therefore lost, though its letters remain. This seal contains the key. Thought, study, and prayer may, for each Master Mason, unlock the secret; and to each who may be found worthy, when the Holy Temple is dedicated, shall this seal and its sacred symbols be given. Meanwhile, and hereafter, as long as Masonry continues,

* 20.   *   *   *   *   *   *

⊙∴ Venerable Brother Azariah, you will take order for conveying these venerated remains to the Temple; and the Most Venerable Brother Adon-Hairōm will cause a Sarcophagus to be carved, to receive it, after the manner of the Egyptians, and a grave to be prepared near the Temple, over which shall be set a tomb of marble, seven cubits in length, five in height, and three in breadth. Also, the letters upon this seal shall be engraven on a triangular plate of gold, and that be-set firmly in one face of a cube of agate, and the whole deposited in a place known to the Masters, that the WORD may, by study, reflection, and prayer, be in due time recovered.

My Brethren, the Lodge is closed.

All the Brethren still standing as they were, the Worshipful Master continues:

⊙∴ Know, thou who hast represented the Master Hairōm, living and dead, that so he died, and so his remains were discovered and disposed of. That the legend was a symbol, was indicated by the ceremonial that followed.

For, when the Candidate, among our ancient Brethren, had seen and heard what has been rehearsed in your sight and hearing, this is what ensued.

Most Venerable Brother Junior Warden, will the dead live again?

O∴ Worshipful Master, the acacia is a symbol of the Master Mason's faith.

⊙∴ How shall this Brother be raised to the new life?

* 21.   *   *   *   *   *   *

To the Glory of the Grand Architect of the Universe, in the name and under the auspices. etc., and by virtue of the powers vested in me as Master of this Worshipful Lodge of Master Masons, I do now create, receive, and constitute you a Master Mason, and member of this Middle Chamber, in the Ancient and Accepted Scottish Rite of Freemasonry; and I do endow you, as a most precious treasure, with the title of "Venerable Brother," which you should always endeavor to deserve and worthily wear.

*   *   *   *   *   *

Then ⊙ hands the new Master an apron, saying:

⊙∴ As a Master Mason, you will wear the apron with the flap turned down. Its material and color signify purity and innocence, and its bordering of blue, which is the color of VENUS, loving-kindness or charity.

Then he returns him his sword, saying:

☉∴ Receive again your sword. Once it was the weapon of a knight and gentleman. As the symbol of Loyalty and Honor, it is the fit weapon of a Master Mason.

Then he returns him his hat, saying:

☉∴ As a Master Mason, you will sit covered in the Lodge. So the Commons of England sit, being the representatives of a free people. The custom is older than the English Commonwealth, having always prevailed among Masons. Hitherto, you have *served* as an Apprentice and Fellow-Craft. As a Master, you are to *command* and *direct.* See that you do not abuse your powers!

Venerable Brother Master of Ceremonies, present this Venerable Brother to the Most Venerable Wardens, that he may be recognized by them in his new dignity.

He is first presented to ⊕, and then to ○. To each he gives the signs, words, and tokens.

○∴ ♪ Most Venerable Brother Senior Warden, all is exact and perfect.

⊕∴ ♪ Worshipful Master, all is exact and perfect.

☉∴ Place the Venerable Brother between the columns, and let him be seated.

XIII.

FINAL INSTRUCTION.

⊙∴ My Brother, we need not, as is sometimes done, tiresomely rehearse the legend which has already been enacted in your sight and hearing. You cannot have failed to understand its *literal* import.

We shall confine ourselves to such explanations as will point to the paths of study, travelling in which you may come, in time, fully to comprehend the meaning of this degree.

The *Word* whispered in your ear is the substitute for the TRUE WORD of a Master. It contains a mystery which you may perhaps hereafter learn. It is said to have been the first exclamation at the grave when the body had been uncovered, and it *covers and contains* the *True Word*. "Seek and ye shall find." "*The Glory of God,*" the Scripture saith, "is, to conceal the Word." "In the beginning was the Word, and the Word was contained in God, and the Word *was* God."

In the French Rite, and also in the English Lodges, the substitute is . . . , which is composed of two Hebrew words, and means, "*the place where the murdered one was concealed.*"

It is said that when the third conspirator was on the point of striking the Master, the latter threw his hands up in front of his forehead, with the palms outward, to protect his forehead against the blow, crying, "O Lord, my God! is there no help for the son of the widow?" Hence Masons are called "Children of the Widow."

The seal found on the body of the Master Hairōm was what is still known among the Arabs and the Hebrews of the Orient as the Light or Seal of Salamah. It is a circular plate of gold, of one-half this size, and with the devices which you see here upon it.

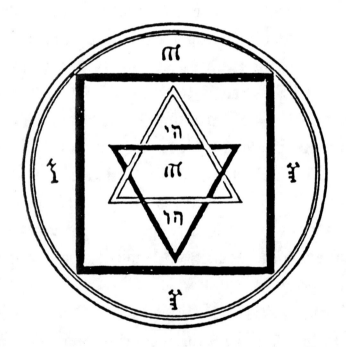

Like the Triangle inscribed within the Square (or on the face of a Cube), and the Pyramid, with its four triangular sides, raised on a Cube as its base, it points out the way, and gives the clue by which the wise may discover the True Word.

By the Square, the Egyptians symbolized matter, or the Womb of things ; by the Triangle, the generative fire. From their conjunction, as in the quadrangular pyramid, their sages held, all things proceeded. Cones were *phalloi*, but pyramids were dedicated to the solar fire, and represented the flame. Jupiter was so represented at Corinth. Vulcan was symbolized by the pyramid ; but it was more exclusively devoted to Dionūsos, Apollōn, and the Sun.

Once more we lead you back to the Ancient Initiations, which, the succession of their Hierophants never interrupted, became the Freemasonry of the Ancient and Accepted Scottish Rite.

" The ceremony of initiation," says the Chief Priest to Lucius, in Apuleius, " into the mysteries, is, as it were, to suffer DEATH, with the precarious chance of resuscitation." The Goddess, he said, selected only such persons as might, through her Providence, be in a manner BORN AGAIN, and commence the career of a new existence.

All initiation is but introductory to the great change of death. Everything earthly must die. Man, like Oïdipos, is wounded from his birth ; his real Elysium can exist only beyond the grave. Death is the inseparable antecedent of life ; the seed dies, in order to produce the plant ; the worm dies to produce the brilliant moth. The death of the seed in giving birth to the plant, connecting the sublimest hopes with the plainest occurrences, was the simple, yet beautiful, formula assumed by the great mystery in almost all religions, from the Zend-Avesta to the Gospel.

The Hierophants of Samothrace assured those initiated into their mysteries, of the rewards reserved for the virtuous after death, by the justice of the Gods. In the mysteries of Eleusis, the Initiate was taught that the Soul was the whole of man ; that earth was but his place of exile; that Heaven was his native country ; that for the Soul to be born is really to die : and that death is for it to return to a new life.

By the ceremonies through which you have passed you have been taught the same great Truth, of the Immortality of the Human Soul ; and that death is but the gateway through which it passes to another sphere of existence. This lesson you could not mistake. You were prepared for it, also, by the instruction received during your seven journeys. Life is a school for the Soul ; an arena in which, amid calamity, suffering, and evil, it may learn to practise the manly and heroic virtues. It is fitted, by the Divine wisdom, for a place of instruction and discipline. Can any better means of instructing, disciplining, and invigorating the Soul be imagined than are afforded by the trials and sufferings, the reverses and disappointments, the triumphs and defeats, the satisfactions and mortifications of this life?

But the Legend of the death of Hûrôm was intended to teach much more. Again, to understand it, you must resort to the Mysteries.

Everywhere, and in all their forms, these were funereal, and celebrated the mystical death and restoration to life of some divine or heroic personage; and the details of the legend and the modes of the death varied in the different countries where the Mysteries were practised.

Everywhere, also, this heroic and mythical personage primarily symbolized the Sun, which, descending southward in Autumn until he reached the Tropic of Capricorn at the Winter solstice, was said then to *die* and be *buried*, for the few days that he seemed undetermined whether to continue to tend further and further southward, until he should leave the world in perpetual night, or to begin again to ascend toward the equator; and this ascent, after the solstice, was called his resurrection, aphanism, or regeneration, and the *salvation* of the world from the malignant powers of darkness, cold, and evil.

The Legend of the Master's degree is but another form of that of the Mysteries, which reaches back, in one shape or other, to the remotest antiquity.

Everywhere, also, the personage of the legend was a beneficent being or Deity, the personification of

LIGHT; a HERO, an INTERCESSOR and MEDIATOR for men, a SAVIOUR and REDEEMER.

In these mysteries was also taught the division of the First cause into an *active* and *passive* cause, of which two, BRAHM and MAYA, OSIRIS and ISIS, the Heavens and the Earth, and the Sun and Moon, were symbols. So the Hebrew Genesis represents the BREATH or SPIRIT of God as brooding on the surface of the Chaos of matter, to create by generation, and man was made male and female after the image of ALOHIM.

Another division of nature has, in all ages, struck all men, and was not forgotten in the mysteries, that of Light and Darkness, ever alternating, overcoming and overcome by turns; an apt symbol of the alternating preponderance of Good and Evil in the world, and in the soul of every man that lives. To the Initiates in the mysteries of Eleusis, as to those of Masonry, the spectacle of these two Principles was exhibited, in the successive scenes of Darkness and Light which passed before their eyes.

The fruit of the sufferings of the God, Father of Light and Souls, slain by the Chief of the Powers of Darkness, and again restored to life, was gathered in the mysteries. *"His death works your salvation!"* said the High Priest of MITHRAS. That was the great secret of this religious tragedy, and its expected fruit; the resurrection of a God, who, repossessing himself of His dominion over darkness,

should associate with Him in his triumph those virtuous Souls, that by their purity were worthy to share
His glory ; those that did not strive against the
divine force that drew them to Him when He had
thus conquered.

Life, rising out of death, was the Great Mystery,
which symbolism delighted to represent under a
thousand ingenious forms. Nature was ransacked
for attestations to the grand Truth, which seems to
transcend all other gifts of imagination, or rather to
be their essence and consummation. Such evidences
were easily discovered. They were found in the
olive and lotus, in the evergreen myrtle, in the
deadly but self-renewing serpent, the wonderful and
brilliant moth emerging from the coffin of the worm,
in the Phœnix, born of its own ashes, the Scarabæus,
the phenomena of germination, the settings and ris-
ings of the Sun and Stars, the darkening and growth
of the Moon, and Sleep, the minor Mystery of death.
The typical death of the Nature-God was a profound
and consolatory mystery. The origin of the doctrine
of the Soul's immortality is as remote and untrace-
able as the origin of man himself.

The Hûrôm of the Masonic legend was not even, so
far as the Bible informs us, a Mason or an Architect.
It testifies to his skill in his occupation, but gives
no hint that he was regarded or valued as anything
more. Comparing the legend of his death with the

others which we have mentioned; seeing that it
occurred in the TEMPLE, which represents the world,
and by THREE blows inflicted at the three gates which
represented the Equinoxes and the winter solstice,
and, remembering that in Masonry the two Solstitial
feasts of June and December are sacred, and that the
Sun, Moon, and Hermes are the great lights of the
Lodge, we are at once forced to conclude that the
legend is neither historical nor traditional, but symbolic. The key to its meaning, and the reason for
the selection of the Hero, are perhaps to be found in
his name.

That name, ordinarily rendered HIRAM, is, in the
book of Kings, Khairōm or Khairûm, but in that of
Chronicles, Khûrōm or Khûrûm. It was either exclusively Phœnician (or Tsûrian), or both Hebrew
and Phœnician, for that of the King of Tsûr was the
same. Adon-Khûrûm (or Adonhiram) was also a
Tsûrian name.

In 2 Chron. ii. 13, the King of Tsûr writes to
Solomon, "I send thee a skilful workman, חורם אבי,"
Khûrûm Abai; which our translation renders, "of
Huram, my father's." In 2 Chron. iv. 16, we find
חורם אבי, Khûrûm Abiu, which our translation renders, "Huram, his father." The last word, *Abiu*, has
been transformed into *Abiff*, and become part of the
name, which it is not. AB, in the Hebrew, meant
not only *Father*, Ancestor, Progenitor, but also *Mas-*

ter. For the meaning of the name of the Master, we refer you to the Morals and Dogma of the Rite.

   *   *   *   *   *   *

Hûrōm may have been selected as the hero of the Masonic legend, solely on account of the symbolic meaning of his name, and its similarity to *Hōr-ra*, *Her-mes*, and *Her-cules*. Though often in political alliance with Egypt, the Hebrews borrowed less from that people than from Phœnicia, Assyria, and Persia. We find among them no Egyptian names of the Deity, no hieroglyphics, no similarity in language. An offshoot of the Arabic stock, the Hebrews never abandoned the names of the Ancient Gods, though they deemed Yehûah greater than any of the *Alohim*. He continued to be to them, *Al, Aloh, Aliun, Adonai*, the *Malakh*, the *Adon-Tsabaoth*, the *Al Shadai*, whom other nations worshipped. It is not difficult to conceive how KHUR-OM should have been substituted for *Hor-ra* and for the God called *Malkarth* by foreigners, that being evidently a corrupted name, and the real one more probably resembling *M'al-Khūr-at.*

The legend of Hûrōm has been also used by the remnants of the Knights of the Temple, to represent the tragical fate of *de Molai*, the last recognized Grand Master; and these have seen in the letters J∴ B∴ M∴ the initials of *Jacobus Burgundus de Molai.* It was also used by the English Royalists, after what they termed the Great Rebellion, to typify the execution of Charles the First, whom they called the Royal Martyr; and by these, it is probable, the names *Romvel* (or *Cromwell*), *Hobhen* (or *Bohun*, the family name of the Parliamentary General, Essex), *Guibs*, *Oterfut*, and *Gravelot* [the latter probably *Argyle*], were given to the assassins. What names are concealed in *Guibs*, *Schterke*, and *Oterfut* or *Otter-foot*, we have not been able to discover.

When Masonry was propagated among the followers of Christ, these saw His crucifixion typified by the death of Hûrōm, who thus became the symbol of the Saviour and Redeemer, the Intercessor and Mediator, who, said to have been born at the winter solstice, was also held to have died at the Vernal Equinox. Then the Lamb became a symbol of Hûrōm, himself a type of Christ; the Sun in the Sign Aries (or the Ram), at the Vernal Equinox, when he begins to move North of the Equator, and Light to overcome Darkness. To the Christians, the three assassins meant the Royal Power, as exercised by *Pontius Pilate* and *Herod;* the Sacerdotal Power, as abused by *Anna* and *Caiaphas;* and the popular brutality, which demanded that *Barabbas* should be released, and CHRIST crucified; the "lamb without blemish and without spot;" "fore-ordained," says Peter, "before the foundation of the world, manifested in the later times, raised up by God from the grave, and invested with glory."

That the legend was meant to be identical at bottom with that of Osiris, regenerated as Hōr-ra, is evident from one of the symbols of the degree, a female, on a platform raised by three steps, with an urn in one hand and a branch in the other, reading a book, a broken column in front of her, while Time, with his scythe and wings, behind her, is manipulating her flowing hair. This is *said* to have been a monument erected by King Solomon over the grave of the Master Hūrōm. You may read the pretended explanation in the Monitors of the English Rite.

*			*			*			*			*			*

The Legend of Hūrōm has also a political interpretation.

The heroes of the other legends are Gods, or the Sons of Gods. Of the *Masonic* legend, the Hero is an Architect, or rather, an Artificer, and so represents the people at large; as Adam, or "*The* Adam," was the symbol of universal Humanity. The Master Hūrōm is a symbol of THE PEOPLE, and of a free STATE, and, therefore, of LIBERTY itself. The three murderers symbolize the chief causes of the loss of liberty of Nations. Usurpation may attempt to gain despotic power in vain, and the Pontificate seek in vain to tyrannize over consciences; the one may strike at the *throat* and the other at the *heart*, and both be foiled, if the people, enrolled as a soldiery, do not become their instruments, and with the *mace* and *hammer* of their united and disciplined force, smiting the *head* of the State, crush its intellect, embodied in its great wise men, who have always been the ardent advocates of rational freedom. The RULE of arbitrary power, the SQUARE of Pontifical infallibility, dictating a creed to consciences, and the MACE of military force, are the instruments and weapons by which nations are enslaved, and freedom expires in agonies. The worst enemy of the People is the People itself.

It has sometimes happened that a free people has lost its freedom, conquered by foreign arms. Sometimes liberty has been sold. But when a free State has ceased to be free, it has generally been because its People have unwittingly connived with a Tyrant or Usurper. It is true that those who, in a free Commonwealth, under the stale pretences of necessity, and the safety of the People, by virtue of their magistracy or military rank, usurp the powers of Dictator, and barbarously violate the most sacred rights of their country, deserve the names of rebels and traitors, not only against the laws of that country, but against Heaven itself. But it is equally true, that wherever an inveterate resolution has been formed to annihilate the liberties of the governed, it is in the power of the people to prevent it, and that history affords examples of successful resistance by force to usurpation by arms.

The usurpation most likely to succeed, because least likely to have its aim or tendency suspected, and also the greatest evil that can befall a nation, is the invasion of the people's rights by the authority of the people's representatives. It is in regard to these that the people are least apt to notice and resist the very beginnings of usurpation. It is likely even to be considered unpatriotic, perhaps treasonable, if the State is beleaguered by danger, to question the motives and doubt the wisdom of the acts of the people's representatives; and yet it is much less dangerous for a Civil or Military Usurper to make his will the law, and confiscate the public liberty, than for those representatives, under the color of law, to put the powers of the State in his hands, and the liberties and rights of the people in his grasp.

Power, without right, is a thing hateful in itself, and ever inclining to its fall. Tyranny is detestable in every shape, but in none so formidable as when it is assumed and exercised by a number of Tyrants.

If you are a Citizen of a free State, ever remember that a paper constitution will always prove insufficient to resist the popular will; that unless there be power to restrain power, nothing can withstand it; and that the people are always inclined to admit necessity as a sufficient plea for unconstitutional action and usurpation. Remember, also, that those who flatter and fawn upon the people to obtain power, will always be the first to urge this plea as an excuse for assuming unlawful power over them.

*   *   *   *   *   *

Seek out the great and wise men, and intrust the fortunes of the Republic, as far as your vote and influence can do so, to their hands. Select those for office who will more add honor to the office than the office will honor them; those who are entitled, by their intellect and learning, to deal on equal terms with the Republic, and to lay her under obligations by accepting her offices. The country that has no such men is indeed a pauper. The State that has them, and does not use their services, is idiotic or insane.

*   *   *   *   *   *

Be always jealous of power, which ever tends to perpetuate itself and to increase. Usurpations generate like vermin. The men of energy are always for burning the parchment. Never listen to those who cry that your free government is too weak and inefficient, and who urge you to give it the power to take the last shilling from your purse, the last drop of blood from your veins. Give this power to no man, or set of men, however worthy he or they may seem of such trust. If a people part with it, they resign their liberties. Even in struggling to attain its independence, a nation may lose its freedom. A people true to itself needs no saviour to achieve its political salvation. If it so wills, it is sufficient for itself

And whatever follies or excesses a Republic, its rulers, or its people may commit, let not these alienate you from a free form of government, and enlist you under the banners of despotism, even in opinion. No government is free from imperfections and evils, and we are always sure to imagine that those under which *we* suffer are the least tolerable of all. The election of unfit and incapable men, in many instances, is inseparable from Republican governments. But petty and base men not only attain power under Kings, but become Kings themselves; and the truly wise and great as rarely govern in Monarchies as in Democracies. It is human nature that is in fault. As yet, free Government is an experiment. After a time it will succeed. It is the only form of government that consists with individual rights and the dignity of human nature; and if it be impossible for a community of freemen wisely to govern themselves, it is absurd for man to claim to have been made a little lower than the angels, and in the image of God.

An explanation of some of the symbols of this degree will, for the present, complete your instruction.

We have already indicated to you the symbolic meaning of the names of the three assassins. JUBELUM, we informed you, has also been called *Abiram*,

Abibal, and *Akirop*. These words, also, like everything in Masonry that belongs there, are symbolic.
אב, *Abi*, as you know, means *father;* and רמה, *ramah*,
means "*overthrew*," or *struck down*. בלא, *bala*, means
Destroyer; balla in Chaldee, or *balah* in Hebrew, "*to
destroy.*"

ABIRAM, therefore, means "*he who struck down our
Father or Master;*" and ABIBAL, "*the slayer of our
Father or Master.*"

עקרב, *Akarab*, means a *Scorpion*, and is the same in
Arabic as in Hebrew. 2,500 years before Christ,
the Sun entered the Constellation or Sign *Leo*, the
Lion, at the Summer Solstice ; *Scorpio*, the Scorpion,
at the Autumnal Equinox, and thence passed through
Sagittarius, the Vindictive Archer, and *Capricornus*,
the filthy and detested He-Goat, the AZAZEL of the
Hebrews, to *Aquarius*, the Water-Bearer, at the
Winter Solstice. The Scorpion was regarded as an
ill-omened and malignant sign ; and it contained the
brilliant but malignant Star Antares. At the Winter
Solstice, which afterwards became the feast-day of
John the Evangelist, the Sun was said to die, and to
remain buried three days.

PLUTARCH says that when *Osiris* was murdered by
Typhon, the Sun was in the sign *Scorpio*, which then
was entered by him at the autumnal equinox. He
had returned from the shades at the vernal equinox,
to assist ISIS and HORUS in warring against TYPHON.

Leaving *Scorpio*, to reach the lowest points of his annual course at the Winter Solstice, he passed through the Signs of the *Archer* and *He-Goat*.

The three gates of the Temple are the two Equinoxes, always called the Gates of Heaven, and the Winter Solstice.

Isis, personified as the *Moon*, searching for the body of Osiris, was accompanied by *Sirius*, or *Kalab-Anubach*, the Dog-Star, the God Anubis. The twelve Fellow-Crafts and nine Masters, sent in search of the body, are also, undoubtedly, astronomical allusions. Nine of the Zodiacal signs did not share in the symbolic slaying of the Sun, and nine great stars, in the Moon's path, and seeming to accompany her, enable nautical men to ascertain their longitude at sea. In the Hyades and Pleiades are twelve stars.

The Master Masons were, at the dedication of the Temple, to receive the TRUE WORD, or the *Master's Word*, to enable them to travel into foreign countries, and there earn and receive wages. The True Word was the symbol and expression of what PLUTARCH calls the HOLY or SACRED DOCTRINE, the knowledge of the one God and the Soul's immortality; the religious *faith* in these, taught by the mysteries, and known to the Hierophants of all nations. Gifted with this knowledge, and armed with this faith, the Initiate would approach, without base fear, the valley of the shadow of Death, to enter into that far distant, unseen, unknown country, from whose bourne no traveller returns, and there to receive the wages of faithful service, the immense boon of Eternal Life.

The raising of the body of Hûrōm symbolizes the reascension and immortality of the Soul. This can neither be proven by the inductions of natural and physical science, *the Apprentice's grip*, nor demonstrated by the processes of the logic of metaphysics and philosophy, *the grip of the Fellow-Craft*, but is only established by the wise analogies of FAITH, the irrefutable convictions of consciousness, which are *the Lion's grip*, that of the Lion of the Tribe of Judah. To the Christian Mason the three grips are symbols of the Pagan Philosophy, Hebraic materialism, and Christianity.

The Caves of Mithras and the Pyramids represented the world. The Initiates were compelled to pass *seven* times through fire, and seven times through water; and we gather from Origen, that the Mithriac Candidate was obliged to pass through seven gates of trial before he arrived at the Ineffable Presence, after which he was proclaimed a Lion of Mithras.

The number *seven*, always divided into, and composed of, *three* and *four*, was represented by the triangle and square, and by the Cube surmounted by the Pyramid. In four and three is the mystery hidden of the Master's Word. The Pyramids were, we believe, edifices built for the celebration of Cavern

Mysteries, like the Caves of Delphi, Trophonius, and Mithras. In the great Pyramid, one main passage divides into three branches, one ascending to a room precisely in the centre, one leading horizontally to the chamber under it, and one descending to the regions of the Dead. Each branch terminates in a distant vault.

The triangular external form of the Pyramids, and the triple internal division, indicate that the rites celebrated there were those of a triple Deity. Hecaté was painted of three colors, and Pluto, like Siva, his prototype, to whom pyramids and tridents are sacred, had three eyes. The Egyptians used only the three primitive colors in their sacred paintings, with which those employed by Moses in the Tabernacle, and by the Brahmans in their twisted girdles, agree. Nothing could be a more beautiful or purer emblem of a triune God than triune light. The seven Hebrew Lights, or Sephiroth, resoluble into one central circle, and surmounted by three radical Lights, or Sephiroth, curiously agree with the phenomena of colors.

Some of the emblems usually exhibited in the Master's degree are ancient, and some modern. The *Beehive*, for example, is modern. The trite explanation given of it does not even merit a passing word. The adherents of the Stuarts, in England and on the Continent, after Charles the First was executed, resorted to Masonry as a means of organization and communication. The Pretender's son, as he was afterwards popularly called, still exercised high Masonic powers, as the lineal inheritor of Masonic Sovereignty, and there is still extant a brief of Constitution of a Chapter of Rose Croix at Arras, in France, granted by him, the unfortunate Charles Edward Stuart. Before the Restoration, the Loyalists were especially active through their secret organization, and the Masonic legend was used by them as a parable or allegory, the interpretation of which was the execution of Charles I., brought about by a rebel Parliament and army, and Scottish Presbyterian treachery. Since then, *English* Masonry, organized at the death of Queen Anne, has always inculcated submission and obedience to the powers of the State, whatever they might be. Thus denaturalized, it adopted the bee-hive as one of its emblems, because it represents a Commonwealth, or a people governed by a King, or the Constitution of the British Government.

This is a key to those "ANCIENT" CHARGES AND REGULATIONS, by which every Master Elect of an English Lodge promises "to be a peaceable *subject*," and not to be concerned in plots and conspiracies against *Government*, but *patiently* to submit to the decisions of *the* "*Supreme Legislature*," *i.e.*, of Parliament, settling the succession to the Crown, and excluding the Stuarts and all Papists.

The three Steps, usually delineated on the Master's Carpet, are said to be emblematical of the three principal stages of human life—Youth, Manhood, and Old Age. They are really symbolical of the same things as the three grips by which it was attempted to raise the body. All the Symbols of Masonry refer to something in the ceremonies. And when the Beehive was interpolated among the Emblems, these three Steps perhaps represented, in the British Government, the Commons, Lords, and Crown, the three degrees of that Monarchical Oligarchy.

The " *Pot of Incense*," said to be an emblem of a pure heart, is really a funereal Urn, such as those in which, anciently, after the body of the dead was burned, its ashes were deposited. It is surmounted by a flame, whose ascent upward is a symbol of the aspirations of the human Soul toward the Infinite and Divine, and therefore of its immortality, of which those aspirations are the most irrefutable evidence.

The *Book of Constitutions* and *Sword* symbolize the obligation taken upon them, and the Duty of the Mason to defend the Rights of Man and the great tenets of LIBERTY, EQUALITY, and FRATERNITY, if need be, by the sword. To these three, also, the three steps allude, these having, like many other symbols, a political as well as a philosophical interpretation.

The *Sword*, pointing to a human *heart*, is a symbol

of the punishment anciently inflicted upon those who violated their obligations, and disclosed the Secrets of the Mysteries. Though no longer inflicted, every Candidate still solemnly submits himself to it, and consents to undergo it in case of perjury.

The *All-seeing Eye* is a symbol of the Deity, as it anciently was, in Egypt, a hieroglyphic of OSIRIS and the SUN. Connecting the legend of HURÔM with that of OSIRIS, by its hieroglyphical meaning, and also because the word *Khūr*, in Hebrew, meant the Socket, or opening of the Eye, it symbolizes that true knowledge of the Deity which was taught in the mysteries, and is the LIGHT, of which the Mason travels in search.

The *Sun, Moon, Comet,* and *Seven Stars* indicate the astronomical symbolism of the legend, and again connect it with that of Osiris. The Sun is Osiris, the Moon Isis, the Comet is a modern substitution in lieu of the five-pointed, or Blazing Star, which represented SIRIUS, ANUBIS, and HERMES. The Seven Stars are those of *Ursa Major*, or the Great Bear, which, connected with BOÖTES, or the *Herdsman*, indicate that this Constellation also symbolized Osiris, and its disappearance in the ocean the death of that deity.

The *Anchor* is a modern symbol, signifying HOPE of that immortality taught by the symbolic resurrection of the Candidate.

The *Ark* is an ancient symbol, denaturalized by being made to represent the vessel built by Noah. It was originally a Chest, like the Ark of the Covenant, and that borne in procession in the Mysteries of Isis, representing the Chest in which the body of Osiris was committed to the waves, and in which it continued when enclosed in the Column cut of the tamarisk tree which had grown up around it.

The *Hour-glass* and *Scythe* are symbols of Horus or Hōr-ra, and again identify the Hebrew and Egyptian legends.

The *Mace* or *Mallet*, the *Spade*, *Coffin*, and branch of *Acacia*, refer, as we hardly need say, to the death of Hūrōm and the discovery of his body, the Spade and Coffin being *very* modern.

The *forty-seventh problem of Euclid*, the only explanation whereof, given in the English Rite, is, that " it teaches Masons to be general lovers of the Arts and Sciences," is in reality one of those Etruscan stones, as it were, builded into the whimsically incongruous walls of that system of Masonry. It is the profoundest philosophical symbol of the whole science. Like a boulder of granite in a great alluvial plain, brought thither at some remote and unknown period from the far-distant mountains, by some cataclysm, or in an iceberg from northern glaciers, when that which is now dry land was covered by the waters of a deep sea, it stands unexplained, a sphinx, its meaning not even guessed at by those who have made trivial so many of the symbols of Masonry. For the true meaning we refer you to the Morals and Dogma.

* * * * * *

The field of study here opened to you is very great. It is because of the Triad in every system of Philosophy and religion, in all the sacred creeds and mystic teachings, from the earliest times to Christianity and Gnosticism, that the number 3 so often recurs in Masonry. We derive the 47th Proposition from our Ancient Masters, the Hindûs, Persians, and Egyptians; and Plutarch, himself an Initiate, has given us the true key to its meaning.

The Mallet of the Master is the Tau Cross of the Egyptian Hierophants. It is held by the Lion, in the symbolic picture heretofore mentioned, and was the symbol of Eternal Life.

In the Egyptian name of Horus (*Har-oeri*), *Oeri* meant *Beautiful;* and while STRENGTH is assigned to HURÔM, King of Tsûr, and WISDOM to SALAMAH, BEAUTY is assigned to HURÔM the Master.

* * * * * *

Revelation of God, the universe is also the one body of which He is in some sense the Soul. It is one. Turn where we will for science, for art, for poetic imagery, for human characteristics, we still find prototypes and models in Nature. She is, in truth, the omnipotent mother, Isis, the fountain-head and well-spring of all life and all intelligence.

The working-tools of a Master Mason are not given alike, even in the same Rite. Some say they are the HOLY BIBLE, SQUARE, and COMPASS; others, that there is but one, the TRESTLE-BOARD; others, that they are *all* the implements of Masonry indiscriminately; but especially the TROWEL. The Hebrews worked in rebuilding the Temple, with the *Sword* in one hand and the *Trowel* in the other. The TROWEL is the chief working-tool of the Master. It is the cement spread by the Trowel that makes solid the walls, and gives the building permanence. Loving-kindness, mutual concession, mutual forbearance, toleration of opinion, may well be termed the cement that binds men together in society. Harmony and concert of action between the departments, each co-operating with the other, each refraining from usurpation of power, or even stopping short of the line up to which it might push its prerogative, are essential to the perpetuity of the State. Sympathy is the cohesive force that binds men together in Orders and Societies; and when it ceases to exist or is weakened, and Selfishness usurps upon it, the Order or the State draws nigh unto its end. When self-interest and self-aggrandizement are deified, as the Roman Emperors were in their lives, the chaos is at hand.

The accomplished Mason applies to their uses the symbolic LEVEL, PLUMB, and SQUARE. He uses also the COMPASS, and other instruments of Geometry, if invested with power or the authority of the intellect, that others may work by his designs; and, if need be, he draws the SWORD as the soldier of Truth and Justice, and the Defender of the rights of man.

* * * * * *

These, my Brother, are hints, and not an essay. So it is, by hints that lead its votaries to think, that Masonry develops the meaning of her symbols. She knows that men do not love the labor of thinking, and that scarcely one in a thousand, of any class, or any country, under any circumstances, can be induced to think at all; since, to most men, to think is a toil and a disturbance that wearies and afflicts them. Yet she addresses herself exclusively in the Ancient and Accepted Scottish Rite to those who can be led to think. These only she encourages to advance into the higher degrees. To these only she opens the Sanctuary. To all others, like Isis, she withdraws the veil from her face, only to reveal a deeper mystery in the expression—eternal silence, and an incommunicable thought; the "*open Secret*" expressed in marble. So NATURE, the great Revelation of God, has always in vain uplifted her veil to the vast majority of men. Nevertheless, remember that solemn warning of the Apostle PAUL, which has probably never fallen otherwise than as an empty sound of words upon your ears, contained in his declaration to the Roman Christians, that God's anger will fall upon all the vicious, because all that can be known in regard to God is manifested and showed to them by God Himself; for all that in Him has been invisible since the creation is clearly visible, manifested by the revelation of creation itself, to wit, His Eternal Power and Divinity, so that they have no excuse.

We are passing through this world into other worlds, perhaps into other bodies. We are passing through, as the old Saxon king said, "like the bird that flies across the hall, entering from the Heavens at one window, departing to the skies at another." We belong to Eternity, and not to Time. Life is little; but its problems are great. Man is nothing; man is infinite. We are all children; but children playing, toiling, suffering, on the shore of the great ocean, across which, from the unknown land, mysterious thoughts come to us, shaping themselves into words whispered by the never-silent leaves. The great problems of God and this world of Nature, and of man, remain and are unexhausted. The human mind can never rest lethargic in the presence of them. If every system taught in the schools, colleges, and temples were swept away, and every echo

of them died away along the sacred walls, there
would, before the sun went down, be some new doctrine thundering from the roof, and a thousand whispered contradictions circling round the pillars and
along the aisles.

*   *   *   *   *   *

In a country where every expression of opinion
is forbidden, and independence, the true national
life, can only be obtained by revolt, revolt can
only be effected by conspiracy. There Masonry
and men must teach, incite, arm, and fight by
conspiracy. It is the dire necessity imposed on
them. They have to earn and win the privilege of debate and discussion. They argue with
an opponent who smites them on the mouth, and
buries them within walls of stone. They must talk
in whispers, assemble in the night, deal their blows
in the shape of insurrection and revolt. Even to
hiss and sting is sometimes nature's great conserv-
atism. The God Vishnu, trodden near to death by a
huge elephant, transforms himself into a snake, that
he may again appear as a divine man. To have
mind, and speech, and *free* discussion, so that the
citizen and the priest may meet each other face to
face, and each hear what the other has to say, Reason
sitting as arbiter and judge, the Soldier must be made
to stand aside, and let the Thinker argue with the

Priest. If you live in a country where the Truth may safely and openly be spoken, so much the more imperative a duty it is for you to speak it. The whole world is the field of that husbandry. Everywhere the good seed may be sown, and, with God's blessing, it may everywhere yield as bountifully as the yellow grain.

It remains only to explain to you the five points of Masonry or Fellowship, on which you received the Sacred Word of this degree. They are so many symbols and solemn pledges. So only you can give or receive that word.

* 23. * * * * * *

(a) . . . Signifies that you will hasten promptly and cheerfully to the assistance of a worthy Brother Master Mason when he needs comfort, assistance, or relief, so soon as you are informed of his need, and without waiting for message or summons.

(b) . . . that you will remember him in your prayers, strengthen his good resolves, and help to raise him from the depths of calamity and affliction.

(c) . . . that you will hold him to your heart by the strong claspings of Loving-Kindness, and, after his death, cherish and protect any who are near and dear to him, who may need protection.

(d) . . . that you will strive to keep him from falling when assailed by temptation or menaced by danger; and upholding and supporting him, ever be to him truly a Brother.

(e) . . . . that you will always give him good counsel, even at the risk of his anger; inform him of any reports to his injury, and give him warning of impending or threatened danger.

And the TRUE GRIP of the Master Mason signifies that even if a Brother has, by sin and shame, sunken, in his own estimation and that of the world, into the depths from which there seems to be no redemption, if he seems dead to the dictates of honor, the demands of duty, the feeling of shame, and the reproaches of his conscience, still you will endeavor to raise him from this death to a new life of manliness, honor, and virtue, not contenting yourself with one trial, nor with two, but using in the third every means and inducement in your power.

Do you now solemnly give and reiterate the pledges contained in these symbols?

✠∴ I do.

☉∴ And do you promise always to renew them when you give or receive this grip and the Sacred Word?

✠∴ I do.

☉∴ There is, then, but a single other lesson. There are recognized truths enough with which to build up a glorious world, if men would but build. That is now your duty. "*It is happier to love than to hate. Forgiveness is wiser than Revenge. Temperance is the line that divides pain from pleasure.*" There is a whole system of morals in these truisms. If that which no one denies as moral truth had but its legitimate sequence in human action, the world would be revolutionized. There is regeneration for mankind in the single words JUSTICE and TEMPERANCE. Industry, activity, and energy, are but our very life itself; the putting forth of the Power that is within us. If men were active to good ends, temperate, just, and equitable, the earth would be peopled with prosperous and contented multitudes. *To meet with all men upon the Level, to act with them according to the Plumb, and to part with them upon the Square,* are the requisitions of the law of Masonry. May you always so meet, act, and part, and may your labors not fail of their reward!

⊙∴ ♫ Rise, and to order, Venerable Brethren! Most Venerable Brethren Senior and Junior Wardens, announce to the Venerable Brethren on your Columns that we are about to congratulate ourselves on the advancement of the Venerable Brother A........ B........, and request them to recognize him as a Master Mason, to give him comfort and assistance, and to applaud his initiation into the sublime degree of Master.

The Wardens repeat the announcement. The battery and ordinary plaudit are then given, all crying HUZZA! HUZZA! HUZZA!

The new Master responds, and the Worshipful Master causes his plaudit to be covered.

The Catechism is repeated, if there be time. Generally it will be postponed to another meeting.

*   *   *   *   .*   *

XIV.

INSTRUCTION.

*   *   *   *   *   *

XV.

TO CLOSE.

When all the business is concluded, and nothing remains but to close, ☉ raps once, and says:

☉∴ ♪ Brother Junior Warden, where is your station in the Lodge?

☉∴ In the South, Worshipful Master.

☉∴ Why do you occupy the South?

* 24.   *   *   *   *   *   *

THE END.